THE RETIREMENT MYTH

WHAT YOU MUST KNOW NOW TO
PROSPER IN THE COMING MELTDOWN
OF JOB SECURITY, PENSION PLANS,
SOCIAL SECURITY, THE STOCK MARKET,
HOUSING PRICES, AND MORE

CRAIG S. KARPEL

HarperCollins*Publishers*

HarperCollins books may be purchased for educational, business, or sales promotional use. For information please write: Special Markets Department, HarperCollins Publishers, Inc., 10 East 53rd Street, New York, NY 10022.

FIRST EDITION

Designed by Irving Perkins Associates

Library of Congress Cataloging-in-Publication Data

Karpel, Craig S.
    The retirement myth : what you must know now to prosper in the coming meltdown of job security, pension plans, social security, the stock market, housing prices, and more / Craig S. Karpel. — 1st ed.
        p.   cm.
    ISBN 0-06-017142-1
    1. Social security—United States.   2. Old age pensions—United States.
    3. Retirement—United States.   I. Title.
    HD7125.K36   1995
    368.4'3'00973—dc20   95-1347

95 96 97 98 99 ❖/RRD 10 9 8 7 6 5 4 3 2 1

This book is dedicated to my mother and father
and to Michael S. Shaeffer

Let every man in mankind's frailty
Consider his last day; and let none
Presume on his good fortune until he find
Life, at his death, a memory without pain.

—Sophocles, *Oedipus Rex*

CONTENTS

ACKNOWLEDGMENTS

I wish to express my gratitude to Ted Barna of Kwasha Lipton; Virginia F. Decker of William M. Mercer, Inc.; Mary Feldman of The Segal Company; James P. Klein, Vice President and U.S. Practice Leader for Retirement Planning and Executive Benefits at Towers Perrin, and his colleague Joseph P. Conway; William McDermott of Hewitt Associates; Robert J. Myers, FSA, MAAA; Mary S. Riebold, FSA, MAAA; Dr. Sylvester J. Schieber, Vice President and Director, Research and Information Center, The Wyatt Company, and his able assistant, Nina Droubay; and Larry B. Wiltse, Consulting Actuary and Director of Planning and Forecasting Services, Buck Consultants.

I learned much from B. Douglas Bernheim, Professor of Economics, Stanford University; Marshall E. Blume, Director, Rodney L. White Center for Financial Research, the Wharton School of the University of Pennsylvania; Robert N. Butler, M.D., Brookdale Professor and Chairman, Henry L. Schwartz Department of Geriatrics and Adult Development, the Mount Sinai Medical School, and his executive secretary, Morrisseen Barmore; Kathleen Christensen, Professor of Environmental Psychology, City University of New York Graduate School; the Hon. John T. Dunlop, Lamont University Professor Emeritus, Harvard University; Eli Ginzberg, Director, the Eisenhower Center for the Conservation of Human Resources, Columbia University; Mark D. Hayward, Professor of Sociology, Pennsylvania State University; Patric H. Hendershott, Professor of Finance, the Ohio State University; Michael D. Hurd, Professor of Economics, State University of New York at Stony Brook; Rosabeth Moss Kanter, Class of 1960 Professor of Business Administration, Harvard University; Laurence J. Kotlikoff, Professor of Economics,

Boston University; N. Gregory Mankiw, Professor of Economics, Harvard University; Daniel L. McFadden, Professor of Economics and Director, Econometrics Laboratory, University of California at Berkeley; Robert C. Merton, George Fisher Baker Professor of Business Administration, Harvard University; Dr. Harry R. Moody, Deputy Director, Brookdale Center on Aging, Hunter College; John Myles, Director, Pepper Institute on Aging and Public Policy, the Florida State University; Karen Newkirchen, Department of Economics, Princeton University; Michael Rendall, Professor of Consumer Economics and Housing, New York State College of Human Ecology, Cornell University; Harold L. Sheppard, Professor Emeritus of Gerontology, University of South Florida; Lise Stark, Centre for Health and Social Policy, Odense University Medical School, Denmark; Richard H. Thaler, Professor of Economics, University of Chicago; Michael Useem, Professor of Sociology (Arts and Sciences) and Management (Wharton School), Karen and Gary Rose Term Professor, University of Pennsylvania; and David N. Weil, Associate Professor of Economics, Brown University.

I would like to thank Senators Pete Domenici, J. Robert Kerrey, Sam Nunn, and William V. Roth Jr.; Dr. Daniel J. Beller and John Turner, Office of Research and Economic Analysis, Pension and Welfare Benefits Administration, U.S. Department of Labor; Polly Dement, Bipartisan Commission on Entitlement and Tax Reform; Stephen C. Goss, Supervisory Actuary, Social Security Administration; Dr. Matilda White Riley, Senior Social Scientist, National Institute on Aging; and Carolyn Wheeler, Equal Employment Opportunity Commission.

Credit is due to R. Theodore Benna, 401(k) Association; Bruce L. Birnbaum, J.D., LL.M.; Michael Clowes, Editor, *Pensions & Investments*; Stephen K. Cook and Mindy Hess of Stephen K. Cook & Co.; Elsie Cosbey, Anne Scully, and Adelaide Flatau of Elder-Share, Inc.; Rob Densen, Vice President and Director of Public Affairs, Oppenheimer Management; Edward W. Davidson, Project Director, Senior Aides/Senior Employment, Department of Community Services, Palm Beach County, Florida; Kim Devore, Interim Personnel; Jennifer Dexter, Employers Council on Flexible Compensation; Robert G. Eggert Sr., Eggert Economic Enterprises; Ellen and Jack Eichelbaum of JDR Financial and Social Services; Joe Famiglietti, Senior Recruiter, McDonald's Corp.; Linda E. Garcia, Communications and Events Manager, SeniorNet; Lou Glasse, Pres-

ident, Older Women's League, and her colleagues Vicki O'Reilly
and Dianna Porter; Margaret Harmon, Director, National Shared
Housing Resource Center; W. K. Ketchum, Vice President—Corpo-
rate Labor Relations and Vice President—Human Resources, Com-
munications Services Group, AT&T, and his assistants Doris Robir-
son and Marilyn Schreiber; Shawn J. Lapean, Assistant Vice
President/Policy Planning, Merrill Lynch, Pierce, Fenner & Smith;
Martin T. Lastowka, Manager of Employee Relations, Raytheon
Engineers & Constructors; George Monahan, Director of Industry
Studies, Securities Industry Association; staff members of the
National Council on Aging including William E. Oriol, Editor, *Per-
spectives on Aging*, and Lisa Stewart, Coordinator, Retirement and
Life Planning Programs and Program Manager, National Institute on
Financial Issues and Services for Elders; John Phillips, Chairman,
Senior Career Planning and Placement Service; Marilynn J. Reid
and Marion Sykes of Yankelovich Partners; Jane Riesterer, Kelly
Services; Brian H. Saffer, Deloitte & Touche; Chester Salkind,
Executive Director, American Society of Pension Actuaries; David
Sarlin, Vice President for Global Finance Development, Citibank;
Barb Shryver, Manpower Temporary Services; Howard "Sandman"
Sims; Philip H. Smyth, Birinyi Associates; Nancy Tenkate, *American
Demographics;* Jean E. Tobin, Research and Planning Division, New
York Stock Exchange; and Joyce Wiegand, R.N., Kelly Assisted
Living.

I am grateful for the aid of James A. Auerbach and Marlene W.
Thompson of the National Planning Association; Dr. Michael C.
Barth of ICF Inc., Dr. Lydia Brontë of the Phelps-Stokes Research
Institute; Dr. Sally Coberly, Director of the Institute on Aging, Work
and Health of the Washington Business Group on Health; M. Cindy
Hounsell of the Pension Rights Center; Cynthia Morris of the Com-
monwealth Fund; Carolyn P. Pemberton of the Employee Benefit
Research Institute; Sarah Priestman of the Omega Institute for
Holistic Studies; and Joan P. Stilwell of the National Bureau of Eco-
nomic Research.

I was graciously assisted by numerous staff members of the
American Association of Retired Persons, including Connie
Capone, Wendy Cater, David Certner, Robert A. Harootyan, Phyllis
Hines-Perdue, Craig Hoogstra, Joan Kelly, Evelyn Morton, Thomas
Otwell, Dr. Sara E. Rix, and Dr. Martin Sicker. I received a warm
welcome from everyone I met at Home Shopping Network, includ-

ing Darryl L. Baker, Mount Burns Jr., Melanie McCarthy, and Dr. Edward M. Vaughn Jr.

To all those who offered encouragement, advice, hospitality, a sounding board, and a helping hand, I am deeply indebted: Cleveland Amory and his guardian angel Marian Probst, Art, Bill, Joe S., Cheryl F., Bob F., Jeff Cohen, Dick, Joe W., Ellen S., Paul S., Joel Fischer, the Rev. Edwin Grant, Jean B., David B., John G., Joy and Larry, Marc Kaminsky, Nancy, Richard Kostelanetz, Donald Lyons, Susan Moldow, Dr. Muriel Oberleder, Orly and Larry, William D. Phillips, Ruth, Ellen C., R. Shmuel, and Susan B.

Carl-Alfred Meier, M.D., Professor Emeritus of Psychology at the Federal Institute of Technology, Zurich, born in 1904, taught me that old age is a time to "get ready." Norman Alfred, whose driver's license says he was born in 1908, was an inspiration. Maxwell Herman provided astute insights.

I wish to express my appreciation to the expert staff of Harper-Collins Publishers, and especially to my intrepid editor, Eamon Dolan, whose enthusiasm and creativity added immeasurably to this book.

Last but most, I thank my family, without whose support this book would not have been possible.

PREFACE

SHELTER

I started volunteering at the Senior Shelter on Monday evenings back in 2014. I got a lot out of helping people my age and usually stayed till lights-out at 9:30. I was thankful that I was doing well financially, still working part-time out of my home office, and I found it satisfying to be able to share my good spirits. But I also received something important in return. Despite the suffering—more than twelve hundred people who'd had it all, the houses, the cars, the vacations, the toys, but now in their sixties, seventies, and eighties had to fit everything they owned underneath the kind of beds they'd slept on in the expensive summer camps they'd gone to and sent their kids to, lined up in endless rows in a cavernous, drafty, echoing building that used to be a defense electronics plant—amid all that misery, there was an odd sense of harmony.

It reminded me a little of the late 1960s and early 1970s, when most of these people were in their teens and twenties. People in the shelter would start talking with you as if they'd known you all their lives. People would put their arms around newcomers to comfort them. Whites who'd known minorities only as their gardeners and maids would hold them and say, "Go ahead and cry. It's nothing to be ashamed of," and then sometimes they'd start crying too. Every once in a while I'd get a little weepy myself. "How can it be that after seventy-five years I feel like a stranger in this world?" a man asked me once, showing me a picture of his dead wife, and my eyes filled right up.

Mostly what I did was shop for them. They'd give me lists of things they needed—writing paper and denture adhesive, lipstick and hearing-aid batteries, Kleenex and Depends. There was a store in one corner of the shelter, but it was poorly stocked, and the residents didn't like going there because a staff member would call you in and say, "According to this printout you've spent more than a hundred dollars in the minimart in the past two months. Now don't tell me you're buying for other people. I wasn't born yesterday— I'm as old as you are. We know from the sign-in database that your grandchildren visit you about once a month. Obviously they've been giving you pocket money. To qualify to stay here, your Maximum Overall Retained Asset Level is twenty-five dollars. Obviously you've had more than that in your possession at various times.

"Now we're here to help you, not hassle you. But I've got to warn you, if the security company the county has brought in to deal with MORAL violations shakes the building down and finds more than twenty-five dollars among your belongings, you're going to end up like those old people who stand on traffic islands in the cold wearing cardboard signs that say WILL WORK FOR MEDICINE. Personally, I don't care if you've got a billion in a Swiss bank and live here because you get off on waiting twenty minutes to use a toilet. But the county's under a lot of pressure from taxpayers. They call this 'the Gimme Shelter.' Plenty of them are people your age who say 'We're the ants, the ones who saved for the winter in Aesop's fable, and a lot of us still have to work to make ends meet. Why should we be taxed to the max to keep a roof over the heads of all those grasshoppers in the Senior Shelters? A lot of them used to live better than we do now!' If it was me, hey. But it's not, it's the Department of Social Services, and if the county fires me, I'll be living in here with you. So spend it outside the building, okay? And if you're going to stash your cash in your shoes—don't take 'em off when you go to bed."

But spending it outside the building wasn't easy because for a resident to own a car would be a gross violation of the twenty-five-dollar MORAL, and every time the county opened another shelter, bus service was cut further. Then there were the homeless people who were camped out in front with signs on their plastic-sheet lean-tos that said things like, IN ONLY 35 YEARS I'LL BE OLD ENOUGH TO SLEEP IN THIS SHELTER. Every once in a while there'd be a scuffle between people from the shelter and the under-sixty-five homeless and someone would wind up in the ER with a black eye or a split lip.

So they'd give me their lists and their pitiful excess "assets," and over the course of the week I'd pick up what they needed. If I was short on time, I'd reluctantly break my rule against setting foot inside a Walkmart (after Wal-Mart merged with Kmart in 2009, I decided it was time to shop in cozier venues) and buy everything in one trip. One night after I parked outside the megastore I found my path blocked by three Senior Sinisters, one of whom stuck a pistol in my belly and grinned, "Time for our cost-of-living adjustment, asshole." It was so incongruous—a woman who looked like Aunt Maude in a Norman Rockwell, and two benign-looking white-haired gents in car coats, except one of them was shoving a Glock in my gut. I gave them my wallet, which had in it the money that belonged to people in the shelter. After my heart stopped pounding I drove home to get my wife's ATM card so I could get enough cash to do the shopping. "And what do they do when they catch people like that here in Blade Runner Land?" she said. "They put them on probation, because so many prisons are being turned into Senior Shelters!"

After I'd deliver their orders I'd sit awhile and listen to their stories. "The day they came to put me out of my house—two boys in a monster pickup with flames airbrushed on the sides, carrying baseball bats—I was never so mortified in my whole life! Imagine what the neighbors must have been thinking. So I pulled myself together and said, 'Put away the sports equipment, will you? This isn't Little League, it's evicting an old man with a wife in a nursing home for falling behind on credit cards he was using to buy food.'"

I'd sit there trying to think of some way to help, but generally, all I could do was hold their hands—usually figuratively, but many times literally.

"I was an account executive at an advertising agency," one woman told me. "My husband's last job was running the management information system for a distributor of office supplies. We made a good living, and we saved a fair amount—at least we thought we did. But by the time we'd put three kids through grad school, we'd sold the place at the lake and borrowed the equity out of our home and were back to square one financially. Then my mother got sick, and my younger daugther got divorced and moved back in with us with her two kids, and then my husband died. . . . Oh, Craig, I don't want to bring you down. It's sweet of you to come here, and if everyone here told you their tale of woe. . . ."

There were tears in her eyes and I reached over and pressed one of her hands between mine.

"I've tried not to just wallow. When they had the Mature Mothers' March in 2015 I dragged myself onto a chartered bus and went. You should have heard us—all those threadbare voices singing 'America the Beautiful.' It reminded me of when I was a kid and demonstrated for civil rights and against Vietnam, except in those days I thought we were going to win, but this time I knew we were going to lose. A lot of politicians came out in front of the Lincoln Memorial and spoke to the crowd—I mean, there were nearly four hundred thousand of us, they couldn't exactly ignore us. The general tone was, 'We'd like to help, but people in their twenties, thirties, forties, and fifties aren't willing to pay any more taxes, and they've discovered that when they get out and vote, there are more of them than there are of you. So enjoy the nation's capital, watch your back for Senior Sinisters, and have a nice ride home.'

"Remember when Bob Dylan sang 'A Hard Rain's Gonna Fall'? We all thought he meant it was going to fall on—I don't know. The Military-Industrial Complex. The Ku Klux Klan. It never occurred to us that Dylan was trying to warn us. The hard rain wasn't going to fall on someone else. It was going to fall on us!"

I heard the sound of rain on the roof, and suddenly I could feel it, not rain exactly but a fine spray, which I thought was strange, and then I remembered I was sleeping next to an open window, and woke up and shut it with an unwrinkled hand.

INTRODUCTION

_.._.._.._.._.._.._.._.._.._.._.._.._.._.._.._.._.._

DUMPIES

I have discovered that one of the most important characteristics of most economic trends is that they are too slow in their motion to be visible to humans. . . . Humans do not get out of the way of that which they cannot see moving.

—R. Buckminster Fuller, _Critical Path_

_.._.._.._.._.._.._.._.._.._.._.._.._.._.._.._.._.._

The preface to this book is fiction, but the plight it dramatizes will be a fact.

Some of us used to be called hippies or yuppies. Many baby boomers who as you read these words are out there driving around in great cars, wearing great clothes, are going to end up picking through dumpsters for cans to sell and scraps to eat. They're so busy shooting the rapids of Decade X that they don't realize they're headed over the falls. They're going to end up as what I call "dumpies": destitute unprepared mature people.

They will be victims of the retirement myth.

Will you?

America's fiscal problems are going to be solved. The deficit is going to be reduced and possibly eliminated. The national debt will no longer spiral upward. But this positive development is going to end retirement as we know it.

Retirement has become a norm so normal, an expectation so expected, that it's hard to imagine what life could be like without it. Yet mass retirement—that's what I call it; until now the assumption that the average person will be able to stop working and turn to a life of leisure has had no name, just as fish have no name for water—is a tradition without a history. All Americans now receiving Social Security based on their own work record are older than the system itself, which was created in 1935 and paid its first benefits in

1940. And when we're older, mass retirement will be thought of as bound to an era, the way we think of Prohibition or fallout shelters.

Human resource executives are in a position to know what their employees' retirement prospects are. The benefit consultants they retain tell them how much their employees will be getting from Social Security. And they have a pretty good idea of how much of a pension each employee will receive—because they're the ones who designed the pension plan.

William M. Mercer, Inc., is one of the nation's foremost benefit consulting firms, with a staff of more than seven thousand in offices in forty-six U.S. cities, serving more than nine thousand corporate clients. It has an entire Social Security Division, headquartered in Louisville, Kentucky. Recently Mercer reported the results of a survey it conducted of human resource executives of major companies. A majority said that their typical salaried employee won't be able to afford to retire at age sixty-five in the year 2000.

Mercer titled its survey report *Retirement Security: Are All Bets Off?* The answer, in a word: Yes.

People whose jobs include thinking about how Americans will provide for their needs when they're older are mostly found at firms like Mercer and at universities, think tanks, and government agencies. They use a shorthand term among themselves: "the three-legged stool of retirement income." For example, a recent Employee Benefit Research Institute report noted, "Over the last three decades the traditional 'three-legged stool' of income security—Social Security, employer pensions, and personal saving—has insured an adequate retirement for an increasing share of Americans." A Pension Research Council publication observed, "An often-used metaphor for describing the retirement-income system in the United States is the three-legged stool. The first leg is Social Security and government welfare programs for the aged, the second is employer- or labor union–provided pensions, and the third is direct individual saving."

Believers of the retirement myth think that the "three-legged stool" is sturdy. So the first thing we're going to do in this book is check it out. If even one of its legs is rickety, we're going to have a problem.

Are any of them less than solid?

Unfortunately, yes.

How many?
All three.

- Social Security benefits may appear untouchable for the moment, but they'll have to be cut before 76 million baby boomers become eligible to receive them.
- Baby boomers' pensions are going to be far from sufficient.
- Their savings will seldom be enough to close the gap.

Yet when the baby boomers are older, they'll require more financial resources than any previous generation, because they're going to live longer than any previous generation. Their need for income is going to cause an unprecedented economic crisis.

The aging of the baby boomers is going to trigger the skyscraper-toppling financial aftershock of what the media of the 1960s called the "youthquake." This time it's going to be the Big One.

When terrorists truly want to make a mess, they set off a small explosion in a downtown street at lunchtime, injuring a few dozen people. The blast draws a crowd of rubberneckers, police, EMS personnel, bomb investigators, media crews, and, if the perpetrators are lucky, political figures to the scene. Then a Semtex-packed van that's been parked near the scene all along is detonated, killing and maiming hundreds. The baby boom generation is an economic truck bomb timed to go off early in the twenty-first century. Its biological clock is relentlessly ticking. In this book, we're going to examine the device and try, ever so carefully, to defuse it.

- We're going to take a rare look at the alarming data contained in the "Pentagon Papers of Social Security," which show why the system's benefits will inevitably be cut.
- We're going to meet the man who, six decades ago, helped create Social Security and find out how he proposes to deal with the system's impending shortfall.
- We're going to find out why the baby boom generation's passage through the private pension system is likely to cause a multidecade economic downturn that will make the Great Depression look like a shallow dip.
- We're going to discover that having enough income when we're older will be literally a matter of life and death.

- We're going to see that it will be vital for us to have the opportunity to work when we're older if we want to or need to.
- Above all, we're going to be relieved to learn that we'll be able to thrive in the future if we start getting ready now.

You can take the first step in preparing for that future by realizing that one of these days, you and I are going to be old.

We know this but often we forget it. It's hard to remember the future, because it hasn't happened yet.

We aren't going to be "senior citizens." We aren't going to be "golden agers." We aren't going to be any kind of euphemism. We're going to be ourselves, older.

I could have said that you and I are going to be old "sooner than we think." But it won't happen sooner than we think. It will happen sooner than we feel. We know we're going to be old, but we don't feel our knowledge. Perhaps we have an inner mechanism that protects us from really feeling that we're going to be old, because the feeling could overwhelm us.

Economists even have a name for the fact that many people behave financially as if they never expect to be old: "myopia." It's the same word eye doctors use when someone's nearsighted.

This book is about realizing that whether we're in our twenties, thirties, forties, fifties, or older, we can begin too late to make sure we have a diversity of economic resources when we're old, but we can't begin too early.

Maybe you have a 401(k) and an IRA. Perhaps you've even sought out information on preparing for your later years. All this is good but not enough. We're living in a time of global political and technological change so swift and sweeping that yesterday's rational retirement plan has become a parachute that won't open.

The purpose of this book is to help you deal with a new reality: That in the rapidly reconfiguring world into which we find ourselves plunging, there's no such thing as a reliable blueprint for retirement. There are only sensible actions we can take now to broaden the range of economic options we'll have in the future.

From now on, attaining a comfortable later life is going to be as much of a challenge as attaining a comfortable earlier life. When you and I are older, people in their sixties, seventies, and eighties will be living just about every way we can imagine. Some will unquestionably be living the golf cart/national park/cruise-wear life we associate with today's retirees. But others will be doing everything from cooking on Sterno under the overpass to jetting into Telluride for the weekend in a Gulfstream IV.

The end of mass retirement will be, on balance, a beneficial phenomenon. Those who don't see it coming will suffer terribly. But if we prepare for it, we'll be able to build opportunities for fulfilling ourselves and contributing to others into every stage of our lives.

CHAPTER 1

2020 FORESIGHT

The current level of Social Security benefits is not sustainable. At today's Social Security tax rate, the system's cash payments will be more than its income starting in 2019. To pay benefits at their current level in 2020, when Americans born in 1955, the middle of the baby boom, turn sixty-five, would require that Social Security taxes be raised to between 25.78 and 30.21 percent of payroll. Action will be taken to bring the system into balance.

The Social Security system is on a collision course with arithmetic.

Hidden in plain sight, on the last page of the last document any American wants to look at—your annual income tax package—is a pie chart showing that "Social Security, Medicare, and other retirement" now eat up the biggest slice of the budget (35 percent), followed by defense (24 percent) and interest on the national debt (14 percent).

And if you're concerned about the spiraling national debt, the numbers speak for themselves. To the left of the pie chart the text indicates a deficit of $255 billion . . . and spending on "Social Security, Medicare, and other retirement" of $500 billion.

By the time the youngest baby boomers turn sixty-five, that biggest slice will have grown to 56.3 percent of the pie if the current Social Security formula remains in place, according to the U.S. Department of Health and Human Services. Less than 4.4 percent of the U.S. budget would then be available to pay for all government functions other than those related to retirement, defense, and the national debt.

If you think that projection sounds bleak, Sen. J. Robert Kerrey (D-Nebraska), chair of the federal government's Bipartisan Commission on Entitlement and Tax Reform, said in 1994: "In 2012, when today's young children are just getting started in the labor force, there will not be one cent left over for education, children's programs, highways, national defense or any other discretionary program." According to the Commission, when the oldest baby boomers turn sixty-six in 2012, "unless appropriate policy changes are made in the interim, projected outlays for entitlements and interest on the national debt will consume all tax revenues collected by the federal government."

There is no possibility whatsoever that the generations currently slated to support aged baby boomers will allow federal spending on everything from the fight against crime to medical research to the war on drugs to air traffic control to food stamps to the national parks to dwindle to a few pennies on the dollar, let alone to nothing. Younger Americans are going to insist on putting an end to the "pay and play" system, in which they pay and older people play.

Those who are already retired should not have their benefits reduced, from the standpoint of either practical politics or simple morality. They played by the rules, and they should be paid by the rules. But the oblong slips of paper that arrive in the mailboxes of Social Security recipients each month are unreality checks.

A 1994 Urban Institute report calculated that "in 2030, additional resources equal to roughly 6.1 percent of GDP [Gross Domestic Product] would have to be diverted from other uses to provide the OASDI [Social Security cash benefits] and Medicare benefits promised under current law. . . . [T]o pay for these costs through taxes would require changes equivalent to a 71 percent increase in individual income taxes."

The Bipartisan Commission on Entitlement and Tax Reform issued an even more startling prediction of the increase in the total federal tax rate that would be required to balance the budget in 2030 if spending were to stay on its present course: 100 percent.

Tomorrow's young and middle-aged will not allow themselves to be taxed at confiscatory rates as each working couple is required to carry one Social Security recipient. Americans in their twenties, thirties, forties, and fifties will be looking at what was once a sacred cow and seeing hamburger.

Here's another way of gauging the unsustainability of leg number one of the "three-legged stool of retirement income": The amount paid out in Social Security old-age cash benefits is today equal to what's being spent on education by all levels of government—federal, state, and local. An analysis by a team including Harvard Professor David A. Wise, area director for Health and Retirement Programs at the National Bureau of Economic Research, has found that by the time the youngest baby boomers turn seventy-five, current law would cause total Social Security old-age cash benefits to be three times more than government spending on schools if Americans adopt optimal control of health risk factors (e.g., high blood pressure, high cholesterol, smoking, lack of exercise) in the years to come. If our NordicTrack, Soloflex, and StairMaster routines work out the way we hope, we're going to end up physically fit and fiscally unfit.

So whether we like it or not, Social Security is going to be scaled down. But the prospect of having to pay the freight for the huge baby boom generation in its old age is so dismal it obscures an ongoing demographic trend that's even more bleak: The proportion of younger people in the population is steadily dropping in relation to the proportion of older people. The Social Security Administration's "best estimates" predict that the fertility rate, now below the population replacement level of 2.1 births per woman, will continue to fall over the next two decades to 1.9. Meanwhile, additional life expectancy at age sixty-five is ratcheting up each year by seventy-two days. Unless productivity rises dramatically, any government that promises an entitlement to affluent relaxation to a growing portion of its people for a growing portion of their lives will spend itself into insolvency. This is not a matter of politics. It's a matter of mathematics.

Social Security's finances are out of whack because life expectancy has gone up more in this century than in all previous history—from forty-six years for men and forty-eight years for women in 1900 to seventy-two and seventy-nine years, respectively, today. In 1935, the year the Social Security Act was passed, it was sixty for men and sixty-three for women. Most potential recipients were expected to be conveniently dead and buried before they turned sixty-five. Few Americans imagined that the program would ever be called upon to support dozens of millions of older people. In 1945 there were only 771,000 retirees, spouses of retirees, and widows or widowers of retirees collecting Social Security. Today there are more than 35 million. In 2045, says the Social Security Administration, there will be 72 million.

The U.S. population in 1945 was slightly over 133 million. The current population is slightly over 262 million. The Census Bureau estimates that the population in 2045 will be slightly under 375 million. So in 2045 there will be almost 100 times as many people receiving Social Security as there were in 1945—yet America's population will have less than tripled. And the number of people collecting Social Security in 2045 will be more than 200 percent what it is today, despite the fact that the overall population is projected to increase by less than 50 percent.

I'm not advocating that Social Security benefits be cut. I'm a weatherman, not a rainmaker. I'm standing in front of the satellite map pointing to a demographic low pressure area moving in from the early 1970s. I'm not in favor of the prevailing winds—I'm just reporting their direction and velocity.

Some government officials are either less knowledgeable or less candid. Social Security Commissioner Shirley S. Chater told *AARP Bulletin,* the American Association of Retired Persons' monthly news report, in 1994, "My children [Cris and Geoffrey, both in their early thirties] feel that [Social Security] won't be there for them in the long term. . . . I ask them if they have U.S. savings bonds. They say of course they do. I point out that Social Security is as safe as those bonds."

Well, I hope Cris and Geoffrey are socking away plenty of those Series EEs for their old age, because their mom, a former university president with no professional background in finance, was mistaken. A savings bond is a legally binding document requiring the government to pay interest linked to the Treasury bill rate, with an unchangeable minimum, unlike Social Security benefits, which can be cut by Congress at any time.

The root cause of the weakness of the check-is-in-the-mail portion of Social Security is that the baby boomers are being followed by much smaller generations. In the pungent words of Nathan Keyfitz, Professor of Demography and Sociology at Harvard, "The situation is that of a chain-letter scheme, in which the first receivers of the letter faithfully send their dollars in the hope of recouping later from others, but not enough people can be found to continue the process."

We've heard that the best kind of money to invest is OPM—other people's money. The Social Security system pays its benefits using OGM—other generations' money. The problem is that the number of younger people from whose salaries the government can take out the payroll taxes it uses to pay cash benefits to older people is shrinking. According to the Social Security Administration, the ratio of "covered workers" to each beneficiary will drop from 3.2 in 1995 to 2.0 in 2030.

This decline means that:

(a) payroll taxes will have to be increased by roughly 60 percent, so that they'll be about 160 percent of what they are today (3.2 divided by 2.0); or

(b) cash benefits will have to be decreased by roughly 37.5 percent, so that they'll be about 62.5 percent of what they are today (2.0 divided by 3.2); or

(c) some combination of (a) and (b) that will have the same effect.

The exact amount of the tax hike, benefit cut, or combination will depend on many factors, ranging from certainties (e.g., the current payroll tax is somewhat higher than is needed to pay for current benefits) to uncertainties (e.g., future economic performance). But dividing 3.2 by 2.0 and 2.0 by 3.2 puts us in the ballpark.

And though half of the payroll tax that goes to Social Security cash benefits is paid by employers under current law, there's no guarantee that in the future workers won't have to pay a higher proportion. In any event, as Nobel Prize–winning economist Franco Modigliani of MIT has pointed out, "[T]here is reason to believe that eventually even the half that is paid by the employer tends to be shifted onto higher prices, and therefore finally into lower real wages."

I want to make it clear that while the term "Social Security" is often used in popular parlance to refer only to the check-in-the-mailbox program whose legal name is Old-Age and Survivors Insurance, we'll be using it as sophisticated analysts do—to include both cash and medical benefits.

Because of a kind of cultural lag, and the catchy name that got tacked onto the medical care programs created by the Social Security Amendments of 1965, there's a tendency to talk about Social Security and Medicare as if they were unrelated except insofar as each is an "entitlement" program. In fact, your Social Security taxes go into four separate trust funds, each with the same Board of Trustees—one for Old-Age and Survivors Insurance (OASI), one for Disability Insurance (DI), and one for each of the programs popularly referred to together as "Medicare": Hospital Insurance (HI) and Supplementary Medical Insurance (SMI).

Experts consider Social Security's cash and medical benefits as a unit. For example, the 1994 Urban Institute report explained:

> Until the mid-1960s, all Social Security payments were in the form of cash. Even after the adoption of Medicare, cash payments were dominant; they comprised about 82 percent of total Social Security expenditures as late as 1970. Today, however, cash payments have fallen to about 68 percent of total Social Security expenditures, and they are expected to fall to about half of total expenditures by 2010.

In *Status of the Social Security and Medicare Programs: A Summary of the 1994 Annual Reports,* the Board of Trustees noted:

> When considering the issue of economic security in retirement, both income and health care must be considered together because resources that are required in one area will not be available in the other. Yet, the research and policy discussion on retirement income issues seldom reflects this interrelationship.

Americans have come to expect that a major portion of older people's medical bills should be paid by somebody besides older people. Even if Medicare is folded into some other framework in a future round of health care reform, the cost of the services it now provides will have to be financed somehow. So as we begin to examine the future of Social Security, let's assume that financing health care for older Americans remains part of Social Security. Any other assumption complicates the question without simplifying the answer.

The combined "cost rate" of Social Security's cash and medical benefits as a percentage of annual taxable payroll has been officially projected as far as 2020, the year in which people born in 1954 will turn sixty-six and be eligible to receive both. Every four years the secretary of health and human services is required to appoint a watchdog group known as the Advisory Council on Social Security. The 1991 Advisory Council was a largely honorific thirteen-member body (one might say, a thirteen-body body) that included such non-experts as the chairman of a drug company, a union president, and the CEO of the American Stock Exchange. But the group took its job seriously. It appointed two "technical panels" of real authorities: one to project the cash-benefit part of the system out to 2020 and one to do the same for the medical-benefit portion. When the Advisory Council met to review the panels' reports, its members added up the percentages of taxable payroll the two panels found would be needed to finance Social Security's benefits in 2020.

The total came to about 25 percent.

The Advisory Council's members were appalled. One-quarter of most salaries and wages earned by Americans gobbled up by Social Security for the baby boomers? The panels' forecast sounded like something out of an op-ed piece by Social Security critic Peter G. Peterson, the former U.S. secretary of commerce who cofounded the antideficit Concord Coalition.

The Council responded by drafting a dream team: the Expert Panel on the Future of Income Security and Health Care Financing. The Expert Panel was headed by Prof. Peter Diamond, chair of the Department of Economics at MIT. Its members included some of the savviest economists and actuaries on earth. They were told to crunch the numbers unflinchingly, and they did.

The group's findings were quietly distributed to a limited number of recipients in December 1991 under the title *Income Security and Health Care: Economic Implications 1991–2020—An Expert Panel Report to the Advisory Council on Social Security*. A copy is about as easy to come by as a Dead Sea Scroll. I got mine by driving on icy roads to a major research university and borrowing the irreplaceable bound original belonging to a member of the Expert Panel, who looked at me like I was asking him to lend me his wife. Two hundred thirty-nine photocopies later, snow-blind from the strobing of the Xerox machine, breathing hard from the dash back to the man's office, I had the feeling that he'd been just about to dial the campus police and have me hauled in for report-napping.

Income Security and Health Care: Economic Implications 1991–2020 is the ultimate inside-baseball account of Social Security. It's more troubling than anything by the system's critics because it comes from those charged with maintaining it, not those who'd like to see it downsized.

This little-known document—I call it the "Pentagon Papers of Social Security"—sounded an alarm that should have been been heard around the nation. Warning that its projections were "dramatic," "alarming," and "dire," the Expert Panel predicted that the correct future cost rate wasn't a grim 25 percent of taxable payroll. By 2020, it said, a brain-numbing 31.57 percent of taxable payroll would be needed to finance Social Security.

The 31.57 percent forecast assumed what the Expert Panel characterized as a rate of medical cost increases "slower than the past decade but consistent with longer-term trends." If there could be a "significant slowing of existing trends" of medical increases, the all-stars explained, the percentage of taxable wages needed to pay benefits in 2020 might conceivably rise to as low as 26.50 percent.

Figures like these had been cited by critics of Social Security for years but dismissed as Chicken Little material by mainstream observers. Now the mainstream observers were being warned by their own blue-ribbon panel that the sky was falling.

To get an idea of the percentage of payroll that would have to be devoted to Social Security in 2020 to keep benefits at current levels, three updates need to be made to the 1991 Expert Panel's forecast. First, when the Expert Panel made its projections, the maximum salary subject to Social Security's Hospital Insurance ("Medicare Part A") tax was $125,000. This cap was removed in 1993, increasing total taxable payroll somewhat and thus lowering the percentage required in 2020. Second, the Expert Panel included in its calculations of the total cost of Social Security's Supplementary Medical Insurance ("Medicare Part B") the premiums paid by people over sixty-five. Congressional practice has been to adjust SMI premiums to cover about one-quarter of the program's cost, which has to be subtracted from the Expert Panel's 2020 forecast. Third, the Social Security Board of Trustees' *1994 Annual Report*'s "best estimates" forecast was that the cost of Social Security's cash-benefit program in 2020 will be 14.96 percent of taxable payroll, 1 percent higher than the 1991 projection used by the Expert Panel. Making these adjustments brings Social Security benefits as a percentage of taxable payroll in 2020 to between 25.78 percent and 30.21 percent.

Let's compare these figures with what we're paying now. Social Security taxes currently consist of the following, split between our employers and ourselves, or paid entirely by us if we're self-employed:

- 12.4 percent of an annually increased maximum amount of wages ($61,200 in 1995), earmarked for paying for Social Security's cash-benefit program ("Old-Age, Survivors, and Disability Insurance" or "OASDI").
- 2.9 percent of our entire salary, earmarked for paying for Social Security's Hospital Insurance (HI) benefits.

In addition, each Medicare Part B enrollee pays a premium, currently $46.10 a month, which the federal government matches out of general revenues on a roughly 3 to 1 basis, i.e., about $1,300 a year per individual sixty-five and over.

The 12.4 percent tax rate brings in more money than is now being paid out in monthly checks. The excess is invested by the Social Security Administration in interest-paying "special public-debt obligations" (SPDOs) issued by the U.S. Treasury. The Treasury immediately spends the cash it receives for these SPDOs on general government expenditures. The SPDOs owned by the Social Security Administration make up the "trust funds" about which so much has been written but so little is understood. The Social Security trust funds constitute the most egregious case of creative accounting in public life today. Destructive accounting, actually, because the very mention of the trust funds has the ability to turn the human mind to tofu.

The best way of thinking about the trust funds is not to think about them at all. The second best way of thinking about the trust funds is to imagine you've got a cookie jar in which you're putting money aside for a rainy day—in this case, a rainy fifty years, because that's about how long it's going to take all the boomers to pass through the Social Security system. Every time you put a dollar in the jar, you immediately borrow it back from yourself to buy gas, rent videos, and have your hair done. Each time you instantly whip out the dollar bill you just put in, you replace it with an I-O-U (more precisely, an I-O-ME) for $1.00.

Question: Is the total value of the markers in the jar too much, too little, or just right?

Answer: Irrelevant and immaterial. On that rainy day, you're going to need folding money, which is going to have to come from somewhere else besides the jar.

The liberal Urban Institute summed up the situation we're facing:

> If Social Security is to pay out the benefits it has promised to the baby boom generation, moreover, the federal government will have to find money to repay what it borrowed from the trust funds, with interest. The only way it will be able to make up for the lost surpluses and repay the trust funds is to increase other taxes, cut other spending, and/or increase the deficit still further.

The lowdown on the trust funds is contained in the Social Security Board of Trustees' *Status of the Social Security and Medicare Programs: A Summary of the 1994 Annual Reports*:

> For the combined OASI and DI trust funds, the year of exhaustion is 2029—in thirty-five years. However, combined OASDI expenditures [Social Security cash benefits] will exceed current tax income beginning in 2013. Thus, current tax income plus a portion of annual interest income will be needed to meet expenditures for years 2013 through 2018, and current tax income, annual interest income, plus a portion of the principal balance in the trust funds will be needed for years 2019–2029.

Social Security's Board of Trustees is warning us that if nothing is done, beginning in 2019, the year after Americans born after 1955—the middle of the baby boom—become eligible to collect cash benefits at sixty-two, the age at which most people begin receiving them, the system will be paying out more than it will be taking in.

But something will be done.

CHAPTER 2

THE UNKINDEST CUTS

Two ways the Social Security system can be brought into balance are by raising taxes and by cutting and postponing benefits. It's doubtful whether taxes can be raised. Benefits have already been cut, and are likely to be cut more in the future.

The financing of the Social Security system is going to be reformed, and reform is going to mean benefit cuts.

Here's what researchers told a conference in Tokyo cosponsored by the prestigious Cambridge, Massachusetts–based National Bureau of Economic Research and the Japan Center for Economic Research in 1993 about leg number one of the "three-legged stool of retirement income":

> Every bit of evidence available to national policy makers today indicates that Social Security will not be able to provide the benefits currently being promised to the baby boom generation. . . . Given the size of the baby boom generation and potential adjustment that may be required in their Social Security benefit expectations, it seems imperative that policy makers begin to address the funding of the baby boomers' benefits as soon as possible so they will have the maximum amount of time to adjust their other retirement savings relative to more realistic Social Security promises.

Actuaries—the experts who calculate insurance and annuity premiums and reserves—agree with the economists. In 1993 the American Academy of Actuaries issued a report entitled *Social Security: Will It Live Up to the Baby Boom Generation's Expectations?*

> How is this program, which affects so many Americans and on which the majority of Americans will rely for a significant portion of

their retirement income, likely to perform in the future? The short answer to this question is that the program will be here for all Americans for the generations to come and that Social Security payout will continue to be a substantial and even growing proportion of governmental expenditures. The more complex answer is that for many Americans Social Security will replace less of pre-retirement earnings than it does now. Even without changes in the current program, this would be true because of an already legislated higher required retirement age for full benefits and the taxation of benefits. But of equal importance are the many pressures that are likely to result in further reductions in benefits.

I asked political consultant James Carville, a key strategist in the 1992 Clinton campaign, how he thinks Social Security's financing problems will be resolved. "It'll be like anything else in politics," Carville replied. "There'll be some kind of compromise. Part of it will involve raising taxes, and part of it will involve cutting benefits."

RAISING SOCIAL SECURITY TAXES?

It's conceivable that Social Security payroll taxes could be increased somewhat. The question is, by how much?

The payroll tax originally passed in 1935 was 2 percent on the first $3,000 in earnings—a maximum of $60 a year. By 1966, the first year after the Hospital Insurance tax, then 0.7 percent, was added, the rate totaled 8.4 percent on a maximum of $6,600 in wages— $554.40 a year. In 1995 the tax totaled 15.3 percent on the first $61,200 of salary—$9,363.60—plus an additional 2.9 percent on earnings above $61,200. So in the past three decades the OASDI tax has gone up by 61 percent, applied against a salary base that has increased by 927 percent (more than twice as much as inflation), while the HI tax has more than quadrupled and is applied to every penny we earn. Somewhere there's a limit.

The limit will be determined by the public's perception of whether it will be getting its money's worth out of government in general and Social Security in particular.

If we haven't already reached the latter limit, it isn't far away.

• A series of surveys by Merrill Lynch has been asking whether people agree with the statement "I don't expect to get out of Social Security anywhere near the amount I have put into it." The number agreeing has increased from year to year. In the most recent poll, published in 1993, it was 76 percent.

• A 1993 survey by Yankelovich Partners for Phoenix Home Life Mutual Insurance found that 80 percent of Americans thirty to thirty-five years old are "concerned that Social Security will be bankrupt"; 76 percent of those aged thirty-six to forty, and 66 percent of those forty-one to fifty feel the same way. While 64 percent said their confidence in Social Security had decreased over the past five years, only 4 percent said their confidence had increased.

• A 1993 Gallup poll found that only 49 percent of Americans "expressed confidence that the Social Security system will be able to pay them a benefit when they retire."

• The National Taxpayers Union's 1993 *Survey on Retirement Confidence* stated, "About two-thirds of Americans over age 25 are not confident that either the Social Security system (65 percent) or the Medicare system (66 percent) will continue to provide benefits of equal value to the benefits received by retirees today. While roughly one-quarter of the respondents indicate being 'somewhat' confident that Social Security (24 percent) and Medicare (24 percent) will provide equal benefits, few [5–7 percent] say they are 'very' confident."

• A 1993 survey by Colonial Life & Accident Insurance and the Employers Council on Flexible Compensation asked one thousand employees, "For every $100 you and your employer pay into Social Security, how much do you expect to get back after you retire?" Only 20 percent answered $100 or more, and 10 percent said $51 to $99. Fifty-two percent expected to get back less than $50, and 18 percent expected to receive nothing at all.

These surveys show that Americans are more pessimistic about Social Security than is called for by the facts. The chance of receiving zero from Social Security is zero. But for many people, the rate of "return" on Social Security will actually have a minus in front of it. Future recipients with relatively high incomes who live in two-earner families or are single are highest on the list of those who won't get out of Social Security what they put into it, the Urban Institute reports.

For example, take a couple in which one spouse earned the highest salary subject to Social Security cash-benefit taxation in 1994 ($60,600) and the other earned the average 1994 U.S. salary (about $24,500). If they retire at sixty-five in 2030, they'll receive benefits worth 26 percent less than the taxes they paid into the system.

And the days when a typical American could "earn" 5 to 6 percent on Social Security taxes—the "investment return" received by average couples who turned sixty-five in 1980—are gone. If the system's benefits were to stay at today's levels, Social Security taxes would "earn" average two-worker couples who reach sixty-five in 2010 a real, inflation-adjusted lifetime annual return of between 1.45 and 2.52 percent. Those skimpy rates are already scheduled by law to drop still further for younger Americans.

The Colonial Life survey asked, "If the government provided for the majority of retirement needs for most people, would you be willing to pay higher taxes and more into Social Security?" A majority said no. Participants were then asked, "Do you think that dollars invested for retirement are better put into Social Security or an employer pension or retirement plan?" An overwhelming 80 percent said they'd rather see their money go into an employer-sponsored plan.

With "returns" so low, and employee resistance to paying into the system so high, not only is it doubtful whether Social Security taxes can be raised by much but pressure may even develop to lower them.

A sobering thought for anyone who believes that when the baby boomers are older they'll be able to use their voting power to impose higher Social Security taxes on younger generations: When most baby boomers are sixty-five and over, they'll make up about 22 percent of the population. But 57 percent of Americans will be eighteen through sixty-four years old. Older people have traditionally been more likely to vote than younger Americans. But if older baby boomers were to try to use raw political power to raise Social Security taxes, an increased proportion of younger people would undoubtedly find their way into voting booths.

CUTTING SOCIAL SECURITY BENEFITS?

To the extent that Social Security taxes can't be raised, benefits will be cut and/or postponed.

There exists a myth of an omnipotent Gray Lobby capable of mobilizing enough votes to make legislators cry, "I've fallen and I can't get up!" This doddering juggernaut supposedly has the clout to crush any politician who would "tamper with Social Security." I know I'm not going to be able to convince everyone that this is pure bosh, because there are plenty of folks out there who firmly believe in the Abominable Snowman, and photos that purport to show the AARP's Washington headquarters are usually in a lot better focus than the snapshots I've seen of Bigfoot. But I'll try.

During its 1977 session, Congress adjusted downward the benefit formula enacted as part of the 20 percent across-the-board increase passed in 1972, because it would eventually have caused benefits to increase faster than inflation. According to economist Gary Burtless of the Brookings Institution, "The 1977 Social Security amendments actually reduced benefits for workers reaching age sixty-five in 1982 and later years below the level received by earlier cohorts of retirees." Having finally, after forty-two years, summoned up the courage to cut Social Security benefits, lawmakers discovered something interesting: The world didn't end. Emboldened by that discovery, Congress has been whittling away at the system's benefits ever since.

• In 1980 Congress reduced benefits to newly disabled workers.

• In 1981 Congress raised the Medicare Part B deductible to $75, eliminated the provision that had allowed expenses incurred in the previous year to be counted toward the current year's deductible, increased Part A coinsurance, and eliminated coverage for alcoholism treatment.

• In 1983 Congress delayed cost-of-living-adjustments (COLAs) for six months, thereby permanently reducing benefits for all current and future recipients; shifted indexing of benefits from being based only on the Consumer Price Index (CPI) to the lower of the CPI or wage growth; raised the age of eligibility for full benefits above sixty-five for everyone born after 1937, with gradual increases to age sixty-seven for people born after 1959; cut benefits for those starting to collect at age sixty-two beginning in 2003 by changing today's 20 percent reduction for early retirement to 30 percent in 2027; and subjected 50 percent of benefits to income tax for those whose "provisional income" (i.e., their income including half their Social Security benefits) was more than $25,000 for an individual or $32,000 for a couple.

• In 1984 Congress reduced Part B's payment for medical equipment required for home health care from 100 percent of "costs" to 80 percent of "reasonable charges."

• In 1986 Congress increased the Part A deductible and ended waiver of the Part B deductible and coinsurance for outpatient surgery.

• In 1987 Congress restricted eligibility for Part B home health care.

• In 1989 Congress reinstated the Part A requirement that skilled nursing facility services be preceded by a hospital stay, and reduced home health services from the previously increased figure of thirty-eight days to twenty-one days.

• In 1990 Congress raised the Part B deductible to $100. More ominously, the Omnibus Budget Reconciliation Act of 1990 cut payments to Medicare health care providers by $34 billion over the following five years. According to a Senate committee report, "A convincing argument can be made that cuts to providers eventually filter their way down to [the] beneficiary in the form of higher costs, reduced access, or lower quality." While there were numerous extensions of Medicare coverage in the 1980s, a legislative study found that between 1981 and 1990 Congress reduced Medicare benefits by a total of 18 percent of what they would have been without the cuts.

• In 1993 Congress cut Medicare payments to providers by $56 billion over the next five years and subjected 85 percent of benefits to taxation for individuals with "provisional income" above $34,000 for singles and $44,000 for couples.

The truth is that Social Security lost its immunity to cuts and postponements in the first year of the Carter administration. Above all, taxation of benefits, introduced in 1983 and increased in 1993, was in effect a benefit reduction based on a means test. Because benefits were raised so many times in so many ways between 1935 and 1972, the public mind has developed an immunity of its own: to comprehending that "tampering with Social Security" has become as much a part of Washington life as lunching at the Jockey Club, and that benefits have taken a haircut every time Congress has touched Social Security since 1977. The House Ways and Means Committee has reported that Social Security cash benefits as a percentage of national personal income peaked in 1983 and have been dropping ever since.

Gerontologist Harry R. Moody deputy director of the Brookdale Center on Aging at New York City's Hunter College, specializes in deflating conventional notions about the role of older people in American society. He has written,

Liberals have portrayed the elderly as the deserving poor. For two generations, the aged have been an ideological loss leader for other liberal social welfare reforms. These reform measures in health care, income maintenance, and so on were originally intended to be universal but in the end were targeted at the aged as a matter of political compromise. Conservatives defeated attempts to extend liberal benefits to the jobless, minority groups, etc. But the elderly, because they were the deserving poor, could legitimately receive public benefits. Thus, national health insurance became Medicare (1965), the Guaranteed Minimum Income became SSI [Supplemental Security Income] (1971), until today age-based entitlements have become the greatest single factor of the domestic federal budget....

The broad question for American social policy in the future and for aging policy in particular, can be phrased in these terms: Will the substantial social spending of the welfare state be used to make older people more productive or will it remain bound to a view of transfer payments defended by competing interest groups in the name of a redistributive ethic?

Robert B. Hudson, Professor of Social Welfare Policy at Boston University, has written: "Policy elites—if not the general public—are pressing for cuts, limitations, and exclusions in age-related programs." It's those elites that will determine the rules of engagement for the general public. The differences of opinion among them are about the why and the how, not the whether. Conservatives determined to curtail government spending want to cut benefits—even eliminate them entirely—for all except the truly needy. Liberals want to cut benefits to people with higher incomes so they can be preserved—even increased—for those with lower incomes. A variety of methods for cutting benefits has already been put forward:

1. *Cut, freeze, or delay cost-of-living adjustments.* According to a Senate report, "In the early days of the Clinton Administration, certain advisers floated the idea of cutting Social Security cost-of-living adjustments. . . ." A similar proposal was put forward by Senators John C. Danforth (R-Missouri) and David L. Boren (D-Oklahoma) in 1993. Their "Bipartisan Alternative Budget Proposal" demonstrated that COLAs are so politically vulnerable that a Republican and a Democrat could join forces to chip away at them even though they were being accused of thwarting passage of the White House's budget merely as an oil-state tactic to prevent a broad-based energy tax. In 1994 J. J. Pickle, a senior Texas Democrat and former chair of the House Social Security subcommittee, introduced a bill to pay COLAs every two years rather than annually. In the summary of Social Security's *1994 Annual Report,* the system's public trustees referred favorably to the Pickle bill.

2. *Reduce age-sixty-two benefits.* Representative Pickle's bill would have permanently reduced by 40 percent the checks of people who choose to start collecting at age sixty-two. They're currently lowered by only 20 percent and present law schedules them to be reduced by 30 percent by 2022.

3. *Tax benefits more.* Increased taxation of recipients with moderate incomes was put in place in 1993 by a Democratic administration and a Democratic Congress. The current tax thresholds aren't indexed for inflation. This means that "bracket creep" will automatically increase the proportion of Social Security recipients subject to taxation each year. Even if future inflation were to average as low as 3.5 percent, the thresholds will drop by nearly a third in real-dollar terms every ten years. Meanwhile, the Democratic Leadership Council, which was headed by Bill Clinton before he became presi-

dent, proposed in 1994 that the insurance value of Medicare coverage be treated as taxable income.

4. *Change the benefit formula.* As a way of reducing benefits to average and higher earners while keeping them about the same for lower earners, this might go down easier than an out-and-out means test. Dallas L. Salisbury, president of the Employee Benefit Research Institute, the private pension community's main think tank, has said that for politicians "the easiest way to do it would be to change the formula because people don't understand the formula."

5. *Means-test benefits.* The Concord Coalition, a nonpartisan organization founded by Peter G. Peterson, former New Hampshire senator Warren B. Rudman, and former Massachusetts senator Paul E. Tsongas, whose goal is deficit reduction, has proposed that as part of a comprehensive means testing of entitlements, Social Security cash benefits be reduced by 10 percent of the amount that would cause family income to exceed $40,000, with the rate of reduction raised by 10 percent for each additional $10,000 in income, up to a maximum reduction of 85 percent. In 1994 the Democratic Leadership Council proposed that benefits be means-tested by denying full COLAs to higher-income recipients.

Not only does support for cutting Social Security cross party lines, but it's the apolitical types who are proposing the most dramatic reductions. The American Society of Pension Actuaries (ASPA) has warned that "the United States faces a looming retirement income crisis. . . . A generational economic conflict is inevitable unless this country takes action."

In 1994, ASPA issued a report recommending sweeping changes in how older Americans are supported. It emphasizes that major increases in other sources of later-life income will be needed to make up for the cuts the actuaries consider necessary in Social Security, and includes a schedule showing the pace at which cash benefits would be reduced:

• People born in 1930 would receive benefits at current levels.
• Those born in 1940 would receive the equivalent of 91 percent

of today's cash benefits in real, inflation-adjusted dollars.
- Those born in 1950 would receive 80 percent.
- Those born in 1960 would receive 67 percent.
- Those born in 1970 would receive 54 percent.

Actuaries tend to be quiet types. It isn't just that they're not known for going public. They're not known for existing. Yet lately they've been doing what for them is, compared to their usual hunched-over-the-books posture, the equivalent of setting themselves on fire in an attempt to get some attention focused on what they see as a disaster waiting to happen.

So in a sense, both Social Security Commissioner Chater and her kids are right. When Cris and Geoffrey are older, Social Security will indisputably "be there" in the sense that there will be a very sizeable program bearing that name. No president, no Congress is likely to violate the principle laid down five centuries ago by Machiavelli: "He who desires or attempts to reform the government of a state . . . must at least retain the semblance of the old forms, so that it may seem to the people that there has been no change in the institutions, even though in fact they are entirely different from the old ones."

But Social Security is going to be gradually restored—indeed, the restoration is already in process—to what it was originally supposed to be: a safety net, not a gravy train. The net's shape, and the number, size, and placement of its holes will be determined by the stars of C-SPAN. Because of what some will see as the political clout of those who are already retired, and others will see as a compelling moral claim, benefits for those now collecting will remain mostly untouched, while the payout to those who are only a few years away from collecting will have to be phased down imperceptibly. The rest of us have to begin planning now for a significant reduction and postponement of our own Social Security benefits. The federal government of the future isn't going to be able to guarantee us a life of golf, motor homes, and cruises to Alaska.

CHAPTER 3

THE GRAND OLD MAN OF OLD AGE

Robert J. Myers, one of the architects of Social Security and the key figure in rescuing it in 1983, emphasizes that the system can and will be adjusted to bring it into balance. Myers favors doing this by raising the age of eligibility for full benefits. His approach is widely accepted, and when the system is rebalanced, increasing the "Normal Retirement Age" is likely to be part of the package.

The man who invented retirement as we know it has no plans to retire.

Robert J. Myers has said that the two institutions for which he has the greatest affection are Lehigh University and Social Security. The first helped create him; the second he helped create. Maybe it's because he loves Social Security so much that, though he was born in 1912, he's still paying taxes into it.

Myers isn't what most people would call a household name. But in the households of those who make policy about later-life income, he's *the* household name. The author of the standard text on the subject, a thick volume called, simply, *Social Security,* Myers has been an adviser to the social security systems of Barbados, Bolivia, Chile, Colombia, the Dominican Republic, El Salvador, Greece, Honduras, Nicaragua, Panama, Peru, Saudi Arabia, Suriname, and Venezuela. One might say that the man is internationally famous, but only among a few people.

Representative Andy Jacobs Jr. (D-Indiana), former chair of the Subcommittee on Social Security of the House Ways and Means Committee, has called Myers "one of the very few living oracles of the Social Security system." Senate Majority Leader Robert Dole

(R-Kansas) has said, "Throughout a remarkable career that stretches back to the birth of Social Security, Bob's advice has influenced Presidents and Congress." Senator Daniel Patrick Moynihan (D-New York) has declared Myers "a national treasure."

Though his celebrity is restricted to those who have a need to know, Robert J. Myers is one of the most influential individuals in American history. It was Myers who, as he puts it, "did the math" that led to fixing Social Security's age of eligibility to receive full benefits at sixty-five. That number, which has come to define "old age" for everyone now living in this country, had no previous biological, social, or legal significance to Americans. Sixty-five was selected because, as Myers has explained, "sixty was too young and seventy was too old. So we split the difference."

Myers began his career in government service in 1934 as a member of the actuarial team hired by the Committee on Economic Security, the agency that made the studies underlying the Social Security Act, which was passed the following year. He immediately went to work for the Social Security Administration if established, and was the system's chief actuary from 1947 to 1970.

Myers resigned from his beloved agency in 1970 after writing a *Reader's Digest* article that warned against Social Security "expansionism," which was being pressed by organized labor. He was worried that if Social Security benefits were increased without regard to cost, the solvency of the system to which he'd devoted thirty-six years of his life would be threatened. In a letter to *The Wall Street Journal,* he warned presciently that "in the 1990s and increasingly in the immediately following decades, the immediate ZPG [zero population growth] conditions will produce fewer individuals at the working ages to support the same number of aged beneficiaries. . . . Eventually, [between 1990 and 2025] the total aged population will rise, . . . an increase of about 55 percent as against a rate of only about 15 percent for the productive population."

Two years after Myers quit, precisely the kind of increases he'd warned against were pushed through Congress. In 1977 he was a consultant to both the House and Senate committees that tried unsuccessfully to put some of the toothpaste back into the tube that had been squeezed in 1972. When in 1982 the Social Security Administration found itself a few months away from bouncing checks to beneficiaries, he was appointed executive director of the federal government's National Commission on Social Security

Reform, which developed the 1983 amendments that shaped today's system. Myers's reputation as a whistle-blower called back to service to undo the damage he predicted gives him tremendous credibility today.

To meet this comeback curmudgeon I take the Washington Metro to one of the capital's suburbs. He meets me at the station in a gleaming white Dodge Intrepid, not ordinarily thought of as an octogenarian's car. Its color matches his hair. He drives aggressively to a modest neo-Tudor house that fits him like an old shoe.

There are piles of paper and books on every horizontal surface in his study. All the certificates an actuary can possess are framed on the walls. Myers, one can readily see, is

Professor Emeritus of Actuarial Science at Temple University, Past President of the Society of Actuaries, Past President of the American Academy of Actuaries, Past President of the Middle Atlantic Actuarial Club, Past President of the Inter-American Association of Social Security Actuaries, President of the International Fisheries Commissions Pension Society, Past President of the Lutheran Church in America Board of Pensions, member of the Board of the Directors of the National Academy of Social Insurance, former Chairman of the Railroad Unemployment Compensation Committee, former Chairman of the Commission on Railroad Retirement Reform, Fellow of the Casualty Actuarial Society, Fellow of the Conference of Consulting Actuaries, Fellow of the Fraternal Actuarial Association, Fellow of the American Statistical Association, Fellow of Britain's Royal Statistical Society, Associate of the British Institute of Actuaries, Corresponding Member of the French Institute of Actuaries, Corresponding Member of the Spanish Institute of Actuaries, and Fellow of the Conference of Actuaries in Public Practice.

He makes himself uncomfortable and testily flings at me, "You haven't been talking to any of those boneheads who think the entire Social Security system is headed over the cliff, have you?"

"Sure I have," I tell him.

"Well, don't pay attention to all that yammering. I'm here to tell you that Social Security will outlive us all. It isn't a contract, like a private insurance policy. Nothing's set in concrete. There are all kinds of adjustments that can be made to bring the system into long-term balance."

"Such as?"

"Such as raising what we call the 'Normal Retirement Age'—the age at which people become eligible to receive full benefits."

"Do you foresee a large number of baby boomers and members of the generations that come after them working later in life?"

"Right on! And if people who read your book want to tar and feather me for saying so, all I can say is, start heating up the tar pot."

"What would you raise the Normal Retirement Age to?" I ask.

"According to my calculations it should be increased to somewhere between sixty-eight and seventy."

"I think I smell some hot tar," I say.

"People shouldn't get it into their heads that they should be able to retire at sixty-seven, which is what the age will be as of 2027, let alone when they turn sixty-five, which is going to be history starting in 2003," says Myers. "Look—I'm a status quo-er. I believe Social Security should always be there. I believe it *will* always be there. But the Normal Retirement Age is the system's demographic safety valve. It should be a dynamic thing, based on your life expectancy, not on when your father retired.

"I wouldn't mind putting a timetable into law right now to raise it in steps to seventy," Myers continues. "If life expectancy doesn't go up as much we anticipate, we can always call off the schedule. It'd be easy to lower the retirement age, but it's hard to raise it. So we should do it now, when we can do it gradually, rather than later when we'd have to do it suddenly. If life expectancy goes up higher, we should go above seventy. Senator Dole had a bill in 1983 that would have indexed the Normal Retirement Age so that the ratio of years in retirement to working years would remain the same as it was in 1990. If you raise the Normal Retirement Age, you should raise the Medicare age while you're at it. Face it—any retirement age is arbitrary. There's no way you can prove it's correct."

"Would you still let people begin receiving reduced benefits at age sixty-two?"

"I don't see any reason why the early retirement age shouldn't also go up with life expectancy," Myers says. "Age sixty-two isn't written in stone. It wasn't part of the original system. Women couldn't get benefits at sixty-two until 1956, and men weren't eligible at age sixty-two before 1961. I've always believed that early retirement was a bad idea. I think people should continue working as long as they can. It's good for them, physically and psychologically. It's a free country, and people can stop working whenever they want. Just don't expect the public to pay for it."

"What if people are physically or mentally unable to work?" I ask.

"If older people can't work for health reasons, that's what Social Security's Disability Insurance program's for!"

"What about the argument that if older people were to continue working, there'd be fewer jobs for younger people?"

"Hogwash. If people work longer, there'll be more disposable income, which means more demand, which means more jobs. It isn't a zero-sum game."

"I find it interesting that the living American most closely identified with Social Security is still working in his eighties," I say.

Myers shrugs. "We never intended Social Security to encourage quitting work at age sixty-five. Keep in mind that the first monthly benefit checks were about seventeen dollars, and people had hardly anything in the way of savings or pensions. To put that seventeen dollars in perspective, the average wage at the time was about a hundred dollars a month. The purpose of Social Security was to provide a floor of protection for older people—period.

"I get a nice pension from the government, but retirement isn't for me. I have substantial income from self-employment. When I'm invited to give a speech they ask me what my fee is. I say, 'Whatever's usual and customary'—I don't ask for more, but I don't want to take less. I'm a director of one of the AARP's mutual funds and a mutual fund that's run by North American Security Life Insurance Company. I'm a consultant to the National Association of Life Underwriters and the American Council on Life Insurance. William M. Mercer, Inc., has a Social Security consulting office in Louisville and I do work for them.

"I also set Bermuda's hospital insurance rates. Every winter I spend four or five days there." Robert J. Myers winks. "It's a tough job, but somebody has to do it."

The idea of raising Social Security's Normal Retirement Age resonates across the political spectrum. The 1994 bill introduced by former House Social Security subcommittee chairman J. J. Pickle, a prominent Democrat, contained a provision raising the Normal Retirement Age to seventy by 2029, and trimming the monthly checks of people who choose to begin receiving them at age sixty-two. The Democratic Leadership Council's 1994 "Progressive Alternative" to the Republican "Contract with America" called for raising the Normal Retirement Age.

Senator Bob Kerrey, chair of the Bipartisan Commission on Entitlement and Tax Reform, and former Senator John Danforth, the Commission's vice-chair, issued a statement in December 1994 advocating gradually raising the age of eligibility for full Social Security cash benefits to seventy.

Meanwhile, conservative Dorcas R. Hardy, commissioner of Social Security under Presidents Reagan and Bush, recently told Dan Cordtz of *Financial World* that "if sixty-five was the proper retirement age in 1940, because of rising life expectancies, it should be seventy-three. A retirement age of sixty-five is a luxury. We don't need it, and we can't afford it." She has proposed moving the Normal Retirement Age to sixty-seven in the next three or four years, and slowly upping it to seventy.

Former Social Security chief actuary A. Haeworth Robertson, with whom Myers agrees on little else, advocates raising the Normal Retirement Age to between seventy and seventy-two. And the American Society of Pension Actuaries' National Retirement Income Policy Committee issued a report in 1994 proposing that a "standard retirement age" for receiving Social Security benefits "be created that would automatically change to reflect current life expectancy. This encourages working longer and controls the retirement benefit liability. It also uncouples the progress of the standard retirement age from political and revenue considerations. Benefits would begin at the standard retirement age regardless of when active work ceases. There should be no gain by deferring retirement and no subsidy for early retirement."

The Social Security system is going to have to be rebalanced, and when it is, raising the Normal Retirement Age will almost surely be part of the package. Increasing the age of full eligibility won't reduce our total lifetime cash benefits because our lifetimes are going to be longer. But you and I will have to do something to make up for the fact that we'll be starting to receive them later.

CHAPTER 4

PENSION TENSION

Because pensions aren't automatically adjusted for inflation, within fifteen years after they start being paid to you, they'll lose half their purchasing power. And pension funds too often don't have enough assets in them to meet future obligations to baby boomers. Meanwhile, plans such as 401(k)s are unlikely to provide adequate later-life income because participants tend to put their money in low-risk, low-return investments, and economists expect that they'll continue doing so.

Employer-sponsored pension plans have been touted as the industrial-strength solution to providing retirement income. Let's leave aside the fact that a majority of American employees aren't covered by such plans. Even for the 47 percent who have vested pension rights, leg number two of the "three-legged stool" of Social Security, pensions, and savings is far from sturdy.

There are two basic types of pension plans:

- "defined benefit," in which an employee is promised a monthly payout determined by earnings and length of service; and
- "defined contribution," such as 401(k), 403(b), 457, and profit-sharing, in which the employer, employee, or both contribute to an investment account managed by the employee, with no promises about the size of the payout.

According to the Employee Benefit Research Institute (EBRI), whose stats are accepted by all the players, defined benefit (DB) plans provide primary pension coverage for 62 percent of participants, and defined contribution (DC) plans are primary for the other 38 percent. In addition, 39 percent of DB participants have a supplemental DC plan.

UNDEFINED BENEFITS

The average "replacement rate" of a typical DB pension plan for employees starting to collect at age sixty-two after twenty years on the job is a meager 22 percent of final salary. One study found that the median private pension replacement rate for workers with thirty years of service is 34 percent for women and 27 percent for men. The average DB pension is $8,040 a year, while the median is $4,830.

Defined benefit plans have a fundamental problem: the way their benefits are defined—in dollars, not in purchasing power. A 1993 study pointed out that "the vast majority of private-sector pension plans offer no automatic inflation protection. . . . Even professional financial planners sometimes fall into the trap of treating pension annuities as if they were adjusted for inflation."

The U.S. Bureau of Labor Statistics reports that 96 percent of pension recipients are in plans that don't have automatic increases in benefits to compensate for inflation. When cost-of-living adjustments (COLAs) are given, they're made on a basis pension administrators call "ad hoc"—that is, at the employer's discretion. During a recent five-year period in which inflation totaled more than 18 percent, 74 percent of pension recipients received no COLA at all. And even when COLAs are provided, they average only one-third of increases in the Consumer Price Index.

A 1991 study for the U.S. Department of Labor by Alan L. Gustman, Professor of Economics at Dartmouth, and Thomas L. Steinmeier, Professor of Economics at Texas Tech University, found that from 1971 through 1986, a fifteen-year period in which consumer prices increased by 181.1 percent, DB pension benefits were increased "ad hoc" by an average of only 63.7 percent.

If future inflation averages a moderate 4 percent a year (the Social Security Administration's "best estimates" scenario, about the average since World War II), over fifteen years the constant-dollar value of your pension will drop by 46 percent. If prices go up 3 percent a year (the Social Security Administration's "low-cost" scenario), the pension's value will decrease by 39 percent. If inflation averages 5 percent a year (the Social Security Administration's "high-cost" scenario—the average inflation rate since 1960) your pension's real value at the end of fifteen years will have fallen by 54 percent. And if we go through another period of late-1970s-style double-digit inflation, which can't be ruled out, your pension could be virtually wiped out. Because of the unpredictability of inflation, another name for defined benefits could be undefined benefits.

Meanwhile, the American pension system is suffering from a neurosis induced by two irreconcilable urges: to tax all employee compensation immediately, yet to give employers a tax incentive to fund pension plans to provide later-life income.

You may have heard about the problem of underfunded pension plans. Yet by an obscure provision slipped into the 1987 edition of the annual catch-all legislation called the Omnibus Budget Reconciliation Act, Congress made it illegal for companies to put enough money into their pension funds to make sure they'll have enough assets to pay promised benefits.

Bizarre? Well, the rationale is that since companies' contributions to their pension plans are tax-deductible, the government can collect more current corporate taxes by forcing them to postpone funding of their plans until their employees approach retirement age.

A 1993 study analyzed the negative impact of the 1987 law on the soundness of the private pension system:

> In the general context of retirement policy it is interesting that there is so much consternation about the long-term prospects of Social Security and the potential underfunding of benefits for the baby boom generation when there is hardly any concern about the long-term prospects of the [employer-] funded pension system. . . . The gross effect of OBRA 87 is that it has significantly delayed the funding of the baby boom generation's defined benefit retirement promises. . . . The need to raise revenues to reduce the federal government's deficit has delayed the funding of the baby boom generation's pension benefits with virtually no consideration of the long-term impact that will have on the cost or viability of those benefits.

The trade-off: more revenue for the federal government in the short term, less retirement-income safety for you in the long term. But relax. Pressure to prevent companies from contributing to pension plans in order to maximize tax receipts may end up being relieved by taxing companies' contributions.

In a barrage of articles in the journal of the Federal Reserve Bank of Boston with titles like "It's Time to Tax Employee Benefits" and "Current Taxation of Qualified Pension Plans: Has the Time

Come?", economist Alicia H. Munnell, a former vice president of the bank, has written, "In an era of large budget deficits and a future that includes the rising costs of an aging society, it is difficult to understand why such a large source of potential revenue is allowed to go untapped." Dr. Munnell is now at the U.S. Treasury as assistant secretary for economic policy, and her ideas have many supporters inside the Beltway. She has proposed not only taxing employers' annual contributions to pension plans and the annual earnings on pension investments, but also immediately taxing away 15 percent of all pension fund accumulations to date to make up for the lack of taxation in the past. Rectifying that lamentable oversight would vacuum more that $600 billion into the federal government's coffers—probably the largest single confiscation of property in the history of civilization, but who's counting?

Speaking of things that are difficult to understand, the idea of meeting the rising costs of an aging society by taxing money that's being accumulated to pay some of the rising costs of an aging society isn't all that easy to comprehend.

Then there are the pension problems caused by the typical baby boomer's job-hopping career path. EBRI has found that an employee who works for three different companies for ten years each can expect only about two-thirds the defined benefit pension of an employee with the same final average salary who worked for one company for thirty years. But even this type of calculation overstates the pension payouts most people are going to receive. The most recent data show that by the time an American female employee reaches age sixty-five, she's held an average of 12.2 jobs; a male employee has had an average of 10.7 jobs. Only 15.3 percent of women and 37.3 percent of men have been with one employer for twenty years or more. In the turbulent labor market we're facing, it's likely that the average number of jobs held will go up, and the percentage with long-term jobs will go down.

Martha Priddy Patterson, director of employee benefits policy and analysis at KPMG Peat Marwick's Washington, D.C., National Compensation and Benefits Practice, says, "It doesn't help when you look at the average job tenure for women, which is 4.8 years in a job, meaning the average woman would never get vested in a pension plan. . . . Employees who change jobs frequently or are out of the workforce for a period of time are especially at risk. Time out of the workforce and job changes can reduce employer-provided retirement benefits in a dramatically disproportionate way. For example, in a forty-year career, three years out of the workforce and six job changes reduces income from an employer-provided retirement benefit by one-half."

I visited the headquarters of a major national pension consulting firm and met with a managing director who specializes in designing lush retirement plans for top management. When I asked her what people who don't have corner offices will be able to expect in the way of pension income, she said with a confident smile: "The Silver Bullet."

Given the way she Capitalized Each Word, I thought that maybe she'd developed some new miracle plan that would solve the pension problem once and for all. *With The Silver Bullet™, your pension worries don't just lay down—they stay down.*

"What," I asked, "is The Silver Bullet?"

She shrugged. "If baby boomers discover they don't have enough money to live on when they're older, they can always blow their brains out."

On the way to the elevator, the firm's PR man, a baby boomer who'd sat in on our meeting and had looked slightly seasick when his boss went ballistic, said to me, "You know, I was at a social gathering a few weeks ago and mentioned that someday I'd like to retire to Costa Rica, but that I wasn't sure I'd have enough money. The people there, who were mostly pretty successful advertising and public relations executives, got to talking about what kind of retirement lifestyle they could expect. The consensus was that even though most of them had been working for thirty years, they hadn't been with one company long enough to receive meaningful pension income, and that their various pensions plus Social Security would total only about twenty percent of their current income."

Worse, DB pensions from previous employers will be especially hard-hit by inflation. Two-thirds of DB plans don't allow an employee who leaves the company to cash out with a lump sum that could be invested for later-life income needs. The day the employee leaves the firm is her benefit's "defining moment." If the employee is, say, thirty-five when she leaves, her payout will be eroded by decades of inflation. At a moderate 4 percent inflation rate, in thirty years it will lose 69 percent of its value, and over the next fifteen years its purchasing power will drop to seventeen cents on the original dollar.

One of my basic journalistic rules is that if you want to know the real story on anything, ask a taxi driver. Here's what Billy, born in 1952, told me: He worked for a food distributor for nearly two decades, driving an eighteen-wheeler under a Teamsters contract, making $30,000 a year. When the company moved to a neighboring state and let most of its staff go, the union went on strike for more than a year, but no one was hired back. Billy had been going to school at night for years, earning a masters in communication. But he hasn't been able to turn his degree into a job, and has been working days on straight commission for a company that telemarkets personal computers whose prices are padded to include a "free" vacation to businesspeople who buy them. Nights, he drives a cab, and he teaches piano and trumpet on weekends. At fifty-five he'll be eligible to receive a pension of $360 a month. If he waits till sixty-five he can collect $620. There are no cost-of-living adjustments, so with 4 percent inflation the $360 will be worth $203 in today's dollars, while the $620 will be worth $233. Not quite a gold-plated retirement for a guy who was an over-the-road trucker for nearly two decades. I gave him a 25 percent tip for not having tried to communicate me into buying a computer system whose peripherals include six days and five nights at a hotel in Cancún.

I've heard it suggested that despite the problems of the DB pension system, married baby boomers will receive more pension income because the rise of the dual-earner couple will result in the rise of the dual-pension couple. But dual pensions won't add much to the baby boom generation's later-life income.

According to the U.S. Bureau of Labor Statistics, 55 percent of sixty-five-plus households now receive some income from employer-sponsored pension plans. That proportion is indeed projected to rise to 88 percent by 2018. But "the percent of total retirement income derived from employer pension plans is projected to increase much less dramatically," from the present 19 percent to 25 percent by 2018.

Urban Institute economists C. Eugene Steuerle and Jon M. Bakija concluded, after evaluating a simulation of future pension recipiency: "The bottom line is that when the baby boom population begins to swell the ranks of the elderly, half of all retirees are still likely to be without significant employer-provided pension benefits or other income sources and will be dependent largely upon Social Security."

Adding to the impending pension shortfall is news that even the most stable companies often have underfunded plans. The most recent data compiled on the DB funds of the largest Fortune 500 companies by Buck Consultants, a pension consulting firm, reveal that 24 percent don't have enough assets to cover their obligations to future beneficiaries. In 1988 only 5 percent of plans were in such sad shape.

But behind the private pension system stands the august power of the federal government's Pension Benefit Guaranty Corporation (PBGC). And behind an agency with such an impressive moniker must stand the full faith and credit of the U.S. government, no?

No. Behind the PBGC, which is supposed to insure the pensions of 32 million employees in 65,000 plans, stands a law authorizing it to borrow up to $100 million from the U.S. Treasury—about what the agency currently spends in fifty-seven days. After that's exhausted, we're talking would-be pension recipients begging for a bailout in a political environment where some killjoy is bound to raise the point that every single one of them is either already collecting or eventually will be collecting Social Security, and that maybe one government check each month is enough for older people in a country where babies are born addicted to crack and Amtrak trains go underwater without benefit of a tunnel.

To get an idea of how secure the PBGC's "benefit guaranty" is, consider that the "accumulated benefit obligation" of single-employer DB pension plans at last count was $926 billion. What do you suppose its net worth is?

$92.6 billion?

$9.26 billion?

$9.26?

How about no net worth at all? How about a *negative* net worth? Dr. Carolyn L. Weaver, director of Social Security and pension studies at the American Enterprise Institute, a moderately conservative think tank, told a recent conference: "Due to the miracles of federal budgeting, the PBGC is running a cash flow surplus—meaning that premium and other income exceeds annual benefits and other expenses—while slipping further into debt on a net worth basis. Sounds like the Social Security system!"

The PBGC is currently paying pensions to 152,000 retirees whose employer plans have gone belly-up. Another 120,000 people are vested in those 1,760 defunct plans and are due to begin receiving benefit checks from the PBGC when they're old enough. The PBGC's liabilities to these 272,000 people total $9.0 billion. To cover those liabilities, the PBGC claims assets worth $6.3 billion, giving it an "accumulated deficit" of $2.7 billion. Isn't it comforting to know that behind those $926 billion in pension liabilities stands an institution that itself admits to being $2.7 billion in the hole?

And it may be even deeper in the hole than that. The U.S. General Accounting Office, which audits the PBGC, has warned that the PBGC's financial statements "have limited reliability," and in 1993 the White House Office of Management and Budget estimated the PBGC's true deficit at $43 billion.

CFO is a magazine for corporate chief financial officers, the executives who are responsible for making the decisions about how much to contribute to pension plans. Here's what *CFO* has to say about the PBGC: "Apart from its growing liabilities, the PBGC's current deficit of $2.7 billion is expected to widen to $30 billion in the next 15 to 20 years as the baby boom generation reaches retirement age." Economists Zvi Bodie, Professor of Finance at the School of Management, Boston University, and author of *Pensions in the U.S. Economy,* and Robert C. Merton, Professor of Business Administration at Harvard Business School, point out that the current PBGC system, in which the government makes sponsors of adequately funded DB plans subsidize the agency's insurance of inadequately funded plans, may result in termination of the solvent ones: "The United States could then be left only with bankrupt defined benefit plans with the benefits financed directly by taxpayers."

But will younger members of tomorrow's public be willing to pay our private pensions when we're older?

If the baby bust generation feels its lifestyle is being cramped by the total income stream to retired baby boomers, including pensions, it will have a technically and politically effortless way of penalizing pension recipients and diverting that income stream back to younger generations. All Congress will have to do will be to broaden and increase the Earned Income Credit (EIC), an already-existing tax mechanism that differentiates between work-derived and non-work-derived income, and between taxpayers who have dependent children and those who don't. Older boomers who have mostly non-work income and no young children will take a hit. Younger busters who are working and have kids will either receive a tax reduction or a "refund" check. Once most of the boomers have died off, it will be easy to adjust the EIC downward by a single, barely noticed act of Congress.

The dean of American management consultants, Peter F. Drucker—born in 1909 and still hard at work—foresaw this intergenerational dynamic in his 1976 book *The Unseen Revolution:*

> The worker who has part of his paycheck put into a pension account foregoes immediate consumption; someone else, already on a pension, consumes instead. In exchange, the worker receives a claim to consumption in the future. But this claim can be satisfied only out of the production of the future. The shoes, automobiles, loaves of bread, and medical treatments today's worker will want to buy with his pension check twenty-five years hence. As a group, the retired people are just as "dependent" as before on the capacity of the people at work to produce a surplus of goods and services for them, and on the willingness of the "productive population" to hand the surplus over against the claims of the retired people.

Above all, DB pensions are a period piece, a relic of a time when U.S. corporations, insulated from foreign competition and operating in a vibrant economy, didn't have to worry so much about controlling employee compensation, and were simultaneously under pressure from powerful unions to grant ever-more-generous benefits. In the new worldwide economy those pressures have reversed. Organized labor is corroding along with the Rust Belt, and foreign competitors have more muscle than ever before. DB plans will be a certain casualty of this power shift as companies cut compensation costs to improve their international competitiveness.

UNDEFINED CONTRIBUTIONS

Defined contribution (DC) plans like 401(k)s seem to be in the money these days. There are plenty of reasons for their popularity—most of which lighten the load of employers, not employees.

• Excessive and constantly changing government regulation of DB pension plans have turned them into a managerial migraine. A PBGC study recently found that employers operating typical DB plans with seventy-five participants have to pay an outlandish $800 in administrative costs for every $1,400 spent on funding benefits. Complex rules that change almost yearly, resulting in high compliance cost, are the most commonly cited reason for terminating DB plans, with the cost of funding the plans a close second. Says Larry Zimpleman, vice president of the American Academy of Actuaries and chair of its Pension Practice Council, "In the current regulatory climate, employers who offer traditional defined benefit plans to their employees face an administrative nightmare."

• DC plans are a more effective way of motivating today's labor force. Employees can watch their 401(k) accounts grow every month, while the value of a DB pension—often called "the hidden benefit" by human resource professionals—doesn't become "defined" until an employee stops working.

• DC plans can be borrowed against for housing, education, and medical expenses, making them attractive to employees who are more concerned about paying for college now than for cruises decades from now.

• Employers with DC plans don't have to pay premiums to the PBGC, which have gone up an average of 2,800 percent and a maximum of 7,200 percent since the agency was established in 1974.

• DC plans are used by bottom-line-conscious companies to lower their "total compensation cost." In the Winter 1992–93 issue of *ACA Journal,* published by the American Compensation Association, Robert D. Paul, chair of The Segal Company, and Dale B. Grant, the pension consulting firm's executive vice president, wrote for their colleagues' eyes only: "Faced [in the 1980s] with the crunch of rapidly rising health costs, employers were eager to limit the costs of retirement benefits. A newly enacted section of the Internal Revenue Code, Section 401(k), gave employers the opportunity to share some of the costs of retirement benefits with their employees. . . ."

• DC plans can be set up so that companies contribute only to the extent that employees do—and many employees don't.

• DC plans shift "inflation risk" to the employee, because while few employers offer COLAs to DB payouts, no employers offer COLAs to DC payouts.

• DC plans, unlike DB pensions, can be structured so that companies don't have to pay one cent into them. Just as most defined benefit plans really offer undefined benefits, most defined contribution plans really offer undefined contributions. Cindy Hounsell, staff attorney and coordinator of the Women's Pension Advocacy Council at the liberal Pension Rights Center in Washington, D.C., told me, "401(k)s aren't pension plans at all. They're just do-it-yourself savings plans, and they're not even necessarily earmarked for later-life income." "There's an unsettling feeling that in the long run defined contribution plans just aren't going to be delivering as much retirement income," says Richard A. Ippolito, the PBGC's conservative chief economist—and chief gadfly.

An American Academy of Actuaries survey has found that more than 30,000 employers have terminated defined benefit plans since 1990: "Of the employers who were known to retain pension coverage after the defined benefit plan termination, 46 percent of the plans were less generous than the terminated defined benefit plan. Since 90 percent of the post-termination plans were defined contribution plans, it is clear that replacement defined contribution plans are less generous." The Academy's Pension Committee noted that "defined contribution plans, as we know them, are seldom as generous as defined benefit plans. Thus, large numbers of workers with defined contribution plans as their primary coverage will be covered by less generous plans than the same employer would provide if defined benefit coverage were selected."

James J. Murphy, executive vice president of the Academy, says: "It is clear that government regulations have gone too far and have helped contribute to the demise of defined benefit plans—the very pensions that helped our parents and those in previous generations retire. The survey findings clearly indicate that not only will the baby boom generation have to retire later or with fewer benefits because of changes in Social Security, but they will also have reduced private pension benefits."

To give you a sense of the "lump sum distribution" (LSD) a 401(k) can pay out: EBRI reported that the average account balance among employees covered only by a 401(k) was $9,705 for women, $15,479 for men. The overall average was $11,154. That's not $11,154 a year for life—it's one check for $11,154 one time, $11,154 to last you the rest of your days.

If you're thinking that average balance must include younger people and others who haven't had a chance to build their accounts, you're right. So let's focus on people aged sixty-one to sixty-four: Their average account balance is $25,011. Anyone who thinks $25,011 is enough of an LSD to provide meaningful income for decades of later life is hallucinating.

But ah, you say, some of those sixty-one-to-sixty-four-year-olds mustn't have been earning or contributing very much. Okay, let's look only at people making $100,000 a year or more. A drumroll, please . . . Average balance: $41,351. I was born in west Texas, and as they say there—it'll turn you loose, but it won't set you free.

An employee whose final salary is $100,000 and is able to earn 8 percent on the LSD from her 401(k) distribution will receive an annual income of $3,308—less than half as much in an entire year as what she was earning in a single month, and every penny of it taxable.

Actually, 23 percent of people whose only employer-sponsored plan is a 401(k) don't need to worry about whether their lump sum distribution will be enough, because they won't be getting one. According to EBRI, that's how many 401(k)-eligible employees aren't putting any money at all into their plans.

As for the 77 percent who at least are in the game, most contribute less to their accounts than the maximum their plans allow, and most of the value of their 401(k)s is in fixed-income investments such as "guaranteed investment contracts" (GICs) issued by insurance companies. Such accounts will stay only slightly ahead of inflation, and stand little chance of providing ample later-life income. For a 401(k) to be able to grow to the point where it could produce generous income, it would have to be aggressively positioned in stocks. Yet U.S. Department of Labor studies show that only 5 percent of employees have have more than half of the value of their 401(k) accounts in stocks. Seventy-five percent have no stocks in them at all.

My favorite 401(k) horror story is about Towers Perrin, one of the biggest pension consulting firms, with five thousand employees and sixty-eight offices worldwide. Towers Perrin has over eight thousand clients, including many of the largest corporations in North America. Naturally, one of the main things Towers Perrin advises companies to do is to try to get their employees to comprehend how vital it is for them to put 401(k) money into stocks. Do I need to tell you that when, in 1992, Towers Perrin analyzed its own DC plan, it found that *76 percent of its employees had no stocks in their accounts?* Appalled, Towers Perrin started a program to convince its personnel to follow their own advice.

EBRI Research Associate Paul Yakoboski testified before the House Subcommittee on Social Security in 1993: "Where worker choice is involved in retirement plans, in particular, 401(k) type arrangements, individuals tend to prefer conservative investments. According to a recent survey by EBRI and the Gallup Organization, 69 percent of individuals preferred low-risk, low-return investments for their pension money, while only 25 percent preferred high-risk, high-return investments."

This caution may have something to do with the need for a feeling of certainty in uncertain times, but there's a more basic, timeless reason. Pep talks about putting more 401(k) assets into stocks will always run up against a phenomenon known among economists as "myopic loss aversion." A 1995 study by Shlomo Benartzi, Assistant Professor of Accounting at the University of Southern California, and Richard H. Thaler, Professor of Economics at the University of Chicago, was summed up by its authors: "First, investors are 'loss averse'—that is, they are distinctly more sensitive to losses than to gains. Second, investors evaluate their portfolios frequently, even if they have long-term investment goals, such as saving for retirement or managing a pension plan. . . . That is, investors appear to choose portfolios as if they were operating with a time horizon of about one year."

Former U.S. Securities and Exchange Commissioner J. Carter Beese Jr. has nevertheless made a mission out of trying to alert baby boomers with 401(k)s to the risk of trying to avoid risk. Speaking at the 1993 Mutual Funds and Investment Management Conference, he said:

How Americans invest with their defined contribution plans will have a much greater impact on their future standard of living than the federal deficit ever will. If you simply take all that we know about retirement planning and extrapolate future retiree income based on current investment patterns, you quickly realize that many workers will not be able to afford a comfortable retirement.

Essentially, Mr. Beese doesn't believe that the average working American can be turned into a pension fund manager: "Taking assets out of the hands of professional money managers and putting them into the hands of individuals almost ensures people are not going to have enough money to retire on. Most Americans know how to save. They don't know how to invest."

Is Mr. Beese unduly pessimistic about the investment acumen of 401(k) participants? Maybe he isn't being pessimistic enough. A 1993 survey by John Hancock Financial Services found that only 25 percent of participants in 401(k)s realize that a rise in interest rates will cause bond mutual funds to decrease in value. Almost half believed money market funds contain stocks and bonds.

On the other hand, Mr. Beese may be too optimistic about the possibility that if 401(k) participants were allocating more to stocks, they'd stand a better chance of having enough retirement income. I often read that from 1926 to the present, Standard & Poor's broad market index of 500 stocks went up an average of 10.2 percent a year—an inflation-adjusted rate of 7 percent. There's no doubt this figure is accurate and impressive. The problem is, is it meaningful? Let's take an index most of us are more familiar with—the one that includes only the bluest chips: the Dow Jones Industrial Average. And instead of looking at the longest of long terms, let's look at some individual decades. From 1962 to 1973, the Dow, adjusted for inflation, went down 1 percent a year. And from 1973 to 1983, it went down 2.2 percent a year. Can we really assume that over, say, the next two decades the real value of our investments will climb by 7 percent a year, compounding to a total growth of 387 percent, when between 1962 and 1983 the Dow Jones average, adjusted for inflation, was *lower at the end than it was at the beginning?*

Of course, that two-decade period included good times and bad, as the next twenty years undoubtedly will. But what if your retirement date happens to coincide with a bad time?

What if about a year before you're planning to retire, the stock market sinks like a stone? I'm not asking what happens if it falls out of bed the way it did in October 1987 but then clambers right back up. Let's say it heads for the Deep South, like it did between April 27, 1981, and August 12, 1982, when the Dow lost 24 percent over sixteen months. How will you feel about cashing out your 401(k) if the southern journey takes stocks down to Tierra del Fuego, off 27 percent over seventeen months, which is what happened between September 21, 1976, and February 28, 1978? What if the market sets out for Antarctica like it did between December 3, 1968, and May 26, 1970, an eighteen-month slide that ended with the market down an icy 36 percent?

It's called volatility, folks, and it's the price we pay for free enterprise, but the question is, will you be sitting there telling yourself, "Not to worry—bad times included, the stock market's total return has averaged 10.2 percent a year since 1926"? We'd all like to think we've got nerves of DuPont Kevlar, but if a major market correction happens to coincide with our planned retirement date, the overall economic atmosphere will seem pretty dismal. The bears will be out in force crying "Woe unto you!"—and as we'll be seeing later on in this book, they may be right. Will you be willing to bet that they're wrong? Or as you watch your life savings setting out by dogsled for the South Pole, will you bail out at the bottom and spend the rest of your life regretting it?

The average maximum decline in the Dow within a calendar year since 1933 has been 14.5 percent. You could end up with 14.5 percent less income a year for life from your 401(k) because you understandably get nervous watching your life savings vaporizing and cash in your chips at an annual low. Worse, when there have been two consecutive years of single-digit declines, in the following year there has been an average maximum decline of 21.1 percent. How many of us will have the stomach to ride that roller coaster when we're in our sixties, seventies, and eighties?

Ray Crabtree, senior vice president for pensions of the Principal Financial Group, recently summed up the DC picture: "For employed workers today, including the baby boomers, cash retirement income risk is being or already has been shifted to the workers from their employers. As we move from defined benefit plans, the predominant form of a pension plan, to defined contribution plans, this risk is going form employers to the employees.

"Our evidence says that within the defined contribution plans, primarily 401(k) programs, individuals are not saving enough today to accumulate enough assets so that they will earn an income replacement ratio in the future high enough to sustain their quality of life in retirement."

The chair of the PBGC's Advisory Committee, Myron Mintz, said in 1993, "A whole generation of people are going to wake up years from now and say, 'God, I wish I had known when I was thirty-two that I should have been putting this money in.' All of these people are not going to have adequate retirement income."

Here's what Donald J. Segal and Howard J. Small of The Segal Company, are telling their fellow pension professionals about 401(k)s in the American Management Association's *Compensation & Benefits Review:* "The lower interest rates, the employees' general lack of understanding of the plan, and the employees' aversion to risk all add to the likelihood that the benefits won't meet expectations. In the end, employees may not be able to afford to retire."

Thomas A. Levy of the Pension Committee of the American Academy of Actuaries sees choppy water ahead: "By the year 2010, the oldest of the baby boom generation will have reached retirement age. That year may also mark the beginning of a generation of retirees without traditional pension plans. Many of the baby boomers who participate in defined contribution plans will find they don't have enough money saved to provide adequately for retirement."

The bottom line on DC plans, as Howard Fine, a partner in the pension consulting firm of Hewitt Associates, succinctly put it in 1994: "If there is not enough money in 401(k) plans, a lot of workers will stay working."

CHAPTER 5

BEYOND SAVING

Increased personal saving is conventionally portrayed as the way the baby boom generation is supposed to bridge the gap between insufficient Social Security and pension benefits and income needs in later life. But the target amounts baby boomers would have to accumulate to allow them to retire comfortably are very high. Baby boomers are typically saving at one-third of the pace that would enable them to reach those targets, and, realistically, few of them are going to multiply their savings rate.

Individual saving is supposed to be the third leg of the "three-legged stool of retirement income." But that leg is so short that the stool could topple.

At a 1993 congressional hearing held on the subject, "Retirement Income Security: Can the Baby Boom Generation Afford to Retire?", Marc E. Lackritz, president of the Securities Industry Association, speaking for brokerage firms and mutual fund groups that account for nine-tenths of the securities business in North America, warned:

> A crisis in financing retirement looms for all Americans unless major efforts are made to set aside significantly more funds for the future. Current trends indicate the likelihood that in the next century, many Americans will spend as much time in retirement as they did working, and must therefore save more in a shorter period of working time for a longer period of retirement. . . .
>
> Over the last three decades, U.S. national savings plummeted almost 400 percent and personal savings as a percentage of disposable income has dropped from an average of 7.8 percent in the 1970s to under 5 percent since 1986. Moreover, baby boomers have failed so far to save as anticipated during their peak savings years. . . .
>
> Over the next few decades, declining growth in the working age population, increasing growth in the retirement population, and spi-

raling debt-service costs will place a tremendous financial strain on the U.S. economy and taxpayers. In order to alleviate this strain we need to do everything we can to revive a culture of savings and foster a renewed sense of personal financial responsibility.

But it's doubtful whether baby boomers can be jawboned into saving more. The U.S. personal savings rate has slipped halfway down from the 9.5 percent of disposable income that prevailed as recently as 1981. By comparison, savings rates in Austria, Belgium, Germany, France, Italy, and Switzerland are more than 12 percent. According to Charles Yuji Horioka of the Osaka Institute of Social and Economic Research, total household saving in Japan is 12.3 percent, including about 7.1 percent for later life—almost twice what Americans save for all purposes.

Americans are now saving at an annual rate of less than 5 percent of their disposable income. By comparison, consumer credit payments are around 16 percent of disposable income. Can people realistically be expected to save for a rainy day if they have to borrow to get through the sunny ones?

"Most Americans today did not live through the Great Depression," says Jon S. Fossel, chairman and CEO of Oppenheimer Management, which runs fifty mutual funds, commenting on abysmal U.S. savings, "but at this rate, that's exactly what most people's retirements will be like. Relatively few Americans will be able to maintain their preretirement lifestyle once they stop working, and many will find themselves struggling simply to make ends meet."

A survey conducted by Merrill Lynch in 1993 found that 74 percent of female baby boomers and 57 percent of male baby boomers are saving nothing for retirement. Fifteen percent of baby boomers said they were saving nothing for any purpose. A 1993 Yankelovich survey of nearly 1,500 women and men between the ages of thirty and fifty with household incomes of $30,000 or more found that 81 percent were confident they'd have enough retirement income, though they were saving a median of only $2,600 a year.

Another 1993 survey, conducted by the Employers Council on Flexible Compensation, is even more alarming. It found that the median amount employees are saving for retirement is $720 a year. The average annual amounts being saved are $1,811 for employees twenty-five to thirty-four years old, while employees thirty-five to forty-four saved $2,098, and employees forty-five to sixty-four saved $2,408. The survey found that the most common amount being saved per year is $0.

No, that wasn't a misprint: zilch.

To get a sense of how awful these savings figures are, you can multiply the amount you think you'll need to stop working by the following factors to find out how much you'd have to save each year to build up the required nest egg. Developed by Fidelity Investments, they adjust for the 4 percent average inflation rate projected by the Social Security Administration and assume you'll earn 8 percent a year on your savings—somewhat below historic levels for stocks, but a handsome return.

> 5 years: .184
> 10 years: .083
> 15 years: .050
> 20 years: .034
> 25 years: .024
> 30 years: .018

For instance, if you were to plan to stop working twenty years from now, in order to accumulate $250,000 in today's dollars, you'd need to save $8,500 every year (.034 x $250,000) in today's dollars for the next two decades. (Note that to keep pace with inflation you'd have to increase the amount of each year's savings by that year's inflation rate.)

B. Douglas Bernheim, Professor of Economics at Stanford University, is one of the country's top experts on savings. He literally wrote the book: *Saving for Prosperity: The U.S. Saving Rate.* Dr. Bernheim has figured out how much savings baby boomers will need to be able to stop working at age sixty-five and maintain their standard of living, and how much progress they've made toward reaching those targets.

His conclusions were drawn from a Merrill Lynch survey of 3,798 baby boomer households and a computerized model he constructed that took into account every factor that could affect retirement income, from earnings profile to family composition to inflation. A description of the variables Dr. Bernheim used fills forty-four pages. His model was, shall we say, a bit more complex than a stool.

The amounts Dr. Bernheim came up with should be a wake-up call, because they look like telephone numbers. Here are some examples:

- For a couple currently earning a total of $40,000 to $60,000 a year: If they have average defined benefit pension coverage, nonhousing financial assets worth $203,790 in today's dollars will be needed at age sixty-five; without defined benefit pension coverage, $270,110.
- For a couple earning $75,000 a year: with pension, $367,800; without pension, $482,910.
- For a couple earning $100,000: with pension, $520,810; without pension, $690,350.
- For a single woman earning $40,000 to $60,000: with pension, $171,290; without pension, $275,150.
- For a single man earning $40,000 to $60,000: with pension, $170,140; without pension, $293,250.

These required savings figures are expressed in 1991 dollars, and have to be increased by about 10 percent to translate them into today's dollars. And to keep pace with inflation, the dollar totals you'll need by age sixty-five will be far higher. For example, if future inflation averages a moderate 4 percent, about the average over the decades since World War II, the target amounts will have to be doubled in eighteen years.

Dr. Bernheim compared the savings targets calculated by his model to the amounts survey participants aged thirty-five to forty-five have actually managed to save. He found that on average they've saved only a third of what they'd have needed to accumulate by age thirty-five to forty-five to have enough to retire on at age sixty-five.

And the more they're earning, the worse they're doing. Couples with total earnings of $40,000 to $60,000 who have pension coverage have saved an average of $12,950—only 40 percent of what they should have accumulated by age thirty-five to forty-five. If they have no pensions, they've saved only 25 percent of what they already should have. Couples earning $60,000 to $100,000 who have pensions have accumulated an average of $17,100. That's less than 34 percent of what they should have saved by age thirty-five to forty-five; if they have no pensions, it's less than 23 percent. Baby boomers who can't drastically increase their savings can forget about Chardonnay and Brie when they're sixty-five. They'll be lucky if they can afford Night Train and Velveeta.

According to Dr. Bernheim, couples now aged thirty-five to forty-four who earn a total of $75,000 before taxes would have to be saving between 8.9 and 13.0 percent of their after-tax income to be on track to accumulating enough to retire on at sixty-five if there were no cuts in Social Security cash benefits (the lower rate would be for couples with pensions, the higher rate for couples without pensions). From age forty-five to fifty-four, they'd need to boost their savings rate to between 19.5 and 23.1 percent of after-tax income. And from age fifty-five to sixty-four, they'd have to increase their savings rate to between 17.1 and 20.9 percent. The required rate of savings for couples or singles with total earnings of $50,000 would range from 5.2 percent of after-tax income at age thirty-five to forty-four to 24.8 percent at age fifty-five to sixty-four.

I spent some time with Dr. Bernheim, whose credentials include being a certifiable baby boomer born in 1958. My overall conclusion is that he twists himself into a pretzel to understate how bad the retirement savings crisis is. In fact, everything about Dr. Bernheim is understated: his office decor, the way he speaks, even how he eats. I took him out to lunch, and what did he order when someone else was paying? No cocktail, a roast beef sandwich, and a Coke. Even the man's clothing is a masterpiece of understatement. Now that I've met him, not only do I know how bad our later-life money problems are going to be, I know how J. Crew comes up with its men's clothing styles. They fly someone to Stanford to take photos of B. Douglas Bernheim and bring them back to Lynchburg, Virginia. End of design process.

Dr. Bernheim told me that, if anything, his numbers minimize the inadequacy of the baby boomers' preparation for retirement. "First," he explained, "the survey figures include all existing household savings. But a substantial portion of those savings will be used for non-retirement purposes like paying college tuition. Or they may be drawn down during a period of unemployment or disability.

"Second, the finding that baby boomers aged thirty-five to forty-five have saved 33.79 percent of what they need to have already put aside to be able to retire at sixty-five is based on a life-cycle model of saving in which the rate of accumulation should increase with age. But the survey showed that baby boomers aren't saving at a higher rate as they get older.

"Third, the simulations used standard insurance mortality tables. But it's probable that life expectancy will continue to rise, in which case typical baby boomers will live beyond the ages in the tables. The longer they live, the more savings they'll need.

"Fourth, there was no variable in the simulations for increases in health care and long-term care costs, because we don't know how much they'll go up. The more they rise, the more money the baby boomers are going to need to save if they want to have a comfortable retirement.

"Fifth, even a moderate tax increase in the future would reduce the percentage of adequacy of current savings below thirty percent.

"Sixth, it's entirely possible that economic and demographic pressures will cause Congress and employers to scale down retirement benefits. For example, a comparatively modest cut in Social Security benefits would reduce the current percentage of savings adequacy to less than twenty percent. So baby boomers really need to save more than the figures generated by the model, as a reserve against cuts in Social Security and pension plans."

Dr. Bernheim wrote in a report on his research that baby boomers need to multiply their savings rate not just three times, not just four times, but probably more. Otherwise, he said, they'll be "forced to accept dramatically lower standards of living during retirement, or else forego retirement altogether."

How dramatic is "dramatically"? "They'll have to cut their spending in half, or more," says Dr. Bernheim.

In 1993 Oppenheimer Management commissioned a report containing simulations of how much retirement income people would have if by some miracle Social Security isn't cut, and if they were to double their savings rate starting now, immediately double the proportion of stocks in their portfolios, and spend half their home equity after they retire.

• A married couple aged forty to forty-four currently earning between $50,000 and $100,000 a year, and willing to spend down 75 percent of their principal during their retirement years, will have retirement income, including Social Security, pensions, 401(k) dividends and interest, investment returns, and dipping into principal, of

44 percent of their average salary during their final five working years.

• If they were to double their savings rate now, their retirement income would increase to 46 percent of final average salary.

• If they were to double their stock holdings now, they'd have 60 percent of final average salary.

• If they were to immediately double both their savings rate and the portion allocated to stocks, they'd have 62 percent of final average salary.

• And if they were to double both their rate of savings and their holdings of stocks, plus spend down half their home equity after they retire, they'd have 67 percent of final average salary.

The models were mathematically elegant, but the variables plugged into them were far-fetched. The fact is that few of us are in a position to save at twice our current rate, most of us would get ulcers if we doubled our stock exposure, and using home equity to buy groceries is a burning-the-furniture-to-keep-warm approach that should be considered only as an absolute last resort.

In any event, learning that even if Social Security benefits were to stay the same, which they won't, and we were to double our savings, double our stock allocation, and mortgage the ranch, we'll still have 33 percent less income than when we were working isn't especially reassuring.

It isn't hard to understand why financial service companies have been going to the moon to document the low savings rate of the baby boom generation. They're trying to scare up some business for themselves. But they aren't under any illusion that their efforts will close the retirement-income gap for most baby boomers. When asked by *Barron's* reporter Leslie Eaton how many people he thought would actually follow his company's advice, Robert C. Doll Jr., Oppenheimer's executive vice president and director of equity investments answered, "Probably not many at all."

The reason baby boomers aren't going to radically increase their savings rate isn't because they're being assailed from all sides by demands on their current income, though they are. It's because of something known as human nature.

A team of economists has observed, "There is widespread myopia with respect to retirement needs. Empirical evidence shows that most people fail to save enough to prevent catastrophic drops to post-retirement income. . . . Not only do people fail to plan ahead carefully for retirement even in the later years of their working life, many remain unaware of impending retirement needs." The late Joseph A. Pechman, Henry J. Aaron, today director of economic studies at the Brookings Institution, and Michael K. Taussig, now Professor of Economics at Rutgers, wrote that in 1968, when the percentage of income Americans were saving was nearly twice what it is today. In the face of the shortsightedness they described, exhortations to double the savings rate from financial service firms trolling for new customers aren't likely to reverse a multidecade trend that has cut the savings rate in half.

Despite all the evidence that baby boomers won't have enough money in later life, it's occasionally suggested that they will. This claim seems to be motivated, perhaps unconsciously, by the hope that by diverting attention from the predicament of middle- and upper-middle-class boomers, public concern—and public dollars—can be directed toward the sizeable minority of baby boomers already living in poverty, who face hunger and homelessness in later life.

I'm troubled by the plight of members of the baby boom generation who are already poor and in danger of becoming poorer. But I don't think the way to help that minority is to tranquilize the majority. If we become dulled to the reality of our own future, how can we be sensitive to the future of others? As Al Franken's Stuart Smalley character on *Saturday Night Live* told Michael Jordan, "Denial ain't just a river in Egypt." Don't fall into it.

For instance, in 1993 a rosy report prepared for a congressional subcommittee showed that baby boomers' median net worth was higher than their parents' net worth in 1962. Alarm bells went off in the heads of nongovernment experts who analyzed the report. For one thing, it was wildly at variance with *The Economic Future of American Families,* a landmark 1991 study by MIT economist Frank Levy and Richard C. Michel, director of the Income and Benefits Policy Center of the liberal Urban Institute, which projected that if current trends continue, "the entire cohort of baby boomers will reach retirement (ages fifty-five to sixty-four) with less than 50 percent of the net worth of their parents' cohort at a similar age: $143,000 versus $293,000."

The report didn't deal with the question of whether it's likely that over the next three decades baby boomers will have as many breaks as their parents did over the last three—a few minor items like the big jump in the inflation-adjusted value of Social Security cash benefits that resulted from legislation passed between 1968 and 1972, the Dow Jones average adding a fourth digit, and a hefty hike in the inflation-adjusted value of their homes, made still sweeter by their ability to pay off their low-interest mortgages with inflated dollars.

And baby boomers had better end up with more later-life income than their parents' generation, because their parents' generation isn't, as is popularly believed, making out like bandits. The Social Security Administration reports that, of households with at least one member sixty-five or above, 19 percent are living below the poverty line. Twenty-nine percent of all older households are classified as "near-poor," with incomes below 125 percent of the poverty line. Of single or widowed individuals sixty-five and over, 32 percent of men and 44 percent of women are "near-poor." A 1993 Urban Institute study found that 12 percent of Americans sixty-five and older have to choose between buying medicine and buying food.

Incidentally, just how Croesus-like is the "household wealth" of the report's typical baby boomers? Among households "headed" (whatever that means today) by someone under age thirty-five: median home equity of $4,800 and "nonhousing wealth" (cars, savings, etc.) totaling $4,200. And those thirty-five and older are really flush: $36,800 in home equity plus $17,400 in nonhousing wealth.

Princely, no? With all that loot, it's a wonder the thirty-five-plus boomers don't cash in their chips now and begin their life of nonstop adventure travel before their joints begin to creak. With no home, no car, and a grand total of $54,200 in liquid assets, they could join Jackie Mason in saying, "I've got enough money to last me the rest of my life, if I don't have to buy anything."

But the desire to believe in a retirement Tooth Fairy—preferably an indulgent sprite who'll be willing to distribute her largesse without our having to put anything under the pillow—remains passionate. Too many baby boomers believe that they're going to be saved from their lack of saving by inheritances from their parents.

"Estimating the Size and Distribution of Baby Boomers' Prospective Inheritances," a 1993 study by Professors Robert B. Avery and Michael S. Rendall of Cornell University's Department of Consumer Economics and Housing, projected that between 1990 and 2040 baby boomers would receive 115 million bequests totaling $10.4 trillion in 1989 dollars. The average bequest would be $90,167. Retirement-income crisis solved, no?

No. The problem is that wealth in this country is extremely concentrated. The richest one-half of 1 percent of Americans, for example, hold about 39.6 percent of all household assets, reports Edward Wolff, Professor of Economics at New York University. As a result, average household wealth is much higher than median household wealth—the middle figure, half of households having more, and half of households having less—which gives a better sense of what typical parents will leave to their boomer adult children. According to a study by Dr. Avery published in the *Federal Reserve Bulletin,* average household wealth is 4.82 times the median. This means the typical bequest will be on the order of $18,707—not enough to keep the wolf away from the door for very long.

The wrap-up on the "three-legged stool" of Social Security, pensions, and savings: Leg number one is going to be partially amputated, leg number two has osteoporosis, and leg number three is one-third long enough to reach the ground.

CHAPTER 6

QUANTITY OF LIFE

The baby boomers' later life is going to be longer and more expensive than that of any previous generation. Yet we've been told that when we're older we'll be able to live on less money than we're earning now. Actually, we'll need at least as much income—if not more.

Twentieth-century America has been about mass attainment of quality of life. Twenty-first-century America will be about mass attainment of quantity of life.

The younger you are now, the longer you're likely to live, because life expectancy at birth has gone up year after year. People who were born in 1965 have a greater probability of living into their seventies and eighties than people who were born in 1935. The older you are now, the higher your life expectancy is, because people who reach fifty have a greater probability of living into their seventies and eighties than they had when they were forty.

Dealing with the challenges and opportunities presented by quantity of life will become the single most compelling national issue, because it will determine our country's budgetary ability to deal with every other issue. How you personally deal with the challenges and opportunities presented by your own increased quantity of life will determine whether you will be able to live comfortably and fulfillingly in your sixties, seventies, eighties, and beyond.

Realizing that our generation is going to live longer than any in the history of the world is like learning that we've each been given a sleek, powerful ocean-going yacht. A marvelous gift, but expensive to maintain. As Marc E. Lackritz, president of the Securities Industry Association, told the House Subcommittee on Social Security in 1993, "Individuals of all ages are simply not financially prepared to meet the increasing costs of living longer."

Life expectancy for people turning sixty-five has already risen to just under eighty-five for women and just over eighty for men. These figures are expected to rise over the next few decades. According to the Census Bureau, if you're a woman, by 2020 you're going to need enough economic resources to live for 20.4 years past age sixty-five. If you're a man, you'll need enough economic resources to live another 16.7 years.

And many experts think the Census Bureau's estimates are too low. A 1993 report by a research team including former UN Adviser on Demographic Statistics Vaino Kannisto, A. Roger Thatcher, the former director of the British government's Office of Population Censuses and Surveys, and James W. Vaupel of the Duke University Center for Demographic Studies observes: "In most developed countries outside of Eastern Europe, average death rates at ages above eighty have declined at a rate of 1 to 2 percent per year for females and 0.5 to 1.5 percent per year for males since the 1960s." The team points out that the current trend will result in the typical girl born today in a developed country living to between ninety and one hundred.

In a 1993 study, Dr. Vaupel and Hans Lundström of Statistics Sweden question the "canonical" view that life expectancy will peak at around eighty-five years because of the inevitability of "natural death (due to senescent frailty)" in the mid-eighties:

> On the other hand, the acceleration of mortality improvement at older ages may continue, so that mortality rates may fall not at 1 or 2 percent per year but at 3 or 4 percent per year over the course of the twenty-first century. Biological, medical, and gerontological breakthroughs could lead to considerable extensions of the human lifespan. The life sciences may be poised at roughly the point the physical sciences were at a century ago, and biological innovations comparable to electricity, automobiles, television, rockets, and computers may be forthcoming. Fundamental advances could occur over the next few decades in genetic engineering, prevention and treatment of such diseases as arteriosclerosis, cancer, or diabetes, and perhaps even in understanding and controlling human aging itself.

Vaupel and Lundström note that as mortality falls, expenses will rise: "If progress can be made, growth of the oldest-old population will quicken, with major economic and social consequences, including escalation of the cost of public health care and retirement programs."

Genetic research that appears likely to blast the canon to pieces is proceeding as fast as cells divide. The Human Genome Project begun in 1990 by the government's National Institutes of Health plans to map the locations of all 100,000 genes in human DNA by 2005. The gene for Alzheimer's has already been mapped, and a gene linked with osteoporosis has been discovered. The gene that causes one of the deadliest cancers, malignant melanoma, has been located, as has one that causes between 5 and 10 percent of breast tumors. Researchers at the University of Milan have discovered a protein called APO A-1 Milano in several dozen residents of the Italian village of Limone who have a gene that prevents carriers with high cholesterol from developing cardiovascular disease. And the work is moving with amazing speed. In late 1993 researchers found a gene believed to cause half the cases of familial colon cancer; in early 1994 genes were identified that may account for most of the other half.

At the same time as scientists are mapping genes that cause death, they're homing in on genes that lengthen life. Dr. Calvin B. Harley of Geron Corporation and Dr. Carol W. Greider of the Cold Spring Harbor Laboratory are isolating and cloning what they call the "immortalizing gene," which produces an enzyme called telomerase. Because it's telomerase that enables single-cell creatures and cancer cells to multiply indefinitely, they believe the enzyme could prevent aging in normal human tissue.

At the University of California at Irvine, biologist Dr. Michael Rose has discovered that strains of fruit flies with higher longevity have a gene that "overproduces" an enzyme called superoxide dismutase (SOD). Fruit flies into which copies of the SOD gene have been inserted live 5 to 10 percent longer than average. Dr. Thomas Johnson of the University of Colorado has discovered that mutating an SOD gene more than doubles the normal three-week lifespan of tiny worms called nematodes. The National Institute on Aging's Dr. Richard Cutler has found that SOD levels are directly related to lifespan in twenty different species of animals. In 1993 Dr. Michal Jazwinski of Louisiana State University reported the discovery of fourteen genes that lengthen the lifespan of yeast cells, which are intriguingly similar to human cells. One of these has been given a name that's self-explanatory: Longevity Assurance Gene 1.

Because our longevity is "in danger" of being assured, we need to take aim at another canonical view: that when we're older we'll need less income.

Retirement-planning guides always inform us soothingly that we'll be able to live on less when we're old, assuring us that because we won't have job-related expenses (transportation, clothes, etc.), and will no longer have to save for retirement or pay Social Security taxes, between 60 and 80 percent of preretirement income will do nicely. The President's Commission on Pension Policy, convened by Jimmy Carter, estimated in 1981 that a couple earning $50,000 would need a "target replacement rate" of 51 percent of total salary to keep up their preretirement standard of living, while low-income retirees were said to require 86 percent. When the Commission's figures were updated to reflect the 1986 tax changes, "target replacement rates" ranged from 74 percent for a couple earning $100,000 to 73 percent for a couple making $50,000 to 88 percent for those with low incomes.

The truth is that most of us will have a hard time making ends come close, let alone meet, when we're older if our later-life income isn't as much as or more than our present income. Yes, we'll be able to save on dressing for success and power manicures. But such sundries will be far outweighed by big-ticket items related to increased longevity: the expense of care for our aging parents, for example, and the escalating out-of-pocket cost of health care for our aging selves.

Not having to save for retirement isn't going to put a lot of money in our pockets when we're older. Our average personal saving rate of less than 5 percent of after-tax income is so minuscule that it's doubtful whether, if we stopped saving it and started spending it, it would do much for our standard of living.

What if your mortgage is paid off? That'll help. But 24 percent of people sixty-five and over rent, and one out of six of the 76 percent who own have mortgages—13 percent of older people. So something like 37 percent of baby boomers will probably still have to make rent or mortgage payments when they're older.

In addition, we're going to need enough later-life economic resources to provide us with a cushion to absorb possible federal, state, and local tax increases . . . probable Social Security cash-benefit

cuts and postponements . . . certain erosion of our defined benefit pensions by inflation . . . and uncertain interest and dividend rates.

Why then does literature from mutual fund groups, brokerage
houses, banks, and insurance companies eager to spur retirement-
dedicated saving stick like glue to a 60-to-80-percent income
replacement rate? I asked an investment executive why her firm
keeps echoing the notion of fractional income replacement rates.

"We had a marathon meeting at which everyone agreed that the
replacement rate for people who are working now is going to actually have to be a hundred percent, if not higher," she said. "If you're
used to fifty thousand dollars a year, will you really be able to live
on thirty-five thousand dollars? What if the spouse needs constant
home health care? Maybe you'll need seventy thousand dollars. But
our marketing people hit the ceiling. They said that with the savings
rate as low as it now is, if we started pushing even eighty-five percent, it would backfire on us. Our VP/advertising started in about a
psychological principle called 'self-efficacy'—that to be motivated
to act, you've got to believe your action is going to be effective.
Customers would figure that even if they sacrifice more of current
consumption in order to save more, they still won't have accumulated anywhere near enough at the end of the day, so what's the
point of saving at all? We decided finally to stay with the replacement rates that are usually cited, because with people saving so little
now, most of them probably won't even save what we've been
telling them to, let alone more. But we're not happy about it,
because if you follow our advice, you're going to be caught short."

Experts in other countries are already scrapping the notion that
fractional income replacement rates will be enough in the future. Dr.
Françoise Forette, director of France's National Gerontology Foundation, told a symposium at 1993's International Congress of
Gerontology in Budapest that even for today's elderly, "Housing
expenses are equivalent to that of other age categories, food expenditures are slightly more important, health expenditures are significantly higher. In the same vein, clothing, education, leisure
expenses which were classically lower now tend to increase and
represent an important part of the budget."

But in the United States, fractional income replacement rates continue to be retailed, despite the fact that older people are already
receiving too little income. A study of couples who retired after
Social Security cash benefits were raised to their current level found

that they were typically spending 14 percent more than their income. And they were spending that much more even though they were reducing their purchases of goods and services by 4.7 percent a year. As one retiree put it to me, "It seems there's always more month than money."

Yet baby boomers are going to find later life even more costly than it is for today's older Americans.

"There is no historical precedent for a majority of middle-aged and young-old [sixty-five- to seventy-four-year-old] adults having living parents," the Census Bureau noted in 1993.

> More people will face the concern and expense of caring for their very old, frail relatives with multiple, chronic disabilities and illnesses. . . . The need for help is likely to come at the very time when the adult children of the frail elderly are near or have reached retirement age. . . . Some of the adult children may bear health limitations of their own. . . . As medical technology provides more ways to save lives, we can expect the duration of chronic illnesses, and consequently the need for help, to increase even more.

Thirty percent of Americans aged fifty to sixty-eight care for older relatives. The policy community calls this "eldercare." Among the general public, it remains nameless because diapering Daddy and mopping up Mommy is too dreadful to think about, let alone talk about.

The Census Bureau estimates that there will be 6.7 million people eighty-five and older in 2020. That means there are going to be a lot of adult children, many of them in their sixties, who are going to want to be there for them—and being there is going to run into money.

Have you heard about the "sandwich generation"—people squeezed between between caring for their children and caring for their parents? Well, for many in the baby boom generation, the sandwich is going to be a double-decker. Baby boomers in their sixties and seventies are going to find themselves faced with the financial needs not only of parents in their eighties and nineties, but of their own grandchildren. "It is increasingly likely," the Census Bureau reports, "that more and more people in their 50s and 60s will have surviving parents, aunts, and uncles. The four-generation family will become common in developed countries. More children will know their grandparents and even their great-grandparents, especially their great-grandmothers." Yankelovich Partners' survey for Phoenix Home Life Mutual Insurance found that 65 percent of Americans aged thirty to fifty say they expect to be paying college expenses well into their fifties.

Yet while families will be adding layers vertically, stacking up expenses, they'll be fracturing horizontally, sapping their economic strength. Lou Glasse, president of the Older Women's League, told me that by the time the baby boom generation is older, more than one out of five older women will be divorced—a 400 percent increase from today. Today's high divorce rates lower the likelihood that Americans in their twenties through fifties will be able to share a spouse's financial resources when they're older. Pension rights are not subject to community property laws and aren't taken into account in divorce settlements. And not only do we have a high chance of divorce, but a high chance of divorce from subsequent marriages. Plus, not only are divorce figures drifting up, but remarriage rates are drifting down, compounding the precariousness of later-life income, especially for women. Even women in intact marriages will have a problem: according to a Senate committee report, seven out of ten baby boom women will outlive their husbands, many by fifteen to twenty years.

Because of their higher life expectancy, women will need greater economic resources in later life. Yet they'll have lower pensions because they're paid, on average, only 70 percent of what men earn for comparable work. Jessie Allen, director of the Project on Women and Population Aging at the Southport Institute for Policy Analysis, and Alan Pifer, the think tank's chair, wrote recently: "There is little to indicate that large numbers of today's younger women—members, for example, of the baby boom . . . —will not later be in the same predicament as so many of today's elderly women. That is, they will eventually find themselves living alone and struggling to get by with inadequate and dwindling resources."

The fractional-income-replacement-rate myth is fed by the notion that we won't need as much income in later life because Medicare will be paying our health care bills. Actually, according to the federal government's Health Care Financing Administration, people sixty-five and above now pay 37.4 percent of their medical costs out of their own pockets, including insurance premiums, deductibles, co-payments, skilled nursing, and outpatient prescription drugs. And the 1991 Social Security Advisory Council's Expert Panel estimated that between 23 and 30 percent of the median income of couples sixty-five and older will have to go for out-of-pocket health care costs in 2020, and between 29 and 40 percent of the income of singles. A 1992 analysis by Northwestern National Life Insurance came up with similar estimates for how much sixty-five-plus households will have to spend: 29 percent of median income in 2011, 36 percent in 2021, and 42 percent in 2031 (the year the youngest baby boomers turn sixty-seven, the age to which eligibility for full Social Security cash benefits is now scheduled to rise). These are disturbing numbers, considering that according to the Bureau of Labor Statistics, the percentage of median income older people are paying today for medical care, which many find burdensome, is 9.4 percent.

Worse, we have to anticipate that the age of eligibility for Medicare may rise. Most of the human resource executives who responded to William M. Mercer, Inc.'s, survey, *Retirement Security: Are All Bets Off?*, said they "expect the Medicare eligibility age to be higher than 65 in the year 2000." Were they just a bunch of Scrooges? In 1994 the liberal Urban Institute recommended "gradually raising the age of eligibility for Medicare [to] orient the system back toward those with greater needs."

Employer-provided retiree health benefits can't be counted on to reduce our need for later-life income. Sixty percent of American employees work for companies that don't provide any medical coverage to retirees. Traditionally generous corporations like McDonnell Douglas, Primerica, and Unisys have recently changed their benefit packages to require retirees to pay the full cost of their health insurance. And the shrinkage goes on. A 1994 survey by benefit consultants A. Foster Higgins & Co. found that 29 percent of large employers who offer retiree health coverage are going to reduce it by the end of 1995, 7 percent are going to eliminate it for future retirees, and 3 percent are going to eliminate it for all retirees. The Mercer survey reported: "For retirement health benefits, the average funding proportion is about 60 percent employer contributions to 40 percent employee contributions. More than 60 percent of respondents expect that balance to shift more heavily toward employee contributions."

A recent report by Towers Perrin, one of the top employee benefit consulting firms, urges companies to communicate a new reality to their employees:

Effective planning of any kind depends on starting with the right assumptions. But in the case of retirement planning, assumptions often reflect a past that bears little relationship to the lives most American employees lead today—and can reasonably expect to lead in the future. For instance:

Americans are living longer than ever before. That fact, coupled with continuing medical cost escalation, means they will spend considerably more on health care than previous generations did. For today's employees, future medical expenses represent a sizable retirement "outgo."

How are we going to pay for long-term care if our income drops when we're older? The risk of a sixty-five-year-old entering a nursing home at some time in life is now 35 percent. About a quarter of those who enter a nursing home will spend a month or less. About half will spend less than six months. Ten percent of men will stay for six years or more, and 10 percent of women will stay for eight years or more. And with increasing longevity, the chances of being institutionalized are going to be greater than they are today.

It's hard to tell which aspect of long-term care is more frightening—lying on a sheepskin for six to eight years, or getting the bill. Nursing home fees range between $30,000 and $125,000 a year. I've got the rate sheet in front of me from a typical nursing home in my area—well-staffed, clean, but no frills: the cost per year for a private room is $88,200; for the more frugal, willing to share a room, $84,600.

The baby boom generation is going to need long-term care coverage and lots of it. With acute medical care for older people already a fiscal black hole, taxpayers aren't going to be willing to pick up our entire tab for long-term care. Medicare pays only 2 percent of long-term care costs. "Elder law" loopholes that used to make it fairly easy for middle-class people to get Medicaid to pay their nursing home bills while keeping most of their assets in the family by putting them in trust or giving them to their children were tightened in 1986 and 1988, and irised down to pinholes in 1993. "We have facetiously described the American approach to paying for long-term care as universal coverage with a deductible equal to all your assets (except your home and a few thousand dollars) and a co-payment equal to all your income (less a few dollars for spending money)," writes Robert L. Kane, Professor of Long-Term Care and

Aging at the University of Minnesota School of Public Health, and Rosalie A. Kane, Professor of Public Health at the University of Minnesota, in 1994.

Long-term care insurance is a sticker-shock item. In 1993 the New York State Department of Insurance established a foundation-supported, public-private Partnership for Long-Term Care. New Yorkers who buy a Partnership policy and use up its benefits are allowed to keep their assets if they go on Medicaid, though they still have to contribute most of their income toward the cost of their care. The minimum Partnership policy for a sixty-five-year-old has an annual premium of about $1,500—for a couple, $3,000. It starts paying $100 a day after the one-hundredth day in a nursing home, for a maximum of three years. The cost of care delivered at home is reimbursed for three years at the rate of $50 a day beginning after the one-hundredth day. The deductible for a stay in a nursing home charging $84,600 a year would be $23,178 for each admission. After the one-hundredth day you'd have to co-pay $131.78 a day. If you had to stay three years, it would end up costing you another $131,121, for a total of $154,299 out of your resources before Medicaid would kick in. A more generous Partnership policy, paying $250 a day for institutional and home care for a sixty-five-year-old couple with a twenty-day deductible costs approximately $5,000 a year. A non-Partnership policy offering identical benefits but letting you keep all your income for the rest of your life costs about $8,500 a year for a sixty-five-year-old couple.

New York tax attorney Bruce L. Birnbaum, an expert on the intricacies of financial planning for later life, told me, "Long-term care policies from top insurers offer excellent coverage, but they don't come cheap. As a baby boomer myself, I can tell you that it's vital for members of our generation who want adequate long-term care insurance to start taking steps now to make sure they'll have enough income to afford the premiums they're going to have to pay when they're older."

But too many people are unconcerned about the cost of long-term care insurance because they mistakenly believe they already have it. A 1993 survey by Colonial Life & Accident Insurance asked one thousand employed Americans whether their companies are providing them with long-term care insurance. Forty-four percent answered yes—a somewhat bizarre response, considering that employer-paid long-term care insurance is virtually never offered as a benefit. The

Mercer survey noted: "Employers currently allocate an average of 45 percent of their retirement benefit outlays to defined contribution plans, 39 percent to defined benefit plans, 16 percent to retiree health benefits and nothing to long-term care."

People may eventually stop fantasizing that they already have commercial long-term care insurance and start actually buying it. The price of long-term policies might come down somewhat if the risk pool became larger and insurance companies developed better experience in calculating their claims exposure. The federal government will undoubtedly step in with some kind of long-term care coverage or tax break. But the heavens aren't going to part and rain down $84,600-a-year nursing home reimbursements. Even the single-payer legislation considered by Congress in 1994—the only approach that included any nursing home coverage—would have required a 35 percent co-payment. Whatever happens, long-term care is going to cost us cash money, and each of us has to start thinking about how we're going to come up with it when we're older. There's no such thing as a free sponge bath.

Our increased and increasing quantity of life means that conventional ideas about income replacement rates have to be replaced. You and I need to start planning to have enough income to pay for unplanned expenses.

But the straw that's going to break the camel's back—and then put the camel on a waiting list to receive veterinary treatment—is age-based medical rationing.

CHAPTER 7

HOW TO SURVIVE GERONTOCIDE

Any program of health care reform will bring with it medical rationing for older people. Baby boomers are going to need enough money when they're older to afford generous supplementary medical insurance and co-payments to enable them to obtain care that will otherwise be denied them.

You and I are going to need much more later-life income than we've been told will be enough because the only way we'll be able to get all the medical care we need when we're older will be to have our checkbooks out. The medical journal *The Lancet* editorialized in 1992:

> Those concerned with planning health care delivery in the developed world face populations that are living longer and technology that is advancing at a pace that will soon make demands on health service budgets impossibly high. Health expenditures in the USA will reach $1 trillion during the next three years. Rationing is inevitable.

The retirement-security survey conducted by William M. Mercer, Inc., found that 95 percent of human resource executives expect that there will be "rationing of health care for older citizens" as early as the year 2000. America's most influential medical ethicist, Dr. Daniel Callahan, director of The Hastings Center, the leading bioethics think tank, has noted, "Already rationing of health care under Medicare is a fact of life, though rarely labeled as such."

We can get a taste of what we'll be up against when we're older by looking at what Medicare is like now, even before demographic push comes to fiscal shove.

In 1983, faced with spiraling Medicare costs, Congress enacted the "Prospective Payment System"(PPS). Under PPS, Medicare pays hospitals a flat fee for each admission. The amount of the fee is determined by which of 487 "Diagnosis Related Groups" (DRGs) the patient's condition falls into, regardless of the number of days she or he is in the hospital. In theory, according to the Senate Special Committee on Aging, "If a hospital can treat a patient for less than the DRG amount, it can keep the savings." In practice, notes the Federal Reserve Bank of Cleveland, Medicare pays hospitals only 88 percent of the cost of treatment. Hospitals have responded, naturally enough, by discharging older patients as quickly as possible. A 1990 Rand Corporation study published in the *Journal of the American Medical Association* concluded, "Overall the fraction of hospitalizations rated both as too short and as resulting in patients discharged in unstable condition almost doubled . . . after PPS was introduced."

This kind of bean-counting doesn't only apply to high-tech hospital care. And we're not talking just about limiting big-ticket heroic interventions that merely prolong suffering rather than add quality time. Cataract removal is the single procedure on which Medicare spends the most—about $3.4 billion on 1.35 million operations a year. Here's an eye-opener: In a 1993 cost-cutting measure, the U.S. Agency for Health Care Policy and Research issued a "clinical practice guideline" advising against cataract surgery "solely to improve vision" as long as "glasses or visual aids provide satisfactory functional vision." According to the American Medical Association's *Physicians' Medicare Guide,* the guideline recommends "simply waiting until the cataract becomes more burdensome." The American College of Eye Surgeons, Outpatient Ophthalmic Surgical Society, and Society of Geriatric Ophthalmology issued the following comment on the guideline: "Doesn't meet current standards of cataract care. Drafted so that rationing could be imposed."

The U.S. General Accounting Office (GAO) then jumped in with a report complaining that one out of six cataract operations are on people with "slight eye problems"—as if old people are going in and having their *eyeballs cut open* to entertain themselves.

I happen not to have such great eyesight and am not looking forward to getting cataracts (which aren't a disease, but part of aging: live long enough and the lens of your eye will turn gray, like your hair). But I look forward even less to having some paper pusher tell me I have to live with cataracts because I only have a "slight eye problem." My first impulse on reading the GAO report was to fall by their headquarters and give whoever wrote it a slight eye problem. On second thought, I decided to simply wait until the agency becomes more burdensome. But you and I had better have enough money when we're older to pay cash on the barrelhead for health care if we don't want to be, so to speak, blindsided.

Will health care reform get rid of age-based rationing? On the contrary: it's going to cause more of it.

Hospitals and physicians have been able to make up for revenue losses caused by PPS and the cap on doctors' fees for Medicare patients that was phased in between 1991 and 1993 by "cost-shifting": boosting charges to non-Medicare patients. Any effective program of health care reform, regardless of whether it emanates from Democrats or Republicans, or relies on a single payer or managed competition, will reduce or eliminate providers' ability to shift part of the cost of treating older patients onto younger patients. The inescapable result will be a lower level of care at higher ages.

For example, securities analyst Joel Zimmerman, who follows the orthopedic implant industry for the investment banking firm of Lehman Brothers, has predicted that in a strict cost-control environment, the number of hip replacement operations could fall by 10 percent, and knee replacements by 25 percent.

Moreover, let's give all of today's reform nostrums the benefit of the doubt and assume they'll really curb the total amount Americans spend on health care. How will that be achieved?

By forcing drug companies to slash prices? If the pharmaceutical industry were to give away all prescription medications for free, health costs would be reduced by a grand total of 8 percent. By putting a lid on physicians' fees? If all doctors were to cut their fees in half, we'd save only 9.5 percent of the nation's health bill.

By having a simple, standardized claim form? I don't want to disappoint the visionaries who believe such an innovation would be a paperwork panacea, but someone should tell them that Medicare, Medicaid, and all other federally financed health programs have been using a simple, standardized claim form since June 1983. It's called an HCFA-1500, makes carbonless copies, and could be filled out by an adequately trained chimp, yet somehow the cost of those programs still manages to skyrocket.

By eliminating fraud and abuse? Medical costs have increased an average of 11.6 percent a year for the past twenty years, far above inflation. The GAO estimates fraud and abuse at 10 percent of health spending. If every last bit of it could be wrung out of the system—and the GAO doubts much can, given what it calls "the high cost of pursuing fraud and abuse"—total health costs would be reduced by less than one year's increase. Health costs in 2000 would be at the level now projected for 1999, and the unbearable rate of increase would keep chugging along.

The only way a significant slowing of that rate can be achieved is by using what we can call the Willie Sutton Principle, derived from the reply of the legendary 1940s bank robber when he was asked, "Why do you rob banks?": "Because that's where the money is."

Where the money is in the health system is the cost of treating older people. Per capita total spending, public and private, for care of Americans sixty-five and over is more than four times per capita spending for younger people. The U.S. National Center for Health Statistics has reported that people sixty-five and above account for 47 percent of all days in hospitals. People seventy-five and older account for 23 percent of hospital days. Between now and when the baby boomers turn sixty-five, the proportion of older Americans is going to practically double. People sixty-five and up already account for 36 percent of health expenditures. The federal government's Bipartisan Commission on Entitlement and Tax Reform projected that, even if revamping the health system were to reduce medical cost increases to where the outlay for each American of a given age were growing no faster than the economy by 1999, the aging of the population would cause federal health care spending to double as a percentage of Gross Domestic Product by 2030. Cost-cutting won't prevent medical rationing for older people, because what's bringing in age-based rationing is precisely the desire to cut costs.

Changing the structure of the health system won't head off age-based rationing. Let's say Medicare ends up being absorbed into some other program—not too likely, but conceivable. The money Medicare would have been paying out for treating older people in 2020 will still have to come from somewhere. If the money comes from employers, the Willie Sutton Principle will still produce age-based rationing. If the money comes from government, same difference.

We don't know yet whether our lives will be in the hands of face-less government officials, faceless insurance company executives, or faceless HMO or managed-care administrators. One thing, though, is certain: Whoever signs off on denying us medical treatment isn't going to want to show us his face.

But wait a second—how do they implement the Willie Sutton Principle in countries where they've already reformed the health system, like England and Canada?

Simple: They put Willie in charge of deciding who gets care.

According to a study published in the *British Medical Journal,* "There are no special British rules about which patients with end-stage renal failure may or may not be treated. Nevertheless, limited facilities for treatment have made it necessary for British physicians to practice selection to a degree which seems strange, even barbaric, to . . . colleagues in other civilised countries."

As described in an article in the *New England Journal of Medicine,* the process is handled with exemplary British tact: "For example, an internist confronted with a patient beyond the prevailing, if unofficial, age at which one's chances of receiving dialysis becomes slight is likely to tell the patient and family that nothing of medical benefit can be done and that he or she will simply make the patient as comfortable as possible."

The United Kingdom's health secretary refused to address a 1993 British Medical Association conference on rationing unless the topic was relabeled "priority setting." Perhaps it would be more appropri-ate, if less politically acceptable, to call systematic lying about whether treatment would help "gerontocide": killing old people.

At any given moment in Britain there's a waiting list with hun-dreds of thousands of names on it for nonemergency operations: U.K. doctors don't come right out and say you can't have your gall bladder removed because you're too old—they just put you at the back of the line. "Rationing, particularly through queuing," medical ethicist James Childress writes in the *Hastings Center Report,* "has been accepted in part because of 'the acceptance of scarcity as a general feature of British society and affection for the National Health Service.'"

The fabled British "stiff upper lip"—except now it's caused by an untreated stroke. In point of fact, Britons are increasingly buying supplementary commercial medical insurance and going to specialists and hospitals that provide private care. The United Kingdom's attempt to provide both universal coverage and cost containment has led to rationing, which in turn has led to a two-tier medical system in which people who can afford to buy their way around rationing get care, and those who can't get the Patient's Charter. Issued in 1992, the Charter gives an indication of what it's like to be on the lower tier: It guarantees surgery such as cataract removal and hernia repair within two years after being wait-listed, and specifies that operations canceled twice must be rescheduled within one month following the second cancellation.

Then there's Canada's much-acclaimed health care system, where, in reality, money talks and anyone who has the cash to get around eighteen-month delays for hip replacement surgery walks. Despite its image as a single-payer system, only a basic package is provided by the government. Whatever the government doesn't cover must be paid for by individuals, either out-of-pocket or through private insurance, which is on the rise. People wait up to a year not only for cataract operations, but for open heart surgery, for which there are 11 centers in the whole nation (the United States has 793). Ontario has decided to limit out-of-country reimbursements to $175 a day to discourage impatient patients from crossing the border to cities like Buffalo, Detroit, and Duluth for MRIs and brain surgery. Winnipeg Insurance Brokers and American Medical Security have teamed to provide insurance to cover the balance on care outside Canada.

Dennis Timbrell, president of the Ontario Hospital Association, defended the Canadian system against a 1992 report that described it as "featuring rationing, shortages, [and] health care waiting lists":

> Bluntly speaking, older people are more intensive consumers of health care resources, and both Canada and the U.S. are anticipating the dire consequences of aging baby boomers. . . .
>
> Health care is like any other resource—it should be used wisely. If that is to be dismissed as rationing, so be it. Care is not rationed on the basis of income or inflammation of the wallet. In fact, overt or covert rationing is a feature in virtually every health care system in the world. The difference between Canada and the U.S. is the difference between rationing based on need as opposed to rationing based on ability to pay. . . . Faced with an aging population, Canada faces a growing need to allocate resources on the basis of need. Triage is not a new concept in health care, it is simply being applied to policy.

Dr. Daniel Callahan (whose degree, incidentally, is in religious studies, not medicine) continues to marshal support for implementing the Willie Sutton Principle in the United States: "How might we devise a plan to limit health care for the aged under public entitlement programs that is fair, humane, and sensitive to their special requirements and dignity? . . . First, government has a duty, based on our collective social obligations to each other, to help people live out a natural life span, but not actively to help medically extend life beyond that point."

What will be the length of your officially determined "natural life span"? "My own view," Dr. Callahan writes, "is that it can now be achieved by the late seventies or early eighties."

How much impact will views like Dr. Callahan's have on your life? Plenty. We can get an idea of which way health policy is moving by considering the testimony of Hillary Rodham Clinton before the Senate Finance Committee on September 30, 1993, as reported in the *New York Times*:

> Mrs. Clinton has argued that the budgetary constraints the Administration plan will put on insurance companies and hospitals may reduce unnecessarily costly treatment. She has repeatedly cited the example of a ninety-two-year-old man given a quadruple heart bypass because the surgeon had depended on a cardiologist who had referred that patient to him, and she suggests that if the system is changed such surgery will not be performed.
>
> She told that same story and offered the same hope today.

We're not talking here about heroic measures that only prolong suffering. Anyone who's had bypass surgery will tell you that it relieves suffering. But let's assume that denying it to ninety-two-year-olds would be humane—though I don't know how many of us would have wanted the plug pulled on George Burns in 1988 when he was ninety-two. Mrs. Clinton has also expressed the "hope" that health care reform will prevent eighty-year-olds from having bypass surgery. Rationing medical care at age eighty would have cramped the style of Michelangelo, who worked on St. Peter's Basilica until he died at eighty-nine, or of Voltaire, who wrote his last play at eighty-three. At age eighty Goethe wrote to a friend, "I work incessantly to the last." He died at eighty-three, a few months after completing his literary masterpiece *Faust*. Harriet Tubman, a key figure in the Underground Railroad that rescued slaves before and during the Civil War, founded a nursing home for African Americans in Auburn, New York, at age eighty-eight. The architect Frank Lloyd Wright produced nearly a third of his lifetime output—300 commissions—between age eighty-two and his death at ninety-one. It's a mercy to know that as age-based rationing is implemented, we won't have to put up with all that creativity.

Do you think the undertow tugging at the overaged out there in the health-policy mainstream is powerful? Let's paddle up one of the tributaries of the river of rationing-rationalization with Prof. Paul T. Menzel of the Department of Philosophy at Pacific Lutheran University in Tacoma, Washington. The author of *Strong Medicine: The Ethical Rationing of Health Care,* Professor Menzel points out that when we give flu shots to nursing home residents

> we are incurring much greater costs than the nominal money for the vaccine and its administration. Per year of life prolonged, modest estimates might easily be another $2,000 of unrelated medical expenditures, $7,000 of Social Security payments, and $20,000 in nursing home fees. [Professor Menzel was writing in 1991, when long-term care costs were lower.] We could easily approach costs of $30,000 for every year of life we save with flu vaccine. This puts it in the same ballpark of admittedly cost-controversial care as kidney dialysis and liver transplants. . . .
>
> There is no general or abstract way to decide whether $30,000 per year of life saved at seventy-five is too high a cost to pay for penicillin for pneumonia or vaccine for influenza. Everything will depend on all the other things we want to do with the resources of our lives. What is clear is that people of integrity, appreciating all the ages they might live into, will not hide their heads in the sand about what the real costs of lifesaving are.

If I were over sixty-five and had to choose between having my care managed by the mainstream Dr. Callahan and the upstream Professor Menzel, I think I'd go with the one who just wants to free up resources for younger age groups by denying me open heart surgery, rather than the one who has his doubts about whether I should get a flu shot because it could end up costing society thirty grand a year. Why not just strangle everyone at birth and save the entire Gross National Product?

Daniel Callahan isn't a villain—he's simply a well-meaning fellow who's making a good living articulating the zeitgeist. It's not his fault that health costs ultimately can't be "contained." It's a matter of supply and demand. The supply of health care will always be limited by the fact that the economy has to produce other things. But unless access is somehow restricted, as it is today by ability to pay—or as it will be tomorrow, by age—the demand will be unlimited, because modern medical care offers the commodity people desire most: life itself.

The late comedian Jack Benny had a classic radio skit in which a robber comes up to his penny-pinching persona and says, "Your money or your life!" No answer. The thief, exasperated, repeats the ancient highwayman's formula: "I said, 'Your money or your life!' " "Wait a minute," says Benny. "I'm thinking." Daniel Callahan is thinking.

Yesterday's Jack Benny routine will be tomorrow's unavoidable choice. In the past, people with more money could afford more amulets or more leeches, but more magic and bloodletting didn't necessarily mean more life. Our generation will be the first in history for which money and life will be fungible. We'll be able to buy life with money. But conversely—ominously—others will be able to buy money with our lives.

The primary purpose of our health care system is to prevent premature death. This effort succeeds, and more people survive to old age. Those who survive to old age need more medical care, which fuels demand for health services, putting upward pressure on medical costs for people of all ages. Age-based rationing, aimed at reducing that pressure, is a form of chronological cleansing. When we're older there will be enormous pressure on doctors to write three letters on our hospital charts: DNR—"Do not resuscitate."

You and I are going to need supplementary health coverage, and lots of it. If U.S. insurance companies can't sell it to us, we'll be able to buy it from top insurers in no-questions-asked places like Switzerland and Singapore. There will be plenty of solid insurance companies out there that will be happy to take our money and give us world-class service anywhere we go to get medical care.

And we'll be going all over to get it. People in Israel, where the government doesn't control health care delivery but the HMOs that dominate the medical system practice British-style "queue rationing," fly to the United States for treatment.

I can foresee massive numbers of older Americans traveling to

Mexico to receive treatment that our system will deny them. There's a long tradition of U.S. citizens crossing the border for medical care. When abortion was illegal in the United States, women drove from California to clinics in Tijuana. American cancer patients who want drugs that don't have Federal Drug Administration approval get them in Mexican hospitals. People who live in El Paso, Texas, and are looking to save money on dental bills drive over the bridge to Juárez to have their teeth fixed.

When we're older, some of the biggest, best medical centers in the world will be in northern Mexico. There are going to be state-of-the-art, American-staffed mega-hospitals with campuslike grounds in cities like Tijuana, Mexicali, Nogales, Hermosillo, Juárez, Monterrey, and Nuevo Laredo, serving not only the West Coast, the Southwest, and Texas by road, but points north by air. They won't be comparable to U.S. facilities: They'll be better, because they won't have their hands tied by inappropriately dubbed "global budgets," which will be, ironically, not global but national.

If Cuba gets tired of being a poor country, all it will have to do is let enterprising American doctors turn Havana into the number one health care center for older Floridians with folding money. Otherwise, the Bahamas, Jamaica, and the Dominican Republic will get all the business.

Health care havens . . . runaway rehab centers . . . does it sound like a sci-fi scenario? What if I were to tell you that the first offshore American hospital has already opened? It's located on a forty-seven-acre site in Glasgow, Scotland, is 75-percent staffed with American doctors, admitted its first patient in March 1994, has 260 beds, cost $200 million to build, and is called, appropriately enough, Health Care International (HCI).

HCI was founded by two former Harvard Medical School pediatric surgery professors, Drs. Angelo Eraklis and Raphael Levey, who expect it to be filled with American patients as care is increasingly rationed in the United States. Financed with seed money from a San Francisco venture capital firm and bonds underwritten by a London investment bank, the hospital is affiliated with the prestigious University of Glasgow, where Sir Joseph Lister originated antiseptic surgery in the 1860s. The medical director of HCI is the former chief of vascular surgery at the Mayo Clinic, and the American physicians who work with him came from top U.S. teaching hospitals.

HCI has nothing to do with Britain's National Health Service—

it's a strictly In-God-We-Trust-All-Others-Pay-Cash operation. Procedures at HCI cost around 25 to 50 percent less than in the United States. Yet doctors receive U.S.-level salaries and more—$300,000 to $1,000,000—so we can see that in the future, American physicians will have ample incentives to practice off the reservation. With 22 percent of HCI owned by Harvard University, this is no sideshow: It's the American Establishment quietly responding to the prospect of tighter controls on health care.

By the way, do I need to tell you that Medicare doesn't pay one cent toward health care received outside the United States?

You and I are going to need additional income in later life to give us the option of being treated at places like HCI, because what we'll be up against at home will be nothing less than rationing of life. Not beginning now to assemble sufficient economic resources to pay your way around age-based rationing will be hazardous to your health.

I can't put it more clearly than this: Having enough income when we're older is going to be a matter of life and death.

CHAPTER 8

THE GREAT DEPRECIATION

As stocks and bonds are sold by pension funds and individuals to support the members of the baby boom generation as they age, there will be strong downward pressure on asset prices. Weakness in financial markets will decrease the value of pension fund holdings, 401(k) accounts, and personal investment portfolios. Falling security prices and real estate values could trigger the deepest, longest, most devastating economic slump in U.S. history.

Because of their huge numbers and lengthened lifespan, the baby boomers are going to need more total income in later life than any previous generation. Yet we've seen that Social Security benefits will be cut or postponed . . . pensions will be insufficient . . . personal savings won't be able to fill the gap . . .

. . . and that's the good news.

Are you sitting down?

On top of the already-established inadequacy of those conventional income sources, there's going to be unprecedented negative pressure on the value of the assets in our employers' pension funds, our 401(k) accounts, and our personal investment portfolios.

Precisely when you and I are going to need every penny we can get our hands on, demographic forces with the power to cause the entire U.S. economy to implode are going to go critical.

In October 1993, two of the foremost authorities on pension economics, Dr. Sylvester J. Schieber of The Wyatt Company, a top pension consulting firm, and John B. Shoven, Professor of Economics and Dean of the School of Humanities and Sciences at Stanford University, presented a report at a Washington conference sponsored by the Association of Private Pension and Welfare Plans and Stanford's Center for Economic Policy Research. Their study, "The Consequences of Population Aging on Private Pension Fund Saving and Asset Markets," presented startling evidence that by the 2020s, when the youngest baby boomers will be in their fifties, "the pension system will cease being a source of national saving," with an impact on stock, bond, and real estate prices that will be decidedly negative.

Drs. Schieber and Shoven constructed a computer model of the pension system as the baby boom generation passes through it. Essentially, the amount paid into pension funds will drop because the generations coming after the baby boom are relatively small. Yet the amount paid out by the pension funds will rise because an unparalleled number of people will become eligible to receive benefits. As a result, while there will be a flow of money from the pension system into financial markets over the next several decades, it will decrease as a proportion of the total economy. And when we're older, there's going to be an enormous, long-term flow of money out of the pension system. The value of pension assets, now pyramiding, will eventually fall by about 50 percent from its peak.

The two analysts factored in everything from the present ages of workers to the years in which they can be expected to receive defined benefit and defined contribution payouts, from years of service to mortality rates. They calculated the amount by which prices of individual stocks, bonds, and other assets owned by pension funds are likely to increase, and included the dividends and interest that will be earned by the funds' assets. They added the contributions employers and employees can be expected to make, figuring in anticipated wage growth. They adjusted these numbers for inflation using the Social Security Administration's "best estimate" of modest increases in the Consumer Price Index. From the total, they subtracted the benefits that will have to be paid out each year. The result was the amount of money flowing into or out of the pension system. To give a sense of the size of this flow in relation to the economy as a whole, they expressed it as a percentage of total payroll.

Drs. Schieber and Shoven displayed the chart reproduced on the following page to the conference's participants. It shows that during

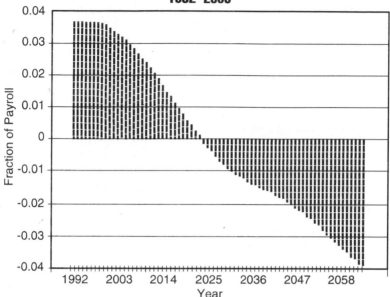

Real Saving of Private Pensions Relative to Total Private Payroll 1992–2065

SOURCE: Sylvester J. Schieber and John B. Shoven, "The Consequences of Population Aging on Private Pension Fund Saving and Asset Markets." Paper presented at a conference, "Public Policy Towards Pensions," sponsored by the Association of Private Pension and Welfare Plans and the Center for Economic Policy Research, Stanford University, Washington, D.C., October 7–8, 1993. Used by permission.

the coming decade, the flow of money from corporate pension funds into markets for stocks, bonds, real estate, and other assets can be expected to be more than 3 percent of payroll. But the proportionate size of the flow will decline until about thirty years from now, when it will go negative. Instead of pumping money into financial markets, the pension system will be selling assets—draining money out of financial markets:

> What [the chart] shows is that under our assumptions the pension system continues to generate significant investable funds for the American economy for the next twenty years or so. In fact, the

decline is very minor for about the next ten years and then it steepens considerably. By 2024, the pension system is projected to cease being a net source of saving for the economy. In fact, the pension system will then become increasingly a net dissaver.

They emphasized that the system's switchover from buying stocks and bonds to selling them is inevitable because of the huge number of baby boomers covered by pension plans.

This change of the pension system from a large net producer of saving to a large absorber of saving or loanable funds will likely have profound implications for interest rates, asset prices, and the growth rate of the economy. . . .

[T]he demographic structure is such that it will by necessity occur. It is not even correct to think of this as a negative development. After all, pension assets are accumulated to provide for the resources needed by the elderly in retirement. It is only natural that when we have an extraordinarily large number of retirees, the real assets of the private pension system will shrink and the system will at least temporarily cease being a source for new investment funds for the economy.

The economists' model predicted that the sell-off of securities by the pension system will begin in the early 2020s, when the baby boomers will be in their sixties and seventies.

The period of time when the pension system begins to be a net seller is more likely in the early part of the third decade of the next century under our conservative assumptions. This could depress asset prices, particularly since the demographic structure of the United States does not differ that greatly from Japan and Europe, which also will have large elderly populations at that time.

Another comment about the asset price effect is that if it occurs, it would likely affect all long-term assets. What we think may happen is high real interest rates which could depress the prices of stocks, bonds, land, and real estate. While this might suggest that a good investment for this period would be short-term Treasury bills, the effect if it occurs is likely to be gradual and last for decades. In the twentieth century the longest stretch of time over which Treasury bills outperformed equities was about fifteen years. We have little else to go on, but we certainly are not advocating that long-term investors invest in short-term instruments to ride out this demographic tidal wave.

Schieber and Shoven concluded with a prediction that the passage of vast numbers of baby boomers through the pension system is bound to put a substantial strain on the American economy.

> We briefly speculated about the impact of the reduced saving of the pension system on asset prices. Even though we don't think the change will be as dramatic as our model predicts (due to adjustments in [pension] contributions and plan design), we still feel that the demographic structure is such that a major change in pension saving will occur. The timing and magnitude of the effect on asset prices is impossible to determine. Capital markets are worldwide, interest rates are determined by both supply and demand, and forecasts of financial rates of return some thirty or more years into the future are futile.
>
> However, the population bulge that we call the baby boom caused considerable strain on the U.S. education system in the 1950s and 1960s. Absorbing those people into the workforce was a challenge in the 1970s and early 1980s and may have been a factor in the slowing [of] the growth in worker productivity. It is probably safe to say that the same numerous cohort will strain the economic system once again during their retirement years, roughly 2010 to 2050.

The chart shows our generation coming over the top of a financial roller coaster. When I first saw it, the way down looked long and scary, so I went to see Dr. Schieber at his office in Washington to find out what, if anything, can be done to smooth out the ride. He turned out to be an even-tempered fellow with a wry sense of humor. With an analysis like his, and as a 1946-vintage baby boomer himself, he'd better be.

Dr. Schieber escorted me into his conference room, picked up a green dry marker, and drew on a glossy white board. "The basic curve can't be changed," he told me. "It's caused by the fact that the huge baby boom generation is going to be drawing money out of the pension system while the not-so-huge generations after it will have to work to put money into it. But the curve can be moved to the right—that is, the sell-off of pension assets could be postponed. And the bottom of the curve can be raised—accumulation of assets would still be at a lower rate, though we wouldn't go into a net sell-off. But the only way the curve can be moved out or up is by expanding the pension system and by turning ourselves into a nation of savers.

"The reason the pension system is stagnating is that it's caught in a double-bind between old-age income policy and tax policy. Until 1981, the emphasis was on pension income security. From 1982 onward, it's been on supposed tax leakages caused by the fact that the money paid into pension funds isn't taxed until it's received as benefits. Those two motives are going to butt heads.

"The other problem is that the United States was endowed with such enormous natural resources that we got slovenly about the need to be thrifty. Also, since the early 1930s there's been a tendency to encourage consumer spending rather than saving. The question now is, can we as a nation save enough to invest enough to make the generations coming on-line productive enough to afford to buy the assets the pension funds will be selling to pay what they owe the baby boomers?"

After I left Dr. Schieber I had a strong urge to call my stockbroker and tell him to sell everything I own and put it in—what? When the demographic tidal wave hits the pension system, what's out there that won't get washed away? Besides, the economists' model doesn't predict a crash in the near future. What it foresees is a sickening slo-mo slide that begins some time between now and 2024 and ends after the last of the baby boomers is pushing up daisies. So I resisted the impulse to dump the whole pile into short-term Treasuries, lay in a supply of freeze-dried food, and head for the hills, and I suggest you do likewise.

But down the road a piece, some kind of evasive action is going to be necessary. Pension funds have poured more than $1.2 trillion into financial markets since World War II. What will happen to those markets when money is hemorrhaging out—which the model says will be the situation around the time the youngest baby boomers turn sixty? Since the early 1980s corporate contributions to pension plans have been low because soaring stock prices made it unnecessary for companies to add money to plans that were funded at legally required levels. But pension-fund buying contributed a lot to that rise. The Federal Reserve Board's periodic *Flow of Funds* reports show that pension funds put $140.1 billion into stocks during the 1980s—about half of all the new money that came into the market. Total pension fund assets are now more than $4 trillion. That's one-third of the $12.4 trillion value of all assets in American financial markets, and twice as much as the $2 trillion held by the runner-up, mutual funds. Pension plans own 32 percent of the stocks in the U.S. economy—by far the biggest institutional chunk. And that percentage is twice what it was in 1975, five times what it was in 1965, and forty times what it was in 1950. It's evident that whether it results in a decrease in future inflows or an increase in future outflows, pensioning off the baby boomers is going to substantially reduce the support pension-fund buying gave to financial asset prices in the decades after World War II.

A plunge of stock and bond prices caused by the demographics of the pension system wouldn't just affect baby boomers. It could trigger a worldwide economic collapse that would make the Great Depression look like a shallow dip. I say "worldwide" not just because today's financial markets are planetary, but because the curves of the private pension systems of the other industrial nations look so much like ours. And I say "collapse" because investment decision making has become so top-heavy. According to a 1993 Wharton School study, the portfolios run by the forty biggest investment managers in the United States contain an astounding 42.8 percent of all U.S. stocks. And a 1994 study by Piscataqua Research proved that "biggest" doesn't mean "smartest." Piscataqua found that between 1987 and 1993, the average investment return of large corporations' pension funds was 9 percent lower than the return on a benchmark portfolio holding 60 percent of its assets in Standard & Poor's 500 stocks and 40 percent in bonds. So as badly as the market will be doing, huge investment managers will probably be doing worse. What if giants like Wells Fargo, Bankers Trust, and Mellon Bank—not to mention the nationwide college faculty pension fund, the New York State teachers' pension fund, and the California public employees' and teachers' pension funds, all of which are among the top twenty investment managers—decide around the same time that, with a demographic tidal wave coming in, perhaps it's time to board up the windows and move inland to Treasury bills?

How long to stay out of stocks and bonds? Oh, a few decades or so ought to do it, considering that the Schieber-Shoven curve shows that the wave will reach full force in the early 2020s, and the coast still won't be clear in 2065. Isn't it comforting to know that as the baby boomers approach their golden years, we're looking at a four-decade blowout in financial asset prices? The Great Depression, which lasted a single decade, bankrupted most American corporate pension plans and brought the world Hitler and Pearl Harbor, the Holocaust and Hiroshima. Can any of us imagine what a multi-decade Great Depreciation will bring?

Feeling a desire to make the specter of the Great Depreciation just go away, I phoned Stephen C. Goss, supervisory actuary at the Social Security Administration and a known optimist, for reassurance.

"What do you think of that curve Schieber and Shoven have come up with?" I said. "Pretty spooky, huh?"

"Reminds me of some of ours," he said cheerfully.

"In fairness to the Social Security system," I offered, "your curves don't go below the zero line."

He laughed. "Oh, ours go below zero. It's just that when we draw them for publication, we stop when we get to the line."

"Do you think Schieber and Shoven's take on the future of asset prices is correct?" I asked.

"Not only do I think it's correct," said Goss, "but what about everything else the baby boom generation is holding—*outside* of pension plans? Stocks. Bonds. Homes. What's going to happen when the boomers start selling off all their assets to raise money to live on?"

Michael D. Hurd, Professor of Economics at the State University of New York at Stony Brook and one of the big guns in the economics of aging, has put some numbers on what will happen. Analyzing responses to the Census Bureau's Retirement History Survey, he found that the elderly "dissave" an average of 3.2 percent of their financial assets each year.

"At this rate," Dr. Hurd noted, "a household with a twenty-year life expectancy will have reduced its bequeathable wealth to about half of its initial level. However, theory suggests that the rate of decumulation will increase with age, so one would expect the wealth level to be less than half after twenty years." Grid this against another of Dr. Hurd's findings: the elderly own about 35 percent of U.S. household wealth. When you consider that the percentage owned by older baby boomers will be higher, because there are so many more of them than of older people today, it becomes apparent that as they spend down more than half their financial wealth, they'll be selling a sizeable proportion of the assets in the American economy. But to whom?

"The consequences of the change in the age distribution of the population are not limited to the Social Security system," Dr. Hurd has written.

The basic problem is how to allocate the output of the economy between the retired elderly, who are increasing in relative numbers, and workers, who are decreasing in relative numbers. Taxation, which is relied on by Social Security and other public programs, is one solution, but it has limits that arise from the political process. Private pensions also have limits imposed by the need of business to show current profit. Private saving is another solution. It too has limits because to finance their consumption during retirement the elderly need to sell their financial assets to someone. As long as the population is growing, they can sell their assets to an expanding pool of workers who are saving for their own retirements. But the changing age distribution means that the pool of workers who want to buy will be shrinking relative to the pool of the retired who want to sell. To induce each person in the smaller pool to hold larger amounts of assets the prices of those assets will have to fall; that is, the return on the assets will be smaller than anticipated. This argument implies that while the fundamental problem of the age distribution can be alleviated by private saving, it cannot be eliminated.

The windows of Dr. Hurd's spacious office look out on the woods that surround SUNY's Stony Brook, Long Island, campus, affording him a long view of both the forest and the trees. "Is the prospect of depreciating asset values as bad as Schieber and Shoven make it out to be?" I asked him.

"It's probably worse," Dr. Hurd said. "When the baby boomers are in their sixties, they're going to need to liquidate their individual holdings of stocks, bonds, and mutual funds. The same thing will happen with real estate. Nobody's assets are going to be worth as much. So pension funds will have to sell more of their assets to meet pension obligations than they currently anticipate selling. If anything, Schieber and Shoven's graph understates the problem."

"What year were you born?" I asked.

"Nineteen forty-one." Like Dr. Hurd's research: slightly ahead of the curve.

"Have you given any thought to how you personally are going to cope with asset depreciation?" I said.

His features clouded slightly. "I've been thinking about it for ten years."

Silence.

"And?"

"What you'd want to do is pre-fund consumption," he said. "The problem is, how can you do that? If you buy a house, for example, you pre-fund your consumption of housing, but you'll own an asset that will be subject to downside pressure on asset prices."

"What do we do with our financial assets?" I asked.

"You've got to sell them before everyone else does," he said. "The problem is—after you sell them, what are you going to hold? The commodity you'd want to hold is labor. But how do you do that?"

"Is this something you've talked about a lot with your friends and colleagues?" I said.

"Yes."

"Any great ideas?"

"No."

How intense will the downdraft on housing prices be? Economists N. Gregory Mankiw of Harvard University and David N. Weil of Brown University predict that "housing demand will grow more slowly over the next twenty years than at any time in our sample [since 1947]. If the historical relation between demand and prices continues to hold, it appears that the real price of housing will fall about 3 percent a year. . . . More formal forecasting . , . implies that real housing prices will fall by a total of 47 percent by the year 2007. Thus, according to this forecasting equation, the housing boom of the past twenty years will more than reverse itself in the next twenty. . . . Even if the fall in housing prices is only one-half what our equation predicts, it will likely be one of the major economic events of the next two decades."

Mankiw and Weil's projections for the U.S. housing market are in line with forecasts for other industrial nations. For instance, Zurich-based Bank Julius Baer reported in 1994, "Demographics from countries within the Organization for Economic Cooperation and Development argue against rising residential housing demand, since individuals at the household formation stage are on the decline." But the work of Mankiw and Weil hasn't been received with universal enthusiasm in the U.S. economic community. For example, Prof. Patric H. Hendershott of the Ohio State University Department of Finance has written, "While real house prices seem more likely to decline than increase over the next two decades, a 47 percent decline seems far beyond the realm of the plausible."

Recently Dr. Hendershott has put forward two somewhat different positions, each more optimistic: "real [house] prices will be either flat or increase," and "the aging of the Baby Boomers between now and 2010 will increase both the willingness to pay for housing and the quantity demanded. Both increases will raise real house price not lower them." But the claim on which he bases both opinions—that housing demand on the part of baby boomers entering their sixties will more than take up any demographic slack in the housing market because "older households are willing to pay a premium for housing"—doesn't jibe with what real estate agents tell me, which is that people entering their sixties generally want to "trade down," cashing out of bigger homes and buying smaller ones. And Dr. Hendershott didn't offer an estimate of how much home prices would go up if they didn't remain flat. Nor did he look beyond 2010, when the oldest baby boomers will be sixty-four and the youngest will be forty-six—all still very much interested in whether the home-equity portion of their net worth will be rising or falling.

If, over the course of two years, a respected economist can disagree not only with two other respected economists, but with himself, then we'd be well advised not to bank on rising housing prices to pay for our retirement.

Meanwhile, in a study for the U.S. National Institute on Aging, Daniel L. McFadden, Professor of Economics at the University of California at Berkeley and head of its Econometrics Laboratory, has developed a sophisticated computer model forecasting housing prices long past 2010. The chart generated by his model, showing home prices from 1869 to 2100, appears on page 92. Dr. McFadden has determined that 1980 will have been the historic peak year for U.S. housing prices, adjusted for inflation. By 2020, home prices will have fallen by 19.2 percent from their 1995 level. By 2030, prices will have dropped by 30.5 percent.

Dr. McFadden notes the crucial role of home equity in the net worth of older people: "Housing equity is the most important asset of most elderly households, and for many is the *only* [emphasis in original] significant asset. . . . [I]n the population aged sixty-five-plus, 69 percent of net worth is in house equity . . . and the median equity among holders was $46,192. The only other assets held by a majority of households [over age sixty-five] are bank accounts and equity in automobiles, and the medians among holders of these assets total less than $17,000."

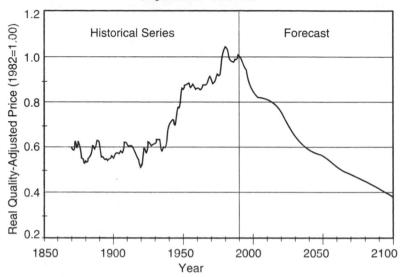

Housing Prices 1869–2100
(Adjusted for Inflation)

SOURCE: Daniel L. McFadden, "Demographics, the Housing Market, and the Welfare of the Elderly." Paper presented at a conference, "The Economics of Aging," sponsored by the National Bureau of Economic Research, St. John, Virgin Islands, May 7–10, 1992. From David A. Wise, ed., *Studies in the Economics of Aging* (Chicago: University of Chicago Press, 1994), p. 278. Copyright © 1994 by the National Bureau of Economic Research. Used by permission.

The rugged contour of Dr. McFadden's graph, a cross-section of the Matterhorn with the summit already behind us, will be a painful sight for anyone who owns a home. Americans have gotten used to the idea of housing as an investment rather than simply a place to live. But the increase in housing prices was fueled by processes that have totally run their course: the post–World War II economic expansion that produced the baby boom, and the fact that once they were grown up, the baby boomers had to live somewhere. The fantasy that, over the long term, society is going to pay us big bucks to live in our own houses is like expecting not merely to have our cake and eat it too, but to have more of our cake after we eat it. In the economy we're plunging into, a home is going to revert to being what it has traditionally been: a place where you hang your hat—and pay for the privilege of doing so.

The effect of weak housing prices in the coming decades will be particularly painful to baby boomers because of four factors.

• First, it will hit those who are counting on receiving bequests. As if the figures in the "Beyond Saving" chapter weren't disappointing enough, consider that 69 percent of the net worth of people aged sixty-five and over consists of home equity. According to Dr. McFadden's figures, inflation-adjusted housing prices will drop by 14.1 percent between 1995 and 2010. This would significantly decrease baby boomers' parents' home equity, and in some cases wipe it out completely. One version of the Mankiw-Weil model forecasts a decline in home prices between 1995 and 2010 of about 37 percent, while another sees prices falling by more than 50 percent. No comment is needed on the effect either of these outcomes would have on baby boomers' inheritances.

• Second, people retiring today routinely sell their homes and use the difference between what they paid for them and what they get for them to buy less expensive housing plus income-producing securities. With prices falling over the long-term, this cash cow will give much less milk to the baby boomers.

• Third, the negative wealth effect of declining housing prices could compound any drag on the economy caused by a long bear market in stocks and bonds. "Wealth effect" is the term economists use to express the fact that when peoples' net worth is higher, they spend more, while when their net worth falls, they spend less. Younger generations, finding themselves living in houses that are dropping in value each year, are likely to go easy on consumer spending. And they may not feel flush enough to bet the depreciating ranch on investing in the stocks and bonds the baby boomers will be trying to unload to make ends meet.

• Fourth, falling home prices will cause a financial cushion today's elderly rely on to become progressively less ample for baby boomers. Professor Jonathan S. Skinner of the University of Virginia Department of Economics has found that "retired households treat housing equity as a form of insurance or precautionary saving. They are unlikely to tap into equity, but when they do, it is because of adverse events, such as widowhood or downturns in income."

I don't believe that Schieber and Shoven's roller coaster and McFadden's alp represent the shape of doom and gloom to come. We shouldn't be jumping out of windows at the prospect of Americans being able to buy stocks at low multiples of earnings, and of housing becoming more affordable each year instead of less. But when top experts are telling us not only that Social Security, pensions, and savings are going to be inadequate, but that both financial assets and real estate will be tumbling into the tank when the baby boomers get older, we've got some serious rethinking to do about our later years.

Economists have identified many kinds of "exogenous shocks"— outside forces that affect the normal up-and-down business cycle. There are monetary shocks, supply (e.g., oil) shocks, technology shocks, liquidity preference shocks, even government policy shocks. It now looks like we're going to be whacked by the Big One: a stupendous demographic shock.

The Great Depression was a prolonged economic contraction driven by a shortfall of demand for consumer goods. That financial calamity of the twentieth century was rooted in what economists call a "distributional" problem: the imbalance between the rich (who, having high incomes, "oversaved") and the poor (who, having low incomes, "underconsumed"). The Great Depreciation, if it comes to pass, will be a hyper-prolonged economic contraction driven by a shortfall of demand for capital goods: machines that manufacture, transport, and process information about consumer goods. The financial calamity of the twenty-first century will also be "distributional," but along a different vector. This time the imbalance will be between generations rather than socioeconomic classes.

The cataclysm we're going to have to live through when we're older will be precipitated by "undersaving" caused by "overconsumption." But that "undersaving" will, in turn, cut consumption by older people, and the resulting "underconsumption" will kick the entire economy when it's down.

Concern about future underconsumption by older people has already been voiced by prescient observers. In 1994 former Securities and Exchange Commissioner J. Carter Beese Jr. said, "For many retirees, the money won't be there, and this will have a direct effect on most Americans' standard of living. A lot of participants in 401(k) plans are not doing a good job. They are not investing well and leagues of them may be retiring at subsistence levels from their 401(k) plans. That has tremendous implications for the economy." Mr. Beese has been warning that the rise of 401(k)s, coupled with the low proportion of equities in 401(k) accounts, reducing the possibility for appreciation, will result in inadequate later-life income, which will slow the entire economy. I don't want to give him an additional headache—the man's been doing the Lord's work—but even if 401(k) participants could be cajoled into loading up on stocks (and given the prevalence and intractability of "myopic loss aversion," I doubt whether they can), sometime between now and the onset of the Great Depreciation, they'd better unload, or the value of their 401(k)s will be brutally hammered. Can you imagine a future Securities and Exchange official telling the public, "Sell your stocks now and avoid the rush?"

A book on "generational equity" a few years back characterized the members of the baby bust as, in the words of Phillip Longman's title, *Born to Pay*. The as-yet-unperceived fate of the baby boom generation is that it is born to sell. And unless there's a profound change in the way we think about the economics of later life, the baby boomers may have to sell for so little that the entire economy will swirl down the drain, taking both the baby boom and baby bust generations with it.

CHAPTER 9

LONGEVITY INSURANCE

We can thrive when we're older despite the inadequacy of Social Security, pensions, and savings, and the high expenses and economic uncertainty we'll be facing. To do so, we must have the opportunity to continue to work into our sixties, seventies, and even later if necessary. When we're older, many of us will be working part-time, others will be working full-time, and some won't be working at all. Today's norm of complete retirement is on the way out. A new norm of semiretirement is on the way in.

If in 1491 you'd asked the smartest people what the shape of the earth was, they'd have told you it was flat.

If you'd asked them what surrounded it, they'd have pointed to a map showing the flat world surrounded by a great ocean. Written around the edges of the ocean would have been the words, "Here be dragons."

The people who keep talking as if you and I can rely on the "three-legged stool of retirement income"—Social Security, pensions, and savings—tend to be pretty smart. But many of them unconsciously continue to cling to that conventional image not because it reflects reality but because the question raised by letting go of it—how is American society going to support such a vast number of baby boomers when they're older?—is too frightening. "Here be dragons."

The smartest people in 1491 had no idea that they were about to encounter a new world. They had no idea that in a few years people would routinely be doing all kinds of things that would previously have seemed. . . . *counterintuitive,* like sailing west to go east.

We are about to enter a new world of old age. Older people—you and I, not that far from now—will be doing all sorts of things that might seem unlikely today. The worldview of 1491 was limited by outmoded ideas about space. Today's worldview is limited by outmoded ideas about time.

Whatever your age today, increased longevity means you're going to need enough financial resources to see you through a longer life than the youth-obsessed culture has been telling you you're going to have. The main risk isn't that we'll fall off the edge of the world: it's that we're going to need enough provisions for an ongoing journey.

Life insurance salespeople are still out there asking prospects, "What if something happens to you?" The real question as we enter the new era of quantity of life is, "What if something *doesn't* happen to you?" What each of us needs now is longevity insurance.

We need longevity insurance because

• Our Social Security benefits are destined to be cut.

• Defined benefit pension payouts, generally inadequate to begin with, will inevitably be eroded by inflation.

• Defined contribution plans won't build enough value unless they're positioned aggressively in stocks, which most 401(k) participants are unlikely to do because of "myopic loss aversion."

• Personal savings are unlikely to close the retirement income gap because, as a practical matter, few people are going to radically increase their savings rate.

• Inheritances will seldom be large enough to add significantly to savings.

• Higher quantity of life will increase later-life financial needs far beyond already inadequate fractional income replacement rates.

• The prospect of age-based medical rationing means that having enough additional income to pay for generous supplemental health insurance and co-payments will be a matter of life and death.

• Downward demographic pressure on asset prices will further reduce the extent to which we can rely on pensions, 401(k) distributions, and personal savings and investment portfolios.

Fortunately, the longevity insurance we must have is available to us: the possibility of doing paid work in later life. Each of us needs to begin to take steps now to make sure we'll have the opportunity of working when we're older if we need to.

In 1776 people sixty-five and above were 2 percent of America's population: one out of fifty, the overwhelming majority of them self-supporting. As late as 1900, the proportion sixty-five and over was only 4 percent. The figure today is 12.7 percent. The Census Bureau estimates that in 2030, when the youngest baby boomers are in their mid-sixties, the proportion of the population aged sixty-five and above will be 21.8 percent—more than one out of five Americans.

No society in the history of the world has ever supported such a huge number of older people for decades in a life of comfortable leisure. There is no evidence that any society *can* support such a huge number of older people for decades in a life of comfortable leisure.

Members of the baby boom generation are going to have two alternatives: give up some of the comfort, or give up some of the leisure.

And the same will go for the generations born after the baby boom. According to the Census Bureau, the percentage of the population sixty-five and over will continue to rise after 2030. By 2080, when it has leveled off, 24.5 percent of Americans will be sixty-five or above, even though the last of the baby boomers will be celebrating their 116th birthdays. "Planners should be concerned not with a one-time phenomenon associated with the aging of this generation, but with a future society in which the ratio of elderly to younger persons has permanently shifted," notes Eric Kingson, Associate Professor of Social Policy at the Boston College Graduate School of Social Work and a member of Robert J. Myers's staff at the National Commission on Social Security Reform, which developed the 1983 Social Security amendments.

The Social Security trust funds' Board of Trustees has five members. Three serve ex officio: the secretary of the treasury, the secretary of labor, and the secretary of health and human services. Two are "public trustees" not on the government payroll. The outgoing public trustees, who finished their four-year terms in 1994, were attorney Stanford G. Ross, who was commissioner of Social Security from 1978 to 1979, and David M. Walker, a former assistant secretary of labor and acting executive director of the federal government's Pension Benefit Guaranty Corporation, now a senior partner in the "Big Six" accounting firm of Arthur Andersen.

The Board of Trustees' *Status of the Social Security and Medicare Programs: A Summary of the 1994 Annual Reports* ended with a four-page afterword printed in italics, signed only by Ross and Walker. It was headed A MESSAGE FROM THE PUBLIC TRUSTEES. This little-noticed section of a little-noticed epilogue to a little-noticed publication contained the following paragraph, little noticed at the time, but destined to be a turning point in the life of our nation:

In order to make informed decisions about what roles Social Security, private pensions, personal savings, and earnings from work should play in providing retirement income in the decades ahead, better information is needed about the needs of future retirees and the resources that will be available to meet those needs.

The Social Security system's trustees had previously issued fifty-three annual reports. Not one of those reports, not one summary of those reports, had included one word suggesting that "earnings from work" would play any role in "providing retirement income."

Indeed, one might think a good definition of "retirement income" would be precisely the income older people receive that doesn't come from work.

Ross and Walker's terminology was perhaps not as exact as it could have been: It's hard to put unprecedented thoughts into words. But the significance of their parting shot was profound:

- Income from Social Security, employer-sponsored pensions, and personal savings will no longer assure that our later years will be filled only with leisure.
- Income from work is going to play a role in the later years of many Americans.

Implicit in Ross and Walker's final message to the American people as the guardians of Social Security was the recognition that the three-legged-stool concept is obsolescent. A role in the income of "future retirees"—you and me—is going to be played by "earnings from work": a fourth leg.

Like any four-legged structure, the coming "chair" of later-life income may wobble a bit unless it's carefully leveled. But four-sided designs tend to be roomier. When was the last time you saw a dinner table with three legs or a triangular house?

Ross and Walker were simply, though courageously, giving official, on-the-record voice to a view I've heard expressed by a wide range of experts.

Robert N. Butler, M.D., is one of the world's most distinguished authorities on human aging. His 1975 book *Why Survive?*, exposing what he called "the tragedy of old age in America," won the Pulitzer Prize. From 1976 to 1982 he was the first director of the federal government's National Institute on Aging. Today he chairs the Department of Geriatrics and Adult Development at New York City's Mount Sinai Medical School, which he founded in 1983. The NIA has predicted that by 2020, people sixty-five and over will compose up to two-thirds of the practices of most physicians and health caregivers. Yet astonishingly, Dr. Butler's department, devoted to teaching doctors how to treat older patients, is the only one of its kind in any of America's 127 medical schools.

At a 1983 conference in Salzburg, Austria, Dr. Butler introduced a concept he called "productive aging." He had been asked to lead a session about dependency in old age. But in every country he'd visited, he had encountered fear of the economic burden posed by the growing proportion and sheer number of older people. So he turned his assigned topic on its head and proposed that alleviating this concern will require encouragement of productive activity among older people—"contributions to family, community, and national life in the form of paid and unpaid services and self-maintenance."

"Societies are afraid this increasing older population will become unaffordable," he has written, pointing to Daniel Callahan's views as an indication of this fear, "lead to stagnation of the society's productive and economic growth, and generate intergenerational conflict." Dr. Butler presented his prescription to the 1993 International Congress of Gerontology in Budapest: "We consider it essential that older people in the industrialized world remain productive in this broad sense and sustain themselves financially."

Dr. Butler's concept of "productive aging"—"the continuing contribution of older persons through work, voluntary services, teaching, sponsorship, and philanthropy"—is now universally embraced by gerontologists in the United States and around the world. Outside that far-seeing circle it is virtually unknown. But eventually the paradigm of "productive aging" is going to become so widely accepted that people won't know or care who originated the phrase, just as people today denounce "ageism" without the slightest awareness that the word was coined in 1968 by a forty-one-year-old psychiatrist named Robert N. Butler.

"The world is in the midst of an all-encompassing change I call 'the longevity revolution,'" Dr. Butler tells me across a table for two at a restaurant on Manhattan's Upper East Side, a few blocks from Mount Sinai. I've snatched him out of his corner office, where he is beset with people who want his ear, because I want his mouth. "Vast numbers of people are living into old age. There's going to be a dramatic increase in the proportion of older people in the population. It's a worldwide phenomenon, and will become a major geopolitical issue in the twenty-first century. The longevity revolution is going to transform all aspects of society—the family, housing, education, medical care, living standards, retirement, the workplace—everything."

Knowing that Dr. Butler was born in 1927, I'd expected a kindly-old-doctor type from Central Casting. Instead, in his blue blazer and bright paisley tie, he looks like a tennis player in his forties who has dyed his hair silver on a dare. Radiating vigor, he seems surprisingly—I was about to write "surprisingly youthful," but why do we persist in considering that a compliment? What he seems is . . . *ageful*. He has just zoomed back from a promotional whirl for a book he coauthored with his wife, psychotherapist Myrna I. Lewis, called *Love and Sex After Sixty*. He appears to be giving and getting a considerable amount of both.

"Life expectancy in the United States has gone up twenty-eight years since 1900—almost what was attained in the previous five thousand years," Dr. Butler tells me. "The longevity revolution is one of civilization's most extraordinary achievements. But it means that when we're older we're going to have to continue to contribute to society, not just make claims on it. People are generally underestimating the number of years they're going to live, and what those additional years are going to cost them financially. The result is that they're underfunding their old age. With all this increased life expectancy, why not an increase in work expectancy?"

In 1994 the American Society of Pension Actuaries (ASPA) issued a report recommending sweeping changes in how older Americans are supported. Few if any of the 3,000 green-eyeshade types who belong to ASPA are probably aware that Dr. Robert N. Butler recently told a symposium of the International Leadership Center on Longevity and Society he founded in Tokyo, "We live longer. We must work longer. We must contribute to our own life and not just depend upon others." Actuaries don't spend much time contemplating the views of prominent medical educators or pondering paradigms like "productive aging." The bottom line with actuaries is—the bottom line. Yet Dr. Butler and ASPA, coming from very different points of origin, have arrived at the same place. One section of ASPA's report, "Working Beyond Retirement Age," begins:

> Traditionally, there have been three sources of retirement income: Social Security benefits, personal savings and private retirement plans. The ASPA National Retirement Income Policy Committee suggests working after attaining retirement age as an optional fourth source of retirement income. Adding work after retirement fulfills several objectives. First, it makes sense to encourage and utilize the experience, skills and vitality of our older citizens. This is a valuable national resource. Second, we must recognize that sixty-five is not "old age" anymore. Life expectancy has been significantly advanced due to medical breakthroughs. Moreover, there is hard evidence that continued work improves the quality of life.
>
> Of critical importance is the practical problem that traditional pension income sources [including Social Security] will be insufficient for future generations. The option to continue productive employment can help fill the unfunded income need.

One way we can tell that work may be part of our later lives is to discover that even now, before demographic overload jolts the retirement system, a significant number of older people are on the job. Some are barely tolerating it; others are having a ball. If there be any dragons out there, they're slaying them.

We can get a sense of the extent to which the backfield of tomorrow's trend is already in motion by looking at the country's largest civilian employer, the Department of Defense (DoD). Sixty thousand of DoD's 912,000 civilian workers could retire immediately on full pension but are continuing to work. Of these, 29,325 are age sixty-two and over; 12,601 are sixty-five and up. One is eighty-nine. In addition, there are 2,000 DoD employees aged sixty-two to eighty-two who haven't yet qualified for pensions. And the assistant secretary of defense for force management and personnel has said that in downsizing its workforce, older employees aren't being targeted, "since there is no correlation between age and a worker's performance."

Right at this moment, more than 3.6 million Americans aged sixty-five and above are in the labor force, according to the U.S. Bureau of Labor Statistics. One out of six men and one out of twelve women sixty-five and over work in paid jobs. Almost 5 percent of women seventy and above have jobs, as do nearly 11 percent of men. Even among people seventy-five and over, about 6 percent of men and 2 percent of women continue to work for a living.

And these figures understate the number of older people who are actually working. Social Security benefits to recipients aged sixty-two through sixty-four are reduced $1 for every $2 earned from work, over a limit of $8,000, and $1 for every $3 earned over around $11,000 from age sixty-five through sixty-nine. The result is what could be called a "gray market" in older employees. Professor Amitai Etzioni of George Washington University, president of the American Sociological Association, told a conference: "I know nine people who work in the underground economy so they will not lose Social Security benefits. Not allowing older Americans to work without penalty decreases Treasury revenues and creates a separate class of people—one that works without fringe benefits in order to augment Social Security income. Removing the penalty would result in an enormous statistical change. Although on the records only 11 percent of Americans over sixty-five work, I would bet at least another 11 to 22 percent work off the record."

As early as 1984 Alan Pifer noted that "age 65 is obsolete." Pifer, born in 1921, is chair of the Southport Institute for Policy Analysis, where he initiated the Women and Population Aging Project, and president emeritus of the Carnegie Corporation, where he organized that foundation's Aging and Society Project and coedited its landmark study, *Aging and Society: Paradox and Promise.* He saw the future with remarkable clarity when, more than ten years ago, he proposed a fundamental change in how society views what he called the "third quarter" of life (ages fifty to seventy-five).

> What is needed to enable third-quarter Americans to be productive in the broad sense is clear enough. First, society needs to look upon them as an asset, rather than a burden. Then, government and business should help them by providing equal access to retraining,

phased retirement, greater flexibility in the use of both public and private pension benefits, greatly expanded public employment similar to that presently existing under the federal Senior Community Service Employment Program and better organized volunteer jobs.

Some of these changes would cost money, but they would also produce substantial savings by using older people's skills, experience and reliability and by cutting health costs. The more active and productive their lives, the healthier they will be. And as older workers, through the challenge provided by new careers, begin to reverse the trend toward early retirement, the growing burden on the Social Security system will be eased.

Little of this has happened so far. But attitudes are changing. The 1993 Health and Retirement Study of 12,600 people aged fifty-one to sixty-one conducted by the University of Michigan Institute for Social Research found that 23 percent expect to continue working full-time after age sixty-five. Seventy-three percent said they "would like to continue doing some paid work."

And a new factor will be coming into play for the baby boom generation. I couldn't agree more with Alan Pifer's overall theme: America needs productive older people. But I want to emphasize that older people are going to need to be productive.

The only "longevity insurance" available to us is keeping open the possibility of continuing to work. When you and I are older, many of us are going to need the opportunity to earn money. Volunteer work will always be rewarding for those who can afford to do it. But it should be a freely chosen option, not dues older people must pay to be considered productive. Volunteerism was how American society used to get the benefit of women's talents without the drawback of having to pay them. A lot of us are going to need paid employment to close the gap between what Social Security, pensions, and savings will bring in and what it will cost us to live. To the model of productive aging I would add this caveat: it also must be solvent aging. We won't be able to maintain our standard of living if our reward for doing forty years of paid work is being sentenced to twenty years of community service.

In 1993 the authoritative Employee Benefit Research Institute, known in policy circles for expressing itself cautiously, reported:

In the future, employees may not desire or be financially prepared to retire early, and employers may attempt to encourage them to stay in the work force past the age of sixty-five. At the same time that work force demographics will shift, leaving fewer younger workers and more older workers, more individuals may find that they do not have sufficient retirement income to retire early or at the normal retirement age. The greater role of defined contribution plans, particularly as primary plans in small to mid-sized employers may result in individuals receiving lower than anticipated investment income and having insufficient retirement funds. These workers may need to stay in the work force longer because they are not financially prepared to retire.

Dr. Sally Coberly is director of the Institute on Aging, Work and Health of the Washington Business Group on Health, and was a senior research associate at the Andrus Gerontology Center of the University of Southern California. In a report prepared for the U.S. Administration on Aging she has written: "Cuts in Social Security benefits, increases in out-of-pocket costs for Medicare, and lower pension/investment returns all loom as possibilities that could result in greater interest in work either through delayed retirement or a return to work after a period of retirement."

Dr. Sar Levitan, born in 1914, a labor market expert who's director of the Center for Social Policy Studies at George Washington University, told a recent conference:

> If anybody in this room aged forty-five or younger anticipates early retirement, forget it. . . . In the short run, if the economy continues to stagnate, we may still anticipate a decline in employment of older workers. Employers are likely to lay off older workers because of their higher costs. However, in the longer run, if and when the economy resumes its historic growth, older workers will have to hold onto their jobs, because employers and workers will not be able to afford the ever-increasing [retirement income] commitment to older workers. . . . Since we keep on living longer, the cost of early retirement will therefore continue to increase, particularly if you factor in the high cost of health care. . . . Pensions have stopped expanding and their value is likely to decline because of inflation. Only 30 percent of retirees collect private pensions, which accounts for 15 percent of total retiree income. Federal Social Security laws are also becoming less generous. The law already raises the normal retirement age to age sixty-six by 2003 and age sixty-seven by 2027. Don't be surprised if later amendments will raise [the age of eligibility for full Social Security benefits] before 2027. . . . If earlier

remarks were on the mark, we should anticipate action by both government and employers to facilitate the participation of older persons in the workplace.

Economist Michael C. Barth, program director of the Commonwealth Fund's "Americans Over 55 at Work" program, is senior vice president and director of the consulting firm of ICF Inc., and was deputy assistant secretary of health and human services for income security policy from 1973 to 1980. Dr. Barth told me, "Social Security was premised on continually increasing economic growth, because contributions aren't invested in productive assets—they're just transferred directly to the people receiving benefits at the moment. The so-called trust funds are used to pay general government expenses. So unless we enter an era of sustained, high economic growth, which doesn't appear to be on the horizon, I don't see how the money is going to be there in the future to sustain the level of benefits we've become accustomed to expecting. Private pensions aren't going to be able to fill the gap. And the baby boomers aren't saving anywhere near enough to meet their need for retirement income."

According to a study by Dr. Barth and economist William McNaught, the Commonwealth Fund's director of research, "It is not unlikely that in the future the usual path to retirement will be a career of full-time work through the late fifties, a partial retirement combining increased leisure and part-time work through the sixties, and full retirement at a much later age than is typical today."

Charles Handy, a leading British management consultant, Visiting Professor at the London Business School, and author of *The Future of Work,* has developed an influential following among U.S. corporate executives through his Harvard Business School Press books *The Age of Unreason,* published here in 1990, and 1994's *The Age of Paradox.* According to Handy, the age structure of work is going to change drastically in the next few years. He predicts that increasingly "clever machines and computers" will reduce the need for human labor, cutting the number of lifetime hours devoted to a full-time job from roughly 100,000 today to about 50,000. His assessment is that after "core workers"—managers and technicians whose functions can't be outsourced—finish their 50,000 hours of full-time corporate employment at around age fifty-five, they will continue to work for another fifteen to twenty years, usually for themselves.

What I call the Berlin Wall between work and retirement will come down because, as Handy puts it, "After all, in the last century no one had heard of retirement—they worked till they dropped, or, as a farmer said once when I asked him what was the difference between farming at 75 and farming at 50, 'The same only slower!' . . . Nor do the self-employed ever really retire, they only slow down."

I'm not going to kid you. The idea of working when we're older may sound about as appealing as being chained to an oar. Those of us who are golf legends may look forward to going out on the senior tour. But not everybody wants a second career. A lot of us would be delighted if we could have avoided our first one! A home run in the stock market, perhaps a major lottery win, and we'd gladly have told the boss, "Take this job and shove it." After years of being hassled by managers, coworkers, and customers, we're beat. We'd love to spend the rest of our lives catching rays.

On the other hand, more than half of the baby boomers are female. The women of the baby boom have fought to enter the workplace out of a determination to become engaged in the affairs of the world. Are these same women going to fight to become disengaged? Are they really going to be so eager to spend twenty years attending ceramics classes? Have they struggled to be the first generation of women to escape the marginalization of housewifery only to find themselves remarginalized as "senior citizens," as trivial a role as any society has ever concocted for its elders?

And male baby boomers, famous for their workaholism, have to ask themselves to what extent their expectation of a later life of leisure springs from a deep inner need, and how much is merely cultural conditioning telling them that when they reach an arbitrary age, they're supposed to switch suddenly to retiraholism. In the great American quest for self-esteem, why is it that you can't look yourself in the mirror when you're forty unless you have a job, while you can't look yourself in the mirror when you're seventy unless you don't have have a job?

In our society, older people have become the keepers of the flame of the "taboo on labor" described by the American economist Thorstein Veblen in his 1899 classic, *The Theory of the Leisure Class*. When I first meet people in their sixties or seventies who've gone back to work and I ask them why, they never say, "Because I need the money, that's why." Later on, they may tell me they started working again because they found themselves dipping into their life savings to buy groceries, but in the beginning they always say, "I just got so bored sitting at home."

When the baby boomers are older, a few will undoubtedly end up like the Polynesian chiefs described by Veblen "who, under the stress of good form, preferred to starve rather than carry their food to their mouths with their own hands." But the rest of us are going to be bored, bored, bored. Old age is just going to be one big yawn, punctuated by dialing in to pick up our voicemail.

Does this mean we're going to work till we drop? The fact is, that's pretty much what most Americans did until about a hundred years ago. Economist Jon R. Moen of the Federal Reserve Bank of Atlanta is an authority on the history of U.S. "labor force participation rates"—the percentage of people in various demographic categories doing paid work. He notes that census data before 1890 showed that wealth had hardly any effect on whether people stayed in the workforce past age sixty-five. The overwhelming majority of men kept working even if, by today's standards, they could afford not to. According to Dr. Moen, census figures show that labor force participation of men sixty-five and above (and it was mostly men who worked for pay) "held steady at about 75 percent until 1890." Professor W. Andrew Achenbaum of the University of Michigan Institute of Gerontology has noted that around 25 percent of American men over sixty-five used to be disabled, which means that just about every male who was physically and mentally capable of continuing to work did so. And in those days, women worked longer than men, because they lived longer—they just seldom got paid for it.

Will this become common again? I don't know. Jessica Tandy, who reached the height of her popularity at age eighty, when she starred in *Driving Miss Daisy,* continued to work until she died at eighty-five in 1994, shortly after finishing *Nobody's Fool* with Paul Newman. Actor Don Ameche, born in 1908, didn't actually expire on the set of his last movie, but no sooner were all his scenes in 1994's *Corrina, Corrina* shot than his life was a wrap.

Julia Child was born in 1912. Hugh Downs (who, incidentally, is a member of the Advisory Council of Dr. Butler's department) was born in 1921. Sir John Gielgud was born in 1904. Mike Wallace, born in 1918, has said, "I'll work until my toes turn up."

Not only are the media models for continuing to work already very much in place, but there are plenty of people outside the limelight who are just doing it. I have numerous friends in their seventies and eighties who work full-time, year-round, love what they're doing, and have no plans to retire. Clinical psychologist Muriel Oberleder, Ph.D., born in 1926, uses her age as a credential and has a busy practice treating older people. "I seem to have this field all to myself," she says. "Younger therapists don't want to treat older people. I think older people frighten them because they haven't come to grips with their own fear of aging." Stockbroker Edgar Dannenberg of Gruntal & Co., born in 1911, is more market-savvy in his eighties than any two analysts in their forties, possibly because he's been through more ups and downs. Blanche Martin, born in 1921, is the office manager of the dancing school where my wife takes her exercise class. She sold her wholesale gift business in her sixties but went back to work after her husband died and she got tired of sitting around worrying about how she was going to be able both to pay the $6,200-a-year taxes on her house and travel to Europe in the summertime. Ear, nose, and throat specialist Lester L. Coleman, M.D., born in 1906, is sought out by recording artists in their twenties in preference to some of his younger medical colleagues because, unlike Dr. Coleman, they didn't take care of Judy Garland's vocal cords, or Cary Grant's.

Annette Thomas, born in 1922, plays Mrs. Bendix, an occasional character on a TV soap opera. "They pay six hundred seventy-five dollars basic," she told me, "plus maybe nine hundred dollars overtime. It can add up to fifteen hundred dollars-plus a day. They call me whenever they decide to throw her in. I worked enough this year so I could collect unemployment.

"I turned pro when I was in my fifties because I got a part in an off-Broadway play where you had to be union. A few years ago I got divorced. We'd been married thirty-seven years. From an economic standpoint, it was a tremendous shock. I'd always relied on him to take care of the finances. I'd been earning money for years, but I'd never handled it. Never paid a bill. Never balanced a checkbook. Suddenly I had to become an investment manager! Widows get respect in this society, plus they get the husband's money. When you're divorced and my age, you get zip. No honor, no cash.

"People say to me, 'You could scrape by if you didn't work. Why don't you quit? You're going to wear yourself out.' But I've got to work. I've got to prove myself. Not to anyone else—to myself. I have to prove myself to myself, every day. I'll work till I drop if I can. My father worked until the afternoon of the day he died."

At the opposite economic pole from Annette is my friend Cleveland Amory, born in 1917, who founded and runs the Fund for Animals, and has authored three bestselling books since he turned seventy: *The Cat Who Came for Christmas, The Cat and the Curmudgeon,* and 1993's *The Best Cat Ever.* "I'll probably work until I just keel over," Cleveland told me. "The retired people I know aren't very happy. There are enough problems when you're old without setting yourself up to feel useless. If I were to get the feeling that people around me were thinking, 'I'm not going to take orders from that old goat anymore,' I might quit. But I'm not in any hurry to get out of their way.

"My father never retired. He was from Boston, the head of a company called Spring Mills. During a blizzard in the 1960s traffic was at a standstill in Manhattan and the whole city was pretty much shut down. I trudged to my assistant's apartment building and threw snowballs at her window till she opened it. I shouted, 'C'mon, Marian, we're going to walk to work.' As we were slogging down Madison Avenue, there was a man ahead of us who was charging into the driving snow. I said to Marian, 'Let's push ahead like that guy.' We overtook him—and it was Dad! He was seventy-nine at the time. I said to him, 'What are you doing out in this weather?' He grumbled, 'Everybody should be going to work today. In Boston, this wouldn't be much of a storm.' The man worked a forty-hour week till he died at eighty-five."

But the way I read the situation, most of the vast number of baby boomers who'll be working far into later life to maintain their standard of living probably won't be doing it full-time, all year. They'll be working either part-time, or full-time at periodic intervals. For the baby boom generation, the norm is going to shift from retirement to semiretirement.

You and I are going to quit working if and when we want to—if and when we can afford to—and we're going to want to reserve the option of reentering the workforce later if we get "bored." No one knows exactly what the economic situation of older Americans is going to be when we're those older Americans. Making sure we have the opportunity to continue working is the only way of hedging against the multiple uncertainties we face. We aren't going to want the Social Security Act of 1935 or our friends and neighbors deciding what's right for us, economically and creatively.

We'll be seeing people in their sixties, seventies, and older working two jobs and working no jobs . . . working full-time in the same line they've been in for years and working part-time in a totally new field . . . being paid more than ever before in their lives and being paid the minimum wage . . . sleeping in refrigerator cartons under highway overpasses and sleeping in shorefront villas on private islands.

The number of older people in the workforce is going to accelerate gradually at first, driven by economic necessity and personal choice. When the demographics kick in as the first baby boomers enter their sixties, the line on the graph will go vertical. Eventually we'll be seeing a large percentage of people sixty-five and older continuing to work, and we'll be thinking it's perfectly normal. In fact, working in our sixties, seventies, and eighties will be like everything else the baby boom generation has done: It will be fashionable.

Anthropologists Pamela T. Amoss and Stevan Harrell of the University of Washington have written that around the world, in all societies and throughout history, "the social rank of the old is determined by the balance between the cost of maintaining them and the contribution they are perceived as making." Reserving the option of continuing to work is essential if we want younger generations to regard us as a resource to be drawn on, rather than a problem to be funded.

Some readers may be saying to themselves, "It's all well and good about actresses of a certain age who are out there today working, but they're doing it not because they need the money but because they love their work." Since the chances are that a lot of us are going to need the money, it's time for us either to learn to love the work we're doing, or learn to do the work we love.

Singer-songwriter Michael McDonald, who has passed through successive incarnations as a pillar of Steely Dan, a Doobie Brother, and a solo performer, has said, "Thank God I do something for a living that I'll still be able to do in my sixties and seventies." It's time for all of us to think about doing things for a living that we'll still be able to do in our sixties and seventies.

For us, quitting paid work in one's sixties and turning to a life of pure play, now a virtually universal middle-class expectation, will become what it previously was in America and still is in most of the world: a dream for many, a goal for some, attained by few.

In the new round world of later-life income for which we have to get ready, a lot of us will be sailing west to go east.

CHAPTER 10

POSTMODERN MATURITY

We'd expect the AARP to be the arch-defender of mass retirement.
Instead, the organization's leaders and staff have quietly come to
the conclusion that retirement as we've known it is on the way out.
One of the AARP's main thrusts is now fighting for the right of older
people to continue working if they want to or need to. If the Ameri-
can Association of Retired Persons is no longer committed to retire-
ment as the norm, how realistic can it be for baby boomers to
assume that retirement will be the norm when they're older?

To help get a sense of the role work is going to play in our lives
when we're older, I visited the headquarters of the AARP.

Does that seem odd to you? Isn't the American Association of
Retired Persons the number-one organization promoting the interests of . . . *retired* persons? Aren't its Washington offices the power-
house of the Social Security lobby, which believes that the only
work older people should do is opening envelopes containing government checks?

In the last decade or so we've seen the rise of a kind of demographic demagoguery. As the gerontological community has come
to embrace Dr. Robert N. Butler's idea of "productive aging," an
assortment of gray-bashers have been pushing a notion that could be
called destructive aging. It's no longer socially acceptable to stir up
group antagonisms based on country of origin, so now it's being
done based on year of origin. From time to time we hear horror stories about adult children beating up their aged parents, evidently
because they don't have the courage to vent their frustrations by
bursting into biker bars and announcing, "You're ugly and your

mother dresses you funny." Scapegoating the AARP has become the political form of elder abuse.

For example, former Colorado governor Richard D. Lamm has satirically proposed forming an American Association of Working People. One of the four planks in its platform would be: "Polls show that a large percentage of workers nearing sixty-five would like to continue working, at least part-time, and it is the position of this organization that it is senseless to deny them that right." Poll results are indeed as he reports them, and I agree strongly with enabling people to work in later life. But Governor Lamm uses his influence not to reconcile older people with younger people, but to polarize. "Simply put," he writes, in the voice of a presidential reelection committee advising the incumbent in 2000, "America's elderly have become an intolerable burden on the economic system and the younger generation's future. In the name of compassion for the elderly, we have handcuffed the young, mortgaged their future, and drastically limited their hopes and aspirations."

Governor Lamm has yet to understand that the way for him to help prevent population aging from bankrupting the government is to stop portraying today's older people as a gray peril and to turn his talents to making sure tomorrow's older people become a resource to be utilized rather than a problem to be funded. He has said, "The elderly lobby in Washington has a single agenda: more." Maybe he'll read this chapter and change his mind.

According to *The Gray Lobby* by Henry J. Pratt, Professor of Political Science at Wayne State University, Detroit, the 1972 Mills-Church Amendments, which set the formula for the enormously increased Social Security cash benefits against which Robert J. Myers warned, and which will be unsustainable when we're older, were pushed not primarily by the AARP, but by the union-sponsored National Council of Senior Citizens: "Its leaders took adamant and highly visible positions on the issue of Social Security reform, whereas the more middle-class AARP, which was willing to accept arguments that major changes would prove inflationary, conse-quently stayed more in the background."

Historian W. Andrew Achenbaum of the University of Michigan Institute of Gerontology analyzed the debate over the 1983 Social Security amendments, which gradually increases the "Normal Retirement Age" to sixty-seven by 2027, and increased the "Delayed Retirement Credit," which increases benefits to people who postpone receiving benefits, from 3 percent at the time, to 8 percent in 2009. "Unlike other old-age lobbyists, moreover," Dr. Achenbaum wrote, "the American Association of Retired Persons (AARP) endorsed a 'work promotion strategy' that would give older people who continued working after age sixty-five more than an 8 percent increase [per extra year of work] in Social Security benefits." The AARP's goal was to make the future Delayed Retirement Credit "actuarily fair," so that average lifetime benefits will be the same even when a person keeps working till age seventy. Dr. Achenbaum noted, "In adopting this view, the leadership of the American Association of Retired Persons has knowingly parted company with other elements of the gray lobby. . . ."

The AARP's 22.6 million dues-payers and five-thousand-plus chapters make it by far the largest organization of any kind in the United States. Counting spouses, which the AARP does, brings total membership to more than 33 million. The group's bimonthly, *Modern Maturity,* has the largest circulation of any magazine in the country. It's neither surprising nor scandalous that an organization that can plausibly claim to speak on behalf of more than one-eighth of the American population is taken seriously by lawmakers.

But the AARP's Social Security lobbying today is directed at preventing cuts, not obtaining increases. The organization has refused, for instance, to be drawn into the campaign for higher benefits for the "notch babies," people born between 1917 and 1921 who, because an error in the inflation-adjustment method was corrected, have received smaller Social Security checks than people born in other years who've inadvertently collected higher benefits. And it didn't dig in its heels against the imposition in 1993 of taxes on 85 percent of Social Security benefits. The only part of the issue its lobbyists "worked hard"—and successfully—was shielding middle- and lower-income recipients from increased benefit taxation.

Far from regarding Social Security's current structure as untouchable, the AARP has published a report called *Lifelong Learning: Investing in People as Social Insurance,* which advocates using the Social Security trust funds as a source of job training loans for midlife and older employees.

According to the AARP newsletter *Working Age,* "AARP has broadened the definition of retirement to include phased retirement, retirement from one job to another, and new careers." The breadth of this "broadening" tells us a lot about how the AARP views the future of retirement. To me, "retirement from one job to another" sounds a lot like what used to be called "changing jobs." And I'd say that a definition of retirement that includes "new careers" is very broad indeed.

Meanwhile, the AARP's financial-planning guides have introduced, emphatically but without fanfare, the idea that many older people are going to have to continue working. Here's a passage from *Planning for Retirement,* published in 1993: "Many people plan to work in retirement, and this may be an idea you want to adopt. The wages that you earn in retirement will most likely keep pace with inflation (unlike fixed income you'll receive from some other sources), and this can help considerably to narrow your retirement income gap. And for some retirees, employee benefits (such as group life and health insurance) contribute to their bottom line as much as the actual income they earn."

It isn't necessary to read between the lines of a mailing the organization sends out to sign up new members to get the new message. The lines themselves do quite nicely. The cover letter describes the AARP only as "the most trusted organization of people 50 and over." Its first selling point: "This is a time for careful planning. AARP's authoritative publications give you the advice you need to secure your future." It certainly seems like they're bending over backwards to avoid the R word: Planning for what? Secure your future how? "This is a time for fairness in America. AARP works to promote fairness for people over 50 in the job market and the health care they receive. Fairness for other generations too." The letter ends, "P.S. You have to be 50 or over to join AARP, but you *don't* [emphasis in original] have to be retired." The reply card has three boxes to check, from left to right: "I work full time," "I work part time," "I am retired."

In his keynote address to a conference called "Resourceful Aging" cosponsored by the AARP and Cornell University, the AARP's former president, Robert B. Maxwell, who served from 1990 to 1992, said, "As a nation, we must rid ourselves of the idea that the day a person turns sixty-five, he or she becomes worn out and no longer useful, like an old shoe. The Depression taught my generation how to be resourceful. You don't have to throw old shoes away. You can resole them: the shoes retain their usefulness, and you avoid having to break in a new pair.

"Older workers are a valuable asset, but we need to continue to resole our job skills. We need to continue to learn, continue to grow. Demographics show that our nation should be pulling older people back into the workforce, not letting them go.

"In the years ahead, there will be significantly fewer potential workers between the ages of sixteen and twenty-four, the traditional pool of workforce replacements. Many people in that age bracket will lack basic job skills, such as reading and math.

"As qualified employees become more difficult to find, business and industry leaders are beginning to see older workers as the valuable asset they really are. Once again, America will need the older generation to remain competitive."

Former AARP executive director Cyril Brickfield has described the organization's mission even more pointedly: "Private pensions are in a state of chaos. First of all, 50 percent of the workforce today has no pension. That alone should be of great concern. And 75 to 80 percent of the other 50 percent have ineffective pensions that pay $55 or $150 or $300 a month—and what does that buy? That's why the AARP says, 'Thank God for Social Security.' It is there; it is universal. . . .

"We all know the old cliché 'The squeaky wheel gets the grease.' The AARP has [33 million] members—and there is power in numbers. We do not seek anything improper, but we certainly want to be heard. And we want the elderly to be heard. We are in a leadership role and equity in the workforce is paramount."

After spending some time at the AARP's headquarters I discovered that a group maligned for supposedly representing a bunch of old fogies is actually one of the most future-oriented organizations I've encountered. It has three separate divisions with a major focus on the prospects of the baby boomers: its Work Force Programs Department, Public Policy Institute, and Forecasting and Environmental Scanning Department. Part of its motivation is that any club taking in more than $180 million a year in dues has an interest in keeping itself relevant far into the future, and the AARP's future "market" is the baby boom generation. What's more, many of the organization's top-level staffers are either baby boomers themselves or close to it. Their concern about the well-being of today's older people is professional; their concern about the well-being of tomorrow's older people is personal.

The AARP recently moved into a complex at the corner of 6th and E Streets in the nation's capital. The epicenter of the gray lobby consists of two ten-story limestone and brick buildings that have been gutted, joined, and suavely decorated in a unifying . . . gray.

Gray wall-coverings. Gray carpeting. Gray partitions. The grayness is so total that the only way you can tell where you are is by the art: If it's the crumpled sheet metal statement airbrushed with iridescent paint, this must be the fifth floor. I make my gray way to see the head of the organization's Work Force Programs Department.

The Work Force Programs Department was founded in 1984. Its Worker Equity Section fights age discrimination in employment. The AARP has led the charge against mandatory retirement for decades, and its efforts have been almost completely successful. When the Age Discrimination in Employment Act was passed in 1967, about half of all workers were subject to compulsory retirement. Since December 31, 1993, it's been illegal to force any employee to stop working because of age. The department's Work Force Education Section teaches companies to give seminars like "Think of Your Future" that offer employees guidance in financial planning for retirement, stressing "the importance of self-reliance and personal responsibility in achieving a secure and fulfilling later life" and "the role that work in retirement can play in enhancing financial security." It presents seminars around the country called "AARP Works" to help older people identify skills and interests that will help them stay in and re-enter the workforce. The Business Partnerships Section works with employers to create programs to recruit, train, manage, and retain older workers and offers a database of such initiatives called the National Older Workers Information System. The department has a staff member in each of the AARP's ten regional offices.

Martin Sicker is director of the Work Force Programs Department. A political scientist, he was associate commissioner for program development of the U.S. Administration on Aging under Presidents Nixon and Carter, responsible for the agency's research, demonstration, and human resource development activities.

I asked Dr. Sicker why an organization ostensibly devoted to retirement devotes so much energy to enabling older people to continue to work.

"The Association's name isn't really descriptive of what it does," he said. "We're not about retirement per se. We're about standing up for the interests of older people, whether they're retired, working, or retired from a previous career and working at something else.

"Retirement as we know it never existed before and will never exist again. It's fading away as we're sitting here.

"The ancient Roman general Cincinnatus was famous for having 'retired' to his farm—that's how rare it was. Retirement came in after World War II because of unprecedented productivity increases and the rise of pensions. For the first time in the history of civilization, average people could put together a package that would let them stop working in their sixties and pursue a life of leisure.

"But fewer and fewer people are going to be able to retire from here on in. I can't envision how a fifty-thousand-dollar-a-year household will be able to retire. Possibly if they're planning to retire soon. Maybe if there are two earners and their total income is a hundred thousand. But the percentage is going to be small.

"By the time members of the baby boom generation begin to enter their sixties very few of them are going to be able to retire. The vast majority of baby boomers will find that Social Security, pensions, and savings won't provide them with enough income. There's no question that they're going to have an increased need to work when they're older.

"The question is whether the jobs will be there for them. For most baby boomers, retirement will be just another name for underemployment. I think we're going to see an increased need for jobs for older people without those jobs being available.

"In the near future half the workforce will be what we call 'contingent'—part-time, temporary, self-employed, and employees of companies providing services that are being outsourced by large corporations. Over the next few decades we're going to see a change in the relation of people to work as dramatic as the shift from agriculture.

"There's going to be massive underemployment. Increased productivity is going to cut the number of working hours in a lifetime in half, from a hundred thousand to fifty thousand. There are only two ways of doing this: either you cut the number of years people work in half, or you stretch it out by making it contingent and reducing the number of hours worked per year.

"Decades ago, we were told that automation was coming, and that it was going to have a catastrophic effect on the labor market. It didn't come, and people came to assume it never would. But that's what contingency is.

"What's going to happen when you start building serious productivity gains into the service economy, where up till now the impact of technology has been negligible? It's going to be as dramatic as the industrial revolution. The implication of a reduced standard of living among contingent workers is pretty daunting.

"The Association's assessment is that the workforce is going to become more and more contingent. We're asking what the role of older workers will be in the contingent workforce. Will they be treated equitably? Or will they be disproportionately pushed out of permanent jobs into contingent work?

"There's a view that in a knowledge economy, older workers ought to be great. When we survey companies, human resources executives all say, 'Older workers are wonderful.' Do you hire them? 'No.' In practice, corporations that are downsizing think it's more humane to let older workers go. But with later marriages, plenty of people in their sixties have kids in college. That's the time when they need the most money! Yet business has found it culturally acceptable to move in that direction. Our department's mission is to counteract that cultural acceptability."

"You don't sound terribly optimistic," I said.

"I'm not pessimistic, because no society has ever voluntarily self-destructed," said Dr. Sicker. "When the crisis hits—and it's going to be a crisis—government will step in to moderate the trend to contingency among workers of all ages. We hear about inexorable market forces, but the reality is that corporations are creatures of public policy. If you have a situation in which people are being underemployed in order to maximize profits, it's appropriate for government to take action. For example, suppose you took unemployment insurance and turned it into a program of public employment. The problem is, the later you intervene, the harder it's going to be."

Robert A. Harootyan is director of the AARP's Forecasting and Environmental Scanning Department. A sociologist and demographer by training, born just before the "official" beginning of the baby boom, Harootyan oversaw preparation of the AARP studies *Lifework: Future Options for Older Workers* and *The Diversity of the Baby Boom Generation: Implications for Their Retirement Years,* and is coauthor of *The Quiet Revolution: Improved Health and Longer Life in the 21st Century.*

"We're going to see the end of what we call 'rocking-chair' retirement," Harootyan told me. "If you look carefully at the Association's literature, you'll see that it uses the logo that just says 'AARP' more than its full name. The reason is that the Association wants to de-emphasize its identification with retirement.

"About one out of five people who are fully retired today express interest in returning to work. The largest number of these are divorced, and three-quarters of the divorced are women. When we ask what the ideal work situation would be, nine out of ten say they'd prefer part-time work. They want more money because they feel economically insecure.

"And it's going to be tougher for older people in the future than it is now. The cost of living in retirement is going to be higher than it was during the good part of the post–World War II period—the 1960s, 1970s, and 1980s. I'm concerned about it personally. I have three kids, all under age ten. I've got years of major expenses ahead of me before I can imagine myself not working.

"A lot of researchers who are thinking about retirement income are underestimating how many baby boomers are going to be living far into old age. As a result, the need to provide income for the very old is also underestimated. The mortality figures that are used as bench-marks today come from what the Census Bureau calls its 'middle series.' I and the people I work with think the 'middle series' is not the most likely scenario. Today's official life expectancy figure—an average of seventy-five and a half years at birth for both sexes—is based on the ages of people who are dying right now. Future advances in medical care and bioscience aren't being taken into consideration. Gregory Spencer, who's in charge of life expectancy figures at the Census Bureau, says he can't make any projections about discontinuous changes—'We're not allowed to.'

"A greater percentage of baby boomers are going to get something in the way of pension benefits—but we don't know how much, and we don't know how many. The rapid change from defined benefit to defined contribution plans is shifting the risk from the employer to the employee. And I'm skeptical about the notion that the 'two-pension couple' will do much to solve the retirement income problem for very many baby boomers. Will they stay married? If they do, will even one partner have a pension?

"What about single, divorced, and never-married people, who are going to make up a greater proportion of baby boomers than of any previous generation? There are a lot of minorities among the baby boomers who've been earning less all along, have been less able to save, and have had less pension coverage. How are they going to live? That's one of the reasons the Social Security system has to be guarded. Social Security was never intended to guarantee adequate retirement income—just to supply a floor. But if anything happens to that floor, a lot of baby boomers are going to be in trouble.

"The younger boomers especially are going to have a struggle when they're older. They won't have had the opportunity to accumulate enough assets. They won't have had the upwardly mobile careers. The glass ceiling isn't just for women. There's a glass ceiling for baby boomers in general, because demand for promotion is so high, yet organizational charts are getting flatter. Even within the Association, we're encouraging people to look for opportunities to make lateral moves, rather than vertical ones.

"I think the trend to early retirement is going to reverse and that labor force participation among older baby boomers is going to go up. I'm convinced they're going to be healthier than older people are today. They'll be disease-free longer, and chronic diseases will be less severe and more treatable. Working when you're older will be a lot more prevalent than it is today. Not full-time work, but part-time and flexible work schedules, probably most of it from one's home. Time has become an enormously valuable commodity to baby boomers with children in dual-earner families. As they get older, they're going to want employment arrangements that allow a balance between work and nonwork. People who are better-educated will have the opportunity to create work situations that are a lot more attractive than older cohorts have had before.

"In particular, we're going to see a lot of older never-marrieds, baby boomers with strong career orientations in the more attractive occupations who are going to continue working because they'll need the money. There are going to be a lot of older lawyers and MBAs in the workforce.

"All American institutions will have that kind of age-heterogeneity— even suburbia. Sun City is an anachronism. Most baby boomers don't envision themselves living in residential environments that thwart interaction with other age groups. Most of them will 'age in place,' as gerontologists put it, or move to slightly smaller places. There will still be clusters of same-age people. But our society as a whole won't be as age-segregated as it is today. People of all generations will live together the way they do right now in Florida: symbiotically."

Moving right along through the corridors of gray power—or should I say, the powerfully gray corridors—I sat down with sociologist Sara E. Rix, a baby boomer who's senior analyst on the Economics Team of the AARP's Public Policy Institute. While at the Center on Work and Aging of the American Institutes of Research in the 1970s, Dr. Rix was coauthor with Dr. Harold L. Sheppard, who pioneered the "economics of aging" in the United States, of the prophetic study *The Graying of Working America: The Coming Crisis of Retirement-Age Policy.*

"I suppose our contribution was that we did the first academic study that questioned whether the trend to earlier retirement would continue," she told me modestly. "Hal and I noted that the aging of the population would increase the burden on the employed. We predicted that as a result the retirement age would eventually be raised, and that there would be downward pressure on retirement benefits."

"Did you get much of a reaction to your book?" I asked.

"Let's put it this way—the phone didn't ring off the hook." She laughed gently. "In 1977 no one in academic or policy circles was talking about older people continuing to work. At that time, retirement ages were dropping. No one had written anything that said, 'You have this large number of people who look good now, but fifty years down the road, the demographic structure is going to change, and who's going to pay?' I mean, this was when the youngest baby boomers were thirteen!"

"And now that those youngest boomers have turned thirty," I asked, "do you feel your conclusions have held up?"

"Pretty much," said Dr. Rix. "Six years after we published our study, sure enough, a phased increase in Social Security's so-called Normal Retirement Age was enacted by Congress. But I'm still rather negative about the future of Social Security. The Social Security age increase that's scheduled doesn't begin to take into account the increase in longevity. The Normal Retirement Age is scheduled to rise from sixty-five to sixty-seven, which is trivial. The increased length of the baby boom generation's retirement will more than undo the savings from raising the Social Security retirement age.

"Also, we're not seeing lifelong stable employment anymore. There's more and more turbulence in careers, which brings with it less of an opportunity to accumulate adequate pensions. So while a larger proportion of baby boomers will be eligible for company pensions, the amounts they receive won't necessarily be so handsome. Two points especially concern me.

"First, we're told that with both wives and husbands working, a higher percentage of baby boomers will be receiving pensions. But how many of those marriages in dual-vested households are going to last into later life? I worry about what kind of pension income divorced women and singles are going to be able to receive.

"Second, self-management of pension investment through 401(k)s is being touted as a great thing. Well, I don't know about most people, but I for one don't have the kind of financial skills to make that money grow enough to provide an adequate retirement income. I had a chart on my office wall of how much savings I'd need to retire at a particular age. I took it down because it was too depressing. I looked at where my investments were going and said, 'If I'm supposed to do this on my own, forget it.'

"We aren't going to see any expansion of public or private retirement programs. The baby boomers and the generations after them are going to be expected to develop their own sources of later-life income. Earnings are going to have to become a major source. People's work lives will have to be prolonged. What I foresee is a greater interest in continued work—a forced interest. We're going to see an awful lot of people around age seventy hobbling around needing jobs.

"For an awful lot of baby boomers, the only alternative will be continued employment—and in many cases, not in what we call 'good jobs.' There's going to be a constant adjustment to lower-wage jobs at age sixty-five and seventy and seventy-five.

"A recent survey found that almost half of companies hire retirees, and that they hire them for professional and managerial jobs. The flip side is that they hire only a few, and that most of the hires are for clerical positions.

"The problem is that the bulk of job creation in the economy as a whole is projected to be in lower-paid service jobs. Look at the occupations that are expected to account for the most employment growth between now and 2005, in order of the number of jobs that will be created," she said, handing me a report from the U.S. Bureau of Labor Statistics.

I read: retail salespersons, registered nurses, cashiers, office clerks, truck drivers, waiters and waitresses, nursing aides, janitors, food preparers, systems analysts, home health aides, secondary school teachers, child care workers, guards, sales supervisors, teacher aides, top executives, maintenance repairers, gardeners, elementary teachers, food counter workers, receptionists, accountants, clerical supervisors, restaurant cooks, special education teachers, practical nurses, fast food cooks, human services workers, and computer scientists.

"The great economic story of the twenty-first century is going to be the emergence of China. A large number of manufacturing jobs are going to move there and to other low-wage countries. Downward job mobility is going to be an essential part of America's adjustment to the new global economy. It's going to affect every age group in the United States. The Association's mission is to see to it that downward mobility doesn't come down disproportionately on older people. There's going to be a change in the image of the AARP to an organization that encompasses more than just retirement. One-third of our membership is in the workforce right now."

"How much progress are you making?" I asked.

"Whenever the Association surveys corporate executives, they've got only good things to say about older workers. They have lower absenteeism. They're less injury-prone. They're more conscientious, loyal, prompt, etc. etc. But companies still force them out during downsizings and are resistant to hiring them. They've simply been conditioned to say nice things about older workers on questionnaires.

"During the 1980s, a lot of analysts foresaw a chronic labor shortage down the road—particularly a shortfall of skilled workers. They thought corporations would start showing greater interest in older workers. But so far, the prospect of such a shortage hasn't been enough to make employers change their policies. On the contrary: Staff reductions during the recession of the 1990s fell more heavily on older workers.

"The job-training picture? Even worse. The same executives who tell us older workers are so great say they focus their training efforts on younger workers. The law now forbids employers to exclude older workers from training programs. But they don't have to encourage older workers to participate in training, and few do so. They see little point in updating the skills of their older employees, because they assume they'll be leaving after a few years. The reality of today's turbulent labor market is that on average, workers only stay with a given employer for a relatively short period, regardless of age. So it makes no economic sense for a company to concentrate on training its younger employees while neglecting its older employees. It's entirely possible that the younger people will be with them fewer years than the older people."

"Dr. Sicker is troubled by the rise of the contingent workforce," I said. "Do you share his concern?"

"Given the fact that contingent workers cost less than permanent workers because they don't usually receive much in the way of benefits, and that contingency enhances companies' competitiveness by giving them more flexibility to fine-tune their payroll to changing market conditions, the rise of the contingent workforce may actually create opportunities for older workers that don't exist now. Contingent employment may turn out to provide the perfect transition between a full-time job and full-time retirement—what we call 'bridge jobs.' Or contingent work may supply the ideal income supplement to fill the gap created by inadequate Social Security, pensions, and savings. On the other hand, older contingent employees are going to find themselves competing with younger workers who'll also be increasingly contingent.

"The rise of contingency means that we should be seeing what we can do to improve the conditions of part-time employment. Part-time jobs have traditionally been low-wage, low-benefit, low-status positions. It's understandable why employers pay part-time workers less. Companies incur fixed hiring and training costs that have to be amortized over a lower number of hours worked by each employee. Some equalization of wages or benefits for part-timers may be in order in an increasingly contingent economy, especially if we expect older people to be able to close their income gap through part-time employment.

"But what we really need is a coordinated set of national policies with the goal of increasing older people's involvement in the world of work, while not forcing employment on older people who are genuinely incapacitated. We should be supporting research on the comparative productivity of older workers, particularly in high-tech industries. We should be encouraging research on cost-effective ways of retraining older workers in new technologies. Companies now have to compete in a rapidly changing world economy, and until they have good data on how to upgrade older people's skills, older employees are going to be underrepresented in private-sector training programs. We should be looking at the pluses and minuses of providing tax advantages to employers who hire, retain, and train older employees. We should be finding ways to make it easier for midlife employees to change jobs and careers. We should be encouraging job redesign to enable older workers with physical limitations to remain on the job.

"The entire federal government should become a laboratory for developing ways of retaining and retraining older workers. Ironically, the government is doing the exact opposite, offering its employees incentives for extremely early retirement that are just about irresistible.

"And I'd like to see encouragement or maybe even requirement of periodic workplace age audits. We can't rely on complaints to the Equal Employment Opportunity Commission as the only mechanism for fostering compliance with the Age Discrimination in Employment Act. Where there's a dramatic difference between the age distribution among a particular company's employees and the age distribution in the local or regional or national workforce, it would be good to have a way of identifying it."

"What do you think the chances are of policies like that being put in place?"

"I'd say they're quite high. Older workers today aren't a potent political force, but the baby boomers have always gotten their way. I know my rights. I know I can't be denied a job because of my age. I know I can't be forcibly retired. I'm more likely to sue my employer. The baby boomers are going to see their need to remain employed. They're going to say, 'I'm not taking this crap. I demand the training and the retraining that will enable me to continue to work.' "

"Do you think you're going to be among the hobblers?"

"I'm going to have to continue to work. But I don't know what I'm going to do. When I was younger I thought I'd want to work forever. I used to say I'd never retire. Gradually I realized there were other things I'd like to do someday. But when I look at what I live on now and analyze my prospects for retirement, they're just not there. As I get older I ask myself, how long will I be able to do this? Doesn't there come a point at which I've said what there is to say? How many papers can I write about older women in the workforce? I've said that already!"

Dr. Rix escorted me to the elevator. She looked around, shaking her head wryly. "These walls," she said. "You'd think they'd have chosen some other color besides . . . gray."

The AARP is popularly identified with the image of golden agers on permanent vacation. It provides a convenient four-letter target for gerontophobia-mongers more interested in accusing today's older people of being dependent than in preventing tomorrow's older people from becoming dependent. In reality, the AARP's most sophisticated staff professionals and activist members have already concluded that the days of retirement as a norm are numbered, and are in the forefront of efforts to make it possible for Americans to have the opportunity to work when they're older. It's time to stop demonizing the AARP for looking out for the interests of its current members and to start listening to what the organization has to say about the interests of its future members.

It's appropriate that even as AARP staffers are fighting hard for the rights of older workers, they're taking a cautious view of their prospects. Sometimes it's good to keep your expectations on the low side. That way, you're less likely to be disappointed by setbacks and by small achievements. But my assessment is that the later-life employment outlook for the baby boomers is a good deal better than some of the AARP's staffers, understandably experiencing some battle fatigue after years in the trenches, may think it is. Like Allied soldiers in the Ardennes forest half a century ago, they are encountering some of the toughest tactical resistance just as strategic victory is at hand.

CHAPTER 11

ROLE REVERSAL

Age discrimination in employment didn't exist until the late nineteenth century. It arose in response to conditions that are now reversing themselves. When you're older, ageism in the workplace will be a thing of the past.

As you begin to think about coping with the inadequacies of Social Security, pensions, and savings by retaining the option to work when you're older, a lot of questions undoubtedly enter your mind.

Will prospective employers tell me I'm overqualified when what they really mean is that I'm overquantified? Will I be physically strong enough and mentally agile enough to continue working if I have to? Will I get paid less than I'm earning now? How will I be able to keep my job or find a new one when companies are constantly downsizing? Will I find myself flipping burgers?

It comes down to this: If I need to or want to work when I'm older, will I find myself on the receiving end of ageism?

I don't think so, because among the major isms, ageism is unique. Every other form of discrimination we can think of has been around forever. Racism. Sexism. Homophobia. Ageism, by contrast, is the precise opposite of the attitude toward older people that has prevailed in most societies most of the time: respect, bordering on awe.

When anthropologists Pamela T. Amoss and Stevan Harrell, authors of *Other Ways of Growing Old*, studied the Coast Salish Indians of Washington and British Columbia recently, they found that "old age did not bring leisure to either sex, but only a shift from the physically more demanding tasks to those where skill, patience, or experience were more important than strength and speed."

How did we get from there to here?

I would suggest that ageism has evolved to justify an exclusion of older people from the workaday life of America caused by technological and economic conditions that have existed only for about a century, and are in the process of being reversed. It's natural for us to be apprehensive about how receptive employers will be to us when we're older because we've lived all our lives in, if you will, the Age of Ageism. But by the time we're older, age discrimination in employment is going to be back there with manual typewriters and vinyl records.

Historian W. Andrew Achenbaum, of the University of Michigan Institute of Gerontology, has written that "older people throughout most of U.S. history were expected to work as long as they were physically able to do so. In the colonial period and the years of the early American Republic, when the economy was underdeveloped, the elderly were perceived as seasoned veterans of productivity. Their advice and contributions were credited with enhancing prospects for social advance."

In the mid-nineteenth century, two-thirds of Americans lived on farms. Most manufacturing was done in workshops in and near the home, and an older craftsperson who could no longer move so quickly could work more slowly. People were usually self-employed and could reduce their hours, if they wished, as the years went on. Those who worked for others were paid by the piece, not the hour, so employers were more interested in getting quality from them than speed.

According to economist Jon R. Moen of the Federal Reserve Bank of Atlanta, the labor force participation rate (LFPR) of U.S. men aged sixty-five and older consistently stayed around 75 percent until 1890. But by 1910, older men's LFPR had fallen to 58 percent, where it remained until the beginning of the Great Depression. What caused that sudden drop?

There appear to have been two major reasons for the decline in older men's LFPR between 1890 and 1910. More than 700,000 Civil War veterans became eligible for military pensions between 1900 and 1910. But more important was the influence of the first "efficiency expert," Frederick W. Taylor. In the 1880s Taylor, an engineer at Midvale Steel Co. in Philadelphia, developed the concept of dividing each industrial job into its component parts and assigning a separate worker to each task. Observers with stopwatches then did a "time and motion study" of every worker to see how the task could be performed more quickly. As factories became more mechanized, the spread of what came to be called "Taylorism" caused fast workers to be thought of as more economical than experienced ones. Companies became eager to replace older employees with younger workers who'd be better able to keep up with the machines.

The new view of older people that had become common among industrialists was expressed most provocatively by Dr. William Osler, the most celebrated medical personality of the day. On February 22, 1905, he gave a farewell speech at Johns Hopkins University before leaving for England, where he was to become regius professor of medicine at Oxford:

> Take the sum of human achievement in action, in science, in art, in literature—subtract the work of the men above forty, and while we should miss great treasures, even priceless treasures, we would practically be where we are today. . . . . The effective, moving, vitalizing work of the world is done between the ages of twenty-five and forty. . . . My second fixed idea is the uselessness of men above sixty years of age, and the incalculable benefit it would be in commercial, political, and in professional life, if as a matter of course, men stopped work at this age.

The address caused a sensation: "Osler Recommends Chloroform at Sixty," was a typical headline. Dr. Osler, as it happened, didn't take his own advice. From age sixty-five to sixty-nine he organized the British medical profession to meet the demands of World War I, for which he was knighted. But "Oslerize" became the term for pushing older people out of the workforce.

During the Great Depression older men's LFPR dropped to 43 percent. At the beginning of World War II it started to rise, reaching a postwar high in 1950, when 47 percent of men aged sixty-five and older were in the labor force. From then on it has fallen steadily toward today's 16 percent figure. Dr. Moen attributes the overall decline in labor force participation of older Americans to three factors in addition to Taylorism:

- Separation of the home and the workplace as industrial employment replaced self-employment.
- The change in compensation from piece rates to hourly wages.
- The rise of Social Security and, after 1950, private pensions as sources of later-life income and deterrents, through earnings tests, to continuing to work.

Happily, just when it's time for baby boomers to begin to confront their need to to have the opportunity to work when they're older, all these factors are doing an about-face.

1. Strength and speed are necessities for a shrinking portion of the workforce.
2. Home and workplace are converging in cyberspace.
3. Time-based pay is being superseded by performance-based pay.
4. Social Security's benefits will be cut, its earnings test is being phased out, and employers are starting to provide incentives for later retirement in order to control pension costs.

When we're older, the factors that precipitated the exit of older Americans from the workforce will no longer be present—so therefore, neither will obstacles to continuing to work.

1. **Strength and speed are necessities for a shrinking portion of the workforce.** First, we aren't going to be all that decrepit. The National Center for Health Statistics reports that more than 70 percent of people sixty-five and older living in the community say they're in good, very good, or excellent health. The U.S. Public Health Service reports that 80.5 percent of noninstitutionalized Americans aged sixty-five and above have no functional impairment. A 1993 study by Prof. Kenneth G. Manton of Duke University's Center for the Study of Aging and Human Development found that "incidence rates for chronic disability for persons sixty-five to seventy-four are low and declining." By the time the baby boomers are older, it's likely that rates of disability will be even lower.

On the other hand, it's true that as we age our physical capacities gradually diminish, our mental processes slow down, and our ability to transfer information from short-term to long-term memory decreases. But in today's workplace these factors have lost much of their importance, and by the time we're older, they'll have lost most of it.

Taylorism with a human face—talking teamwork but still stressing speed—is alive and well in the manufacturing sector. Christian Berggren, Associate Professor of Work Science at the Royal Institute of Technology in Stockholm, commented recently that when he visited Japanese-owned auto plants in the United States, he found that "the rhythm and pace of the work on the assembly line is more inexorable . . . than it ever was before."

But only a small percentage of Americans work on assembly lines. As Dr. Moen has observed, "The share of jobs in manufacturing has been declining since the late 1970s, while the share of service jobs has been increasing. Because service and nonmanufacturing jobs tend to be less demanding physically and in many cases do not require employees to follow a fixed schedule or a routine imposed by an assembly line, retirement may become less imperative." He has written: "The changing mix of jobs away from manufacturing toward services will make it physically easier for older people to remain in the labor force. Like laborers who worked for piece rates, older workers in service jobs will have some flexibility to set their own pace. The widespread decline of labor force participation among older male workers during the middle twentieth century may eventually emerge as a unique event in our economic history."

And you and I don't have to worry that the labor market will deteriorate when most jobs shift to the service sector—because most jobs have already shifted. Manufacturing now provides fewer than 16 percent of U.S. jobs. So most of the trend toward service employment is already behind us.

What's more, even in the manufacturing sector, most of the jobs are really service jobs. Seventy-eight percent of General Motors' employees are white-collar and salaried. At Mobil, the proportion is 62 percent, 57 at DuPont, 60 at GE. Professor Theodore Levitt of Harvard Business School recently said, "There are no such things as service industries. There are only industries whose service components are greater or less than those of other industries. Everybody is in service."

Concern that the service employees are poorly-paid is based on a disparity that used to be sizeable but no longer is. The U.S. Bureau of Labor Statistics reported in 1994 that median full-time wages in the service sector are only 3.8 percent lower than in manufacturing. The highest-paid tenth of service workers earn only 1.9 percent less than the highest-paid employees in manufacturing. The lowest-paid service employees earn 8.2 percent less. The weekly pay gap is narrowing, and is now one-quarter of what it was in 1980. And much of the difference is caused not by lower hourly pay but by fewer hours worked. Long-work-week jobs are concentrated in manufacturing, while jobs with fewer hours are more common in retail and health services. Except in retailing, all industries in the service sector have shown increases in the work-week since the 1980s. It's possible that by the time we're older, the service and manufacturing sectors' hourly pay and hours worked will have equalized. But even if they don't, let's keep in mind that a shorter work-week may be exactly what we want when we're older.

If we've already made most of the move to a service economy, why is there still so much ageism among employers? One reason is that many of today's older workers have been slow to learn computer skills—or perhaps employers have been slow to teach them—reducing their value in the service workplace. Above all, subjective attitudes change more slowly than objective reality. But neither of these negatives will be present for us.

When the baby boomers are older, not only will they already be computer literate, but they'll be experienced in adapting to successive generations of hardware and software. And a basic skill of the computer age—typing—has been found to be unaffected by age. Though older people tap the keys more slowly, they compensate by reading further ahead in the text, pausing less often.

Dr. James F. Birren, born 1918, is one of America's most distinguished experts in the psychology of aging. In the 1960s he established the first major U.S. academic center on aging at the University of Southern California, and at age seventy-one founded the Borun Center for Gerontological Research at UCLA. He and Marion A. Perlmutter, Professor of Psychology at the University of Michigan, have written that "the healthy older brain continues to gain information," pointing to a study that found that the vocabulary of college-educated adults doubles from about 22,000 words at age twenty-one to around 45,000 at sixty-five. Drs. Birren and Perlmutter note that older people who exercise have quicker reaction times. This is a finding that bodes well for fitness-conscious baby boomers who, I've been thinking, may be showing an aerobic response to an unconscious premonition that they'd better take care of their bodies because they're going to be in them for a long, long time.

It's going to be a while before employers' feelings about older workers catch up with older workers' actual productive capacity in what could be described as the new "low-impact" workplace— maybe another 10 years. But that attitude adjustment will have largely been made by the time the first members of the baby boom generation are in their sixties.

In the meantime, older employees have a secret weapon—so secret they don't yet know they have it. It's called the Americans with Disabilities Act. The ADA, which went into effect for companies with fifteen employees or more in mid-1994, prohibits discrimination against employees or applicants who are physically or mentally impaired—who have difficulty, for example, in walking, seeing, hearing, speaking, or learning, who suffer from alcoholism, epilepsy, or tuberculosis, or who are "regarded" as having an impairment—for instance, people who are obese. Employers are required to make "reasonable accommodation" for such people if they otherwise have the "skill, experience, education and other job-related requirements" to perform the "essential functions" of the job. Unless a company can show that the expense of making "reasonable accommodation" for an individual would cause it an "undue hardship" given the size and nature of its business, it has to do everything from rescheduling jobs so disabled people can perform them to modifying equipment, to providing readers.

The employment provisions of ADA are enforceable under the same procedures used for race, sex, national origin, religious, and age discrimination, as provided by the Civil Rights Acts of 1964 and 1991: through the U.S. Equal Employment Opportunity Commission, state human rights agencies, and lawsuits brought by individuals. Remedies include hiring, reinstatement, back pay, promotion, attorney and expert witness fees, and court costs. You can sue for compensatory damages, including future monetary loss, emotional pain and suffering, even "inconvenience" and "loss of enjoyment of life." And if an employer acted with "malice or reckless indifference," you can ask a jury for punitive damages.

ADA was passed as the result of a campaign by organizations representing what might be called the "working-age" disabled. So far, most older people aren't aware of the law's existence, and few have filed complaints under it. But as ADA becomes widely known, its synergy with the Age Discrimination in Employment Act (ADEA) is bound to result in a revolutionary improvement in the employability of older Americans.

After all, what are the decreased physical and mental speed that come with increased age but disabilities? If a young job applicant is in a wheelchair as the result of an injury, an employer must make "reasonable accommodation" for her. How will it be possible for an older person in a wheelchair to be treated differently? If an employee's vision is getting worse, lighting can be improved and bigger computer screens can be installed. If there's hearing loss, background noise can be reduced. Companies are going to have a hard time convincing juries that people in their seventies whose short-term memory is slipping can't be "reasonably accommodated." If getting older is making it harder for them to write to their mental hard disks, companies can give them access to free-form databases like Info Select that let them save new information on a computer's hard disk and retrieve it by keyboarding any word or number sequence they remember. An employee's hands shake because of Parkinsonism? Nikon has developed a vibration reduction system for its cameras to prevent blurred pictures by inducing counter-movement to compensate for side-to-side, front-to-back, and up-and-down movement. Employers who don't want to find themselves in court are going to be scrambling to bring that kind of technology into the workplace.

You can get an idea of which way things are headed by looking at a brochure describing seminars on employee relations law held in fourteen cities in 1995 by the Institute for Applied Management and Law. Block II, at $775, includes such topics as: "An examination of the effect of legislation that lifts the damage ceilings in the Civil Rights Act of 1991. . . . A thorough examination of the Americans with Disabilities Act, and the effective handling of the disabled employee. . . . An update on developments in the law under the Age Discrimination in Employment Act."

Or there's this one from the Council on Education in Management, announcing a $495 conference called "Personnel Law Update 1995": "THE MOST IMPORTANT MANAGEMENT CONFERENCE IN AMERICA TODAY! . . . Management policies and procedures that were sound a few years ago may now leave employers open to charges, lawsuits, and fines. The financial risk is enormous! . . . *ADA—The Courts Finally Deliver Answers:* . . . Learn how these decisions affect your company's ADA policies. . . . *The EEOC's New ADA Interview Guide:* . . . What can and cannot be asked of an applicant under the EEOC's new Preemployment Disability-Related inquiries. . . . *'Happy Birthday, You're Fired':* . . . Age discrimination lawsuit jury awards today average over $450,000—far more than awards for sex, race, or disability discrimination. The number of lawsuits will continue to grow as baby boomers age, downsizing continues, and job competition continues. You'll learn how to control the new wave of employer liability arising from seniority, early retirement, reduced productivity, and other age-related issues in workforce management today."

And as high as age discrimination awards have been, judgments for disability discrimination against older people are likely to be higher. The largest number of ADA filings with the EEOC up to now haven't come from people with visible impairments that could command a jury's sympathy, but from workers who complain of back pain. Once people start suing on the dual grounds that they're (a) older employees being discriminated against because of (b) disabilities that are a normal part of aging, the combination of ADEA and ADA is going to be synergistic.

Attorney David A. Copus, a partner with Jones, Day, Reavis & Pogue in Washington who specializes in defending companies in suits alleging disability discrimination, told a 1994 seminar hosted by the National Employment Labor Institute that ADA is "another arrow in the quiver of the terminated employee." "If you fire someone," he warned employers, "you'd better have a good reason and you'd better document it." Professor Charles Fried of Harvard Law School says that as baby boomers become older, "age discrimination is going to be the bread and butter of a lot of lawyers."

When baby boomers need the opportunity to work when they're older, not only will employers find it unnecessary to demand strength and speed as a condition of employment—they'll find it illegal.

2. **Home and workplace are converging in cyberspace.** The workplace moved out of the home because firms found it less expensive to conduct productive activities in central locations, with workers concentrated. Now it's moving back to the home because firms are finding it less expensive to conduct productive activities in decentralized locations, with workers dispersed.

Moving the workplace out of the home made it much harder for older people to participate in the economy. Moving the workplace back to the home will make it much easier for even the oldest people to participate in the economy.

Many of us will be physically able far into our later years. But for those of us who may have difficulty in getting around, consider my experience with Sam.

Recently I visited Sam at the luxurious "lifecare" facility where he's living—a residence for very old people that combines the features of an apartment hotel, a resort, and a nursing home. Sam was born in 1903 and is extremely frail. "I've got so many diseases," he told me, "it's a good thing one of them's Alzheimer's, because at least I can't remember how sick I am." His wife died not long ago and he's very lonely. He employs attendants from a home care agency—all of them women in their sixties, what gerontologists call the "young-old" looking after the "old-old"—to cook, clean, and just generally be on the premises twenty-four hours a day, seven days a week.

Sam is a wealthy man. When he retired in 1968, Sam was executive vice president of one of America's largest corporations, and had exercised enough stock options to make him a millionaire many times over. But when I visited him, his life was, in the truest sense, "impoverished." None of the things that had mattered the most to Sam were in his day-to-day life anymore—his wife, his children, his friends, his work. He wasn't living in his comfortable apartment. He was haunting it.

After leaving Sam, I got an idea. The company he used to work for has been having problems lately. I called his eldest son, who's in his early sixties and is a senior manager at the company, whose headquarters are about a thousand miles from where Sam lives. I suggested that he arrange for his father's former employer to buy him a computer with a fax/modem and to ask him to be available as a managerial resource in return for a small retainer.

At first Sam claimed that there was no way he could learn to use a computer. But his son hired one of the lifecare facility's staff members to spend some time teaching him how to log onto the corporation's e-mail system and retrieve and send messages.

I had a telephone conversation with Sam a few weeks ago. His voice, which had sounded distant when I'd been sitting in his living room, was strong. He told me that he now gets as many as several dozen computer messages and phone calls a day from company executives who want his advice, that he spends several hours answering their questions, and that his memory has improved. "Most of the kids who e-mail me thought I was dead before this started," he said animatedly, "so for them, asking me what to do about this and that is like getting helpful hints from the spirit world. My son says that since this began I've made or saved the company hundreds of thousands of dollars. He's probably either exaggerating to make me feel useful, or understating so I won't ask for a raise."

The image of the forlorn man in his nineties who's been redis-covered, to its profit, by the world of the living, is a powerful one for me. In thousands of apartments in America with the curtains drawn and most of the lights off there are brilliant, forgotten people padding around feeling sorry for themselves. In the future, it isn't going to be that way.

Link Resources, a New York market research firm, reported in 1995 that 7.6 million Americans now work from home at least part-time. Compaq Computer's entire sales force of 224 has been home-based since 1993. Revenue-per-salesperson has tripled. Bell Atlantic has two thousand employees working from home for its telephone companies in seven states. Days Inns of America decided to allow a seventy-five-year-old telemarketer to work out of his home. With $3.5 million in annual revenues, he became the company's group sales department's most productive employee. By the time we're older, the proportion of the workforce based at home will have increased exponentially, and many of those home-based workers will be in their sixties, seventies, eighties, and beyond.

I haven't used the word "telecommuting" because it's one of those terms like "horseless carriage" that tries to define where we're going by where we've been. "Telecommuting" conjures up the old auto-mobile/railroad/straphanger image of shuttling back and forth to and from a remote location to a central location. But the distinction between "remote" and "central" is evaporating as you read these words. All cyberspace is created equal.

"Telecommuting" has already been superseded by the so-called virtual office or VO, a vogue term that presupposes no transit from here to there, but rather an omnipresent everywhere. I'll use VO here, though it wouldn't surprise me if the concept of an office even-tually becomes as much of a relic as the concept of a reliquary, swept away by the generations of technology that will supersede each other by the time the generation of the baby boom is older. The VO is created by simply giving employees mobile communications and computing equipment, selling the trophy headquarters building, and setting up "hoteling" office facilities where mobile employees can touch base periodically. Xerox's four thousand sales reps, for exam-ple, no longer have assigned offices. They're expected to spend less time in the "nonterritorial" office space they now share with their colleagues and more in the field, talking with customers. About eight hundred IBM employees who used to work out of five office buildings are now assigned to a open-floor, no-cubicle hoteling facility in Cranford, New Jersey, where not even the general manager has a private office.

VOs are being set up to reduce companies' occupancy costs, which are often their biggest expense after labor. Michael Bell, director of corporate real estate at Dun & Bradstreet, says the cost-per-employee of a conventional office is around $15,000 a year, while the cost-per-employee of a hoteling facility is about $1,000. By comparison, the amortized cost of a notebook computer and home-office furniture, plus phone expenses, comes to another $1,000, for an annual total of $2,000. Susanne Cannon, Professor of Finance at DePaul University in Chicago, told the 1994 annual meeting of the Association of Foreign Investors in United States Real Estate in Washington, D.C., that VOs will significantly reduce the need for conventional office space. This is great news for any baby boomer who doesn't own an office building. Just when we're going to want to be able to continue earning a living without a long commute, what I call the new version of NIMBY that's the motive behind VOs will be in full tilt: "Not In My Building—Yours." The virtual office is going to lead to virtual retirement.

Microelectronics is now collapsing space the way it previously collapsed time. PC-based videoconferencing systems have recently come on the market, but they're expensive and only connect two sites at a time. But my friend David Sarlin, Citibank's vice president for global finance technology development, told me he's already telechatting from his home computer with groups of people all over the world via an Internet program developed by Cornell University, called C.U.–See Me, that splits the screen of his monitor into eight video images. His total cost, over and above Internet access: $98 for a video camera.

Self-employed management consultant Peter G. W. Keen charges companies such as British Airways, Continental Insurance, and Coopers & Lybrand $5,000 a day for the work he does for them in his house on a dirt road inside the U.S. Virgin Islands National Park on the island of St. John. Keen, who formerly worked out of Washington, D.C., established his home office overlooking the Caribbean on a bet. At a 1990 dinner party, he told a group of fellow consultants that he could work from the island without any of his clients knowing where he was. His colleagues dared him to try. Using voicemail on his Washington phone, fax, and e-mail, Keen operated out of his small vacation home on St. John for five weeks. When none of his clients realized he wasn't in Washington, Keen decided to buy a larger house on the island and set up shop there year-round. Keen is now in his fifties. What will stop him from continuing this work-style into his sixties, seventies, and eighties?

Technology is moving so quickly that we can't even imagine the cyberspatial freedom that will be ours to work when and where we want when we're older. Sheldon Laube, national director of information and technology at the accounting firm Price Waterhouse, is already planning to acquire wireless systems that will soar above the "information superhighway." According to Laube, "It's going to change the world of computing as we know it. The way people now have cellular phones and pagers, they will have palm-size devices that can send and receive digital data." I recently dialed an accountant friend of mine at his vacation home and found myself talking to him on the cell phone on his sailboat, to which my call had been sent by call-forwarding. He happens to be about sixty, but from the standpoint of his ability to intersect with the world of getting and spending, what difference would it make if he were seventy, eighty, or ninety?

Motorola is building a system called Iridium that's expected to be operational at the end of 1998. Iridium will be the first world-wide mobile communications system, enabling users to make and receive voice, data, fax, and paging calls over hand-held equipment, using a network of sixty-six satellites. It's being financed by an international consortium of financial, manufacturing, and service companies. A sign of the times is that a group led by the Industrial Development Bank of India has acquired the rights to operate the Iridium service in Bangladesh, Bhutan, India, Maldives, Nepal, and Sri Lanka. In a few years it will be as easy to telephone a mountain-climber standing on the peak of Mount Everest—or, perhaps more pertinent, the manager of a factory employing Himalayan workers—as to call around the corner for a pizza. And the age of the person calling or being called will be less than irrelevant.

The Internet is an intergenerationet. There have been scare stories about children presenting themselves on-line as adolescents and young adults and falling into the crazed clutches of cyberweirdos. The flip side of this is that it demonstrates that cyberspace is opaque to age differences and that in the future, no one will know or care whether they're on-line with people older or younger than themselves. In cyberspace there is only cybertime, and we're going to be judged not by our biological age but by our cyber-age. No one will know or care if we're telecomputing from a wheelchair or a Western saddle. We're headed for an era of cyberretirement.

3. **Time-based pay is being superseded by performance-based pay.** The question of whether older employees perform as well as younger ones is going to be made increasingly irrelevant by the rise of what's known in human resource circles as "performance-based compensation." Earnings won't depend on the number of hours worked—or, as in the seniority system we're used to, the number of years worked. Because an older employee who may produce less in a given amount of time will be paid less, the disadvantage to the employer will be eliminated. At the same time, an older employee who produces more will be paid more, eliminating the disadvantage to the older employee. Elements of "alternative reward systems" now being introduced include

- "Knowledge-based pay" or "pay-for-knowledge," which pays employees more for learning more: precisely what we're going to have to do to stay employable
- "Skill-based pay," which provides incentives for developing new skills or enhancing existing ones
- "Pay-for-quality," which rewards employees who achieve quality benchmarks
- "Small group incentives" or "team incentives," which award more pay to members of a high-performing work group
- "Team member incentives," which add to the pay of team members who've made an extraordinary contribution to a group's performance
- "Gainsharing," in which pay goes up when profits go up
- "Key contributor retention grants," designed to retain high-performers by linking pay to continued employment for a specified number of years

"Alternative reward systems" aren't being put in to increase the employability of older people. Their purpose is to enable companies to compete more effectively with other companies. But they're going to enable older employees to compete more effectively with other employees. For instance, "key contributor retention grants" can be used to transcend the question of whether older employees will remain with a company long enough to justify the cost of hiring and training them. Instead of paying an older employee a bonus to quit—that's what an ERIP really is—she'll be paid a bonus to stay.

Ironically, performance-based compensation was originated by the Japanese auto industry to attract younger workers. Faced in the 1960s with young employees who objected to the slow pay progress mandated by the *nenko* or "long service" system, Japanese companies shifted to a system called *shokunoshikaku* ("competence status") in which salaries are based on performance. Pay levels overlap, so that higher-rated employees in a lower grade may be paid more than lower-rated employees in a higher grade. A line worker can be paid more than her foreman, a bookkeeper more than his supervisor. Many American businesses are now implementing a made-in-the-U.S.A. model of *shokunoshikaku* known as "broadbanding," with salaries determined by contribution to the enterprise rather than just hierarchical position. Broadbanding is going to help our employment prospects when we're older. The Age Discrimination in Employment Act makes it hard for companies to lower an older employee's pay simply because of age, which from a moral standpoint is precisely as it should be. But the seniority system has caused companies to put pressure on older workers to retire so they can be replaced with more affordable younger ones. Broadbanding will relieve that pressure.

Another Japanese import that's going to improve our employability when we're older is outsourcing. A prevalent feature of Japan's economy is the vertically integrated corporate *keiretsu* ("group"). The vertical *keiretsu* originated with Toyota's decision in the 1940s only to assemble cars, not to manufacture their components. I remember visiting Ford's River Rouge plant in Detroit in the mid-1970s and seeing iron ore and sand being delivered by ships at one end and driven out as automobiles at the other end. By contrast, Toyota kept costs down by obtaining parts through a pyramid of *sh'tauke*—suppliers, sub-suppliers, and sub-sub-suppliers with lower wage levels than the unionized core company.

There's a myth that once a young person is hired by a Japanese corporation, the job is for life. In reality, not only don't large Japanese companies guarantee lifetime employment, but they force all employees into early retirement, most commonly at sixty, a perfectly legal practice in Japan. The more productive workers—37 percent of male employees and 60 percent of female employees—are then immediately hired back at three-quarters to four-fifths of their previous salaries. Many of the rest are helped by their former employers to get jobs with *sh'tauke* that are part of their former employers' *keiretsu* at about two-thirds of their previous salaries, while others find jobs on their own with smaller companies, usually in the same field, or join "Silver Talent Centers" run by local governments, which contract with corporations to provide services such as bookkeeping, translation, proofreading, building maintenance, and gardening. Of employees who are let go because of age, 17 percent would like to work but can't find a job. Only 15 percent retire in the American sense.

Because of the flexibility of this system, the percentage of Japanese aged sixty-five and older who hold paid jobs is about twice what it is in the United States: 35.8 percent for men, and 15.8 percent for women, compared to our rates of 15.8 percent for sixty-five-plus men and 8.6 percent for women. Not only do Japanese companies value the productivity of older employees, but they view their movement to firms inside or outside the *keiretsu* as improving communication within the business community, increasing Japan's ability to compete in world markets. And it's interesting that in a society we think of as preoccupied with fear of "losing face," older Japanese workers are able to take a salary cut without feeling degraded, while older Americans are made to feel that rather than accept lower wages, they should commit *hara-kiri*.

As U.S. business reinvents the Japanese wheel and dubs it "outsourcing," it's creating an American breed of vertical *keiretsu* that will open the way to the kind of employment opportunities older people have in Japan. The number of American companies in Dun & Bradstreet's database that provide outsourcing services ranging from computer programming to payroll rose from 89,000 in 1989 to more than 146,000 in 1994, employing 7.4 million people. There's even an American "Silver Talent Center": KOPE (Keep Older People Employed), Inc., of St. Paul, Minnesota, a nonprofit organization with about one hundred people working for it part-time, which contracts to do packaging assembly for the Thermo-King subsidiary of Westinghouse and several divisions of 3M. I'm confident that by the time we're older, a system analogous to Japan's will have developed in the United States, based not on mandatory retirement but on older employees' desire to cut down on job responsibility and create space for personal pursuits.

We're already moving from retiring to rehiring. Almost three-quarters of major companies surveyed by Louis Harris and Associates say they hire back their retired employees as consultants or seasonal workers. Some corporations—Aerospace Corporation, Aetna Life & Casualty, GEICO, John Deere, U S West, Varian Associates, and Wells Fargo, for example—have established "job banks" of their own retirees to be on call for temporary and long-term assignments. Xerox has piloted a program that allows employees over age fifty to transfer to a less demanding job at a salary that's halfway between their previous pay and the usual pay for the new position. An official of one of America's largest companies told me, "Please don't attribute this to us, but we offer older employees the opportunity to take a lower-level job at a reduced salary rather than be downsized out of a job entirely. We do this even with unionized workers. In this economy, unions don't complain, because at least they'll have a dues-paying member with a job."

In the future, companies are going to think twice before they tell older job-seekers they're "overqualified." In *Binder* v. *Long Island Lighting Co.*, a man whose job was eliminated sued his former employer under the Age Discrimination in Employment Act because all the other positions he applied for there were filled by younger people. He was told that none of the openings were suitable for someone at his pay level. The court found for the employee on the grounds that the company hadn't asked him if he'd be willing to accept a position at a lower salary. ADEA will simultaneously prevent your employer from forcing you to accept a lower salary, and protect your employability if you're willing to accept a lower salary. An employer who tells you you're "overqualified" is now legally in the same position as an employer who tells someone she can't be hired or retained because she's a Latino or a woman.

You can get a feel for what managers are thinking about older employees from this passage, which appeared in 1994 in a newsletter called *Sales and Marketing Executive Report:* "There's no question that older workers—those with years of valuable experience who have been laid off in a big-company downsizing—can make a major contribution to a smaller firm. The question is, can you afford to hire them? The answer is, yes. Some older workers only want to work part-time and may require fewer benefits. Some are now receiving retirement benefits, so they needn't earn the highest salaries. Some don't even expect to earn salaries comparable to their old jobs."

I call the notion that the more years people have lived the less they should be paid the "age wage" theory. Personally, I think people should get paid what they're worth, regardless of how old they are. But the reality is that employers are always going to try to pay people as little as they can, and that when we're older, some of us may need the work enough to settle for an "age wage." If so, we'll have every right to be annoyed, but no reason to be ashamed. The idea of working when we're older won't be to support ourselves entirely—it'll be to close the gap left by inadequate Social Security, pensions, and savings: to turn the three-legged stool into a four-legged chair.

As compensation becomes based more on performance, will older employees end up being paid less? Some will and some won't. The relationship between age and job performance varies with occupation. Studies of printers, mail sorters, sewing machine operators, and air traffic controllers, for example, have found performance becoming worse with age, while studies of such occupations as salespeople, paraprofessionals, office workers, and quality inspectors have found performance becoming better.

In a recent Yankelovich survey of employers, older employees were rated lowest on "feeling comfortable with new technologies." But difficulty in learning new skills as people age is primarily not an effect of aging, but of aging's place in our culture. Employers have been understandably reluctant to spend money teaching new skills to people who plan to retire before the cost of teaching them has been fully amortized.

According to a recent study by three of the world's foremost experts on the mental aspects of aging, Paul B. Baltes, director of the Max Planck Institute for Human Development and Education in Berlin, Steven W. Cornelius of Cornell, and Ursula M. Staudinger of Germany's Academy of Sciences and Technology, "Whereas the cognitive mechanical system of many older adults remains generally intact, its temporal effectiveness, or speed, is reduced." Let's leave aside the fact that, as one authority has observed, "When time pressure is not a relevant factor, the performance of older people tends to be as good, if not better, than that of younger people." The hard reality is that when time is relevant, their performance isn't as good. For example, as people become older, their scores on intelligence tests, which must be completed in a limited time, drop. But Drs. Baltes, Cornelius, and Staudinger have reported, "On tests of fluid intelligence that typically show a decline with age, older adults are able to significantly improve their performance following relatively brief training programs. The magnitude of performance improvement following training is roughly comparable to the magnitude of decline observed between the ages of sixty and eighty in long-term longitudinal research."

This laboratory research is being confirmed by reports from the workplace. Since 1986, Days Inns of America has made a point of hiring older workers to lessen turnover at its reservations centers, which was 70 percent a year. At first, training older people on the reservations software took three weeks, compared to two weeks for younger employees. But the company has found that if older new hires are given a half-day orientation session, they can be trained in two weeks also—and then stay with the company an average of three years, compared to one year for younger employees, which means that training-cost-per-worker is lower for older employees. "Our experience with older reservations agents has been great," says John Snodgrass, Days Inns' CEO. "Based upon our positive experience, many of our hotels nationwide have also hired seniors."

Much of employers' current negativity toward older workers is caused by the fact that older people plan to stop working in a few years. As more older people choose to continue working, more hardheaded businesspeople will decide that it's worth their while to stop bellyaching about the performance of their older workers and start doing something to improve it.

4. **Social Security's benefits will be cut, its earnings test is being phased out, and employers are starting to provide incentives for later retirement in order to control pension costs.** The New Deal was really the Old Deal. The Social Security Act of 1935 was its centerpiece and is its most enduring and consequential legacy. And the reduction of labor force participation by older people caused by Social Socurity wasn't a side effect. The essence of the deal it offered the old was that they'd stop competing to be producers in return for having a floor placed under their ability to consume.

The idea that became Social Security was advanced in the United States by a small number of post–World War I activists who became known as the "pension crusaders." Most prominent among them was Abraham Epstein, who coined the term "social security" when, at the beginning of the Great Depression, he changed the name of his group, the American Association for Old Age Security, to the American Association for Social Security. The name change reflected a broadening of Epstein's goal: to bring European-style "social insurance," including not only monthly checks for older people but unemployment compensation, to America. Epstein hoped to eliminate what he called the "economic insecurity" of capitalism while preserving capitalism itself.

President Roosevelt embraced Epstein's basic concept as a way of protecting American capitalism's beleaguered left flank by incorporating just enough socialism into the U.S. system to give it a measure of immunity against the charge that it was abandoning the unemployed elderly to destitution. For Roosevelt, Social Security was like today's polio vaccine, which generates antibodies against the disease-producing virus by inoculation with a weakened version of the organism.

Above all, Social Security was enacted as a long-term way of shifting chronic unemployment from the potentially explosive young to the more docile old. Mechanization of agriculture and industry had drastically reduced the demand for labor. Epstein wrote in 1933, "A constructive and immediate method of considerably alleviating the problem of unemployment in the United States would be to remove the extreme age groups from the labor market. This can be accomplished through further restrictions on child labor and through a system of [public] pensions for the elderly. . . . [A]t least half of these aged and child laborers could be eliminated from the labor market and thus afford better opportunities for those between these ages." According to James H. Schulz, Professor of Economics at Brandeis University and author of the standard textbook *The Economics of Aging*, "Public and private pensions have been designed to encourage retirement to help deal with America's chronic unemployment problems. . . . Paradoxically, the major motivating force behind the passage of the Social Security Act of 1935 was probably not the provision of adequate retirement income but the creation of jobs [for younger people]. . . . Old age pensions were promised in future years to help the elderly financially but were also legislated to *encourage older workers to leave or remain out of the workforce* [emphasis in original]. . . . In the original 1935 act, benefits were not to be paid to persons receiving any 'covered wages' from regular employment."

The "removal" of older people from the labor market has turned out to be a magical recipe for cooking the books on employment. Gösta Rehn, former director of the Swedish Institute for Social Research and director for manpower and social affairs at the Organization for Economic Cooperation and Development, wrote recently, "The 'pensioning off' of elderly workers has been one of the main methods for 'reducing' officially registered unemployment."

If Americans sixty-five and over today who aren't working but would be if their labor force participation rate were what it was in 1890 were counted as being unemployed instead of retired, the U.S. jobless rate would be higher by 13 points. When unemployment drops to a reported 5.5 percent—about as close as we ever come to "full employment"—it's actually more like 18.5 percent.

By comparison, in the year Social Security was passed, the official unemployment rate was 20.1 percent. So from the standpoint of the true percentage of Americans employed in a productive capacity, the Great Depression has never ended—it was simply defined out of existence. America's squandering of human resources is as profligate today as it was in the dark days of the 1930s. When we see the sad state into which our public infrastructure and amenities have fallen despite decade after decade of supposed prosperity, it's interesting to consider that in a certain sense, we've lived all our lives during a chronic depression.

The "Old Deal" brilliantly parried the blow to the labor market that was struck by the unprecedented productivity increases of the early twentieth century. The idleness created by mechanization and mass production, which was portrayed by the American Left as a disaster demanding revolutionary change, was converted not merely into something bearable, but something enticing. Unemployment among older people was cleverly repackaged as "retirement." Americans were coaxed into dreaming of joblessness in later life rather than dreading it. In retrospect, one has to admire the genius of the maneuver. Unemployment, the least desirable economic situation, was alchemically transmuted into leisure, the most desirable. The main conservative criticism of social insurance—that its availability would induce people not to work—was turned into a virtue: Social Security recipients were required not to work.

Private pensions provided more "encouragement" to older people to leave the workforce. They first became common in the 1950s, after it became legal for unions to bargain for them. Unions had long wanted employers to provide pensions as part of a strategy to recruit younger, more assertive members. Listen to Senator Robert Wagner, one of organized labor's major champions: "The incentive to the retirement of superannuated workers will . . . make new places for the strong and eager."

Today it's hard for us to conceive of the extent to which retirement was sold to Americans as the scrumptious dessert of life, rather than demanded by them. For instance, there exists a widespread—and condescending—impression that blue-collar workers (unlike world-class cellists, etc.) have always had a desperate urge to stop working the moment they reach a certain age because their jobs are so stultifying. But here's the real story, as told to a 1987 symposium by Douglas A. Fraser, president of the United Auto Workers from 1977 to 1983: "The American industrial workers' quest for retirement began a little over thirty years ago. Then employers could not force a worker to retire because he or she had seniority. When we negotiated our first contract, employers resisted a pension, and the quid pro quo was that we would agree to compulsory retirement at age sixty-eight. I can recall those first meetings, when we advised these people—some of them in their seventies—that they had to retire. They had never even thought about it and were bitterly disappointed that they were forced out of the workplace."

But the combination of Social Security and private pensions still didn't provide adequate retirement income to most people. According to Dr. Robert C. Atchley of the Scripps Foundation Gerontology Center at Miami University, Ohio, in 1967, 60 percent of people sixty-five and over were beneath the poverty line.

Mass retirement as we now think of it dates only from 1968, when the first of four double-digit increases in Social Security benefits was enacted, culminating in the 1972 amendments, which raised benefits 20 percent and provided for annual cost-of-living adjustments. After 1972, Social Security cash benefits increased dramatically. The monthly check of a recipient who started collecting at age sixty-five in 1995 after being credited with maximum taxable earnings in all previous years of employment was 52.2 percent higher in real, inflation-adjusted dollars than in 1972.

The combination of higher Social Security benefits and corporate pensions made it socially acceptable for employers to replace "inefficient" (read: "higher-paid") older workers with younger, cheaper ones. The word "retirement" developed such a positive connotation that corporations downsizing over-fifty-five workers onto the street were able to call the practice "early retirement" and watch older employees react as if by subjecting them to age discrimination, someone had done them a favor—what economist Dr. Michael C. Barth calls "the lemming effect." The AARP's Public Policy Institute has said that Early Retirement Incentive Plans (ERIPs) should really be called "Older Worker Termination Plans." The State University of New York's Prof. Michael D. Hurd has written, "Early retirement is associated with lower resources during the retirement years." The so-called "golden handshake" is often a golden footprint on the rear end. But the most powerful ideology that ever existed is euphemism. How blatant of Arthur Miller (born in 1915 and still getting plays produced) to have described the story of sixty-three-year-old Willy Loman as "Death of a Salesman." Wouldn't it have been more palatable to call it "Early Retirement of a Regional Marketing Representative"?

But Social Security itself is going to be downsized, reversing one of the underlying forces that resulted in lower labor force participation by older Americans. We can get an idea of the extent to which older baby boomers will need to work from the fact that today, with cash benefits higher than they'll be in the future, 63.2 percent of households with members aged sixty-five and older have a yearly income of less than $10,000 from sources other than Social Security.

I predict that the downsizing of Social Security will have a positive effect on the employability of older Americans. The current, unsustainable entitlement to decades of leisure will be compensated for by a morally-based entitlement to job opportunity, regardless of age.

And there's more good news: Social Security's "earnings test" is already scheduled to be phased out for the baby boom generation. Current law provides that starting in 2009, when the oldest boomers turn sixty-three, cash benefits for those beginning to collect after "Normal Retirement Age," which will then be sixty-six, will be increased by a "Delayed Retirement Credit" of 8 percent for each year you wait after the NRA to begin collecting them, up from today's 4.5 percent. So if you were born in 1943 or after, the DRC will be "actuarily fair," which means that, based on your life expectancy, the odds are you'll receive the same total lifetime benefits regardless of whether you stop working at the NRA or later.

The Senate Special Committee on Aging reported in 1993: "Age discrimination in the workplace plays a pernicious role in blocking employment opportunities for older persons. The development of retirement as a social pattern has helped to legitimize this form of discrimination." But under the heading "Prognosis," the report concluded: "As the nation's population ages, there will be additional pressures to maintain an older workforce. This will likely result in the eventual conclusion by the business community that it is to their advantage to modify their current employment practices and provide incentives for older workers to remain on the job."

This "eventual conclusion" is already being reached, as I found out when I went to AT&T's headquarters in Basking Ridge, New Jersey, to meet with W. K. Ketchum, who serves as vice president—corporate labor relations and vice president—human resources of the company's huge Communications Services Group. Bill Ketchum, born 1940, is responsible for keeping 310,700 employees productive during the most aggressive downsizing campaign by any healthy company in the United States, cutting 83,500 employees in a staff reduction program nosed out only by IBM's 85,000. In addition to being AT&T's top human resource executive, he's one of the most influential figures in national HR circles—a trustee of the Employment Policy Association, the Labor Policy Association, and the Boston University Human Resources Policy Institute, as well as a member of the National Planning Association's New American Realities Committee and a contributor to NPA's journal *Looking Ahead*.

"We'd like the average age of retirement at AT&T to go up," Ketchum explained to me. "Today it's fifty-eight to fifty-eight-and-a-half. It's a function of our current retirement plan. We've used ERIPs to get people to retire earlier by offering what we call 'pension enhancements.'

"But our goal in the future is to get our retirement age back up, because we've gotten worried about security of our pension fund. Right now we have three workers supporting one retiree. We want to move it to five workers supporting one retiree. We don't want to get like the steel industry, where one Bethlehem worker is supporting five retirees."

In other words, as companies downsize, they're going to have to up-age.

CHAPTER 12

THE WISDOM ECONOMY

Our society has suffered for decades from the absence of older people in productive roles. The baby boom generation's ongoing participation in paid work will have a positive effect on every aspect of American life.

Our continued involvement in paid work as we get older is going to transform America.

We're told that we now live in a knowledge economy, as if this were big news. In fact, the term dates from 1969, when management expert Peter F. Drucker observed in his book *The Age of Discontinuity* that "from an economy of goods . . . we have changed into a knowledge economy." We can't now be entering an era that began more than a quarter-century ago. I would submit that, on the contrary, we're in the process of leaving it. America is going to become what I call a wisdom economy.

In 1969, Drucker wrote of what he called "knowledge workers." From now on we're going to need wisdom workers. And I believe that not far down the road, we're going to have them.

A knowledge worker is an artisan. A wisdom worker is an artist. The artisan is assigned a task. The artist assigns the task. The artisan is paid for doing what was asked for. The artist is paid for doing what no one could have imagined asking for.

A knowledge worker answers questions. A wisdom worker questions answers.

Knowledge workers have developed unprecedented means of collecting and quantifying data on every conceivable economic, political, and social factor. But only as we become older can we fully grasp the interaction of chaotic multiplicities of factors. This integrative faculty has been missing from our institutions for decades, and we have paid a terrible price for its absence.

If I were to go to an elder of any indigenous tribal culture in the world and tell her or him that in America we pay most of our older people to cut off their involvement in the affairs of society and encourage them to move to special places where old people live, that elder would say, "Then you're doomed. No society can function properly without the participation of those who have lived a long time."

Deep down we know this. We know that, as the Kung San hunter-gatherers of Africa's Kalahari Desert say, "The old people give us life." We know in our chromosomes that it's the old man who wears the antlers on his head. We know that it's the ancient woman, the wise crone, who has the power to heal.

It's there in the Yoda character in *The Empire Strikes Back*. It's there in the Pat Morita character in the *Karate Kid* movies. It's there in the Sean Connery character in *The Untouchables*. It's there in the Angela Lansbury character in *Murder, She Wrote*. But our veneration of vintage people is confined to the mythic substrate of the media. In real life, we feel they should all move to Arizona and wait for us to call them on Sundays, when the rates are cheaper.

> *Where is the wisdom we have lost in knowledge?*
> *Where is the knowledge we have lost in information?*

T. S. Eliot wrote those lines more than half a century before a glut of information began to cause us to go ever-so-slightly microsoft in the head. I think I know where the wisdom is that we have lost in knowledge. I think I know why it is that as our machines have become smarter, the society operating them has become dumber.

The most damaging deficit today isn't a budgetary deficit—it's an experience deficit. One of the main reasons so many of our institutions don't function effectively is that not enough of the people who are supposed to be running them are old enough to know better. Mass retirement is the greatest waste of human capital the world has ever known. With sloppily maintained airliners falling out of the sky, schools where the teachers ought to be wearing flak jackets, and highways you can drive on only in off-road vehicles, we convince our most seasoned technical and managerial talent to book passage on a permanent cruise to nowhere. We've become concerned about recycling everything except people. Bottles we save and sort by color. Wisdom we throw away.

The result of this experience deficit is a relentless downward spiral: The expectation that people are supposed to retire at a particular age forces experienced people out of the economically productive roles . . . a lack of experienced people causes organizations to be dysfunctional . . . the prevalence of dysfunctional organizations results in a less productive society . . . an underproductive society is unable to adequately finance public or private needs . . . and conspicuous among the needs a society suffering from an experience deficit can't finance is the upkeep of all the experienced people who've been exiled from its mainstream.

But you and I have the power to eliminate that deficit. We're going to bring our experience to bear on the problems of the future, both because of our own economic need and the economy's need for us. Members of the baby boom generation have always prided themselves on their willingness to stay after 5:00 to get the job done. I believe that when we're older, we'll think of continued productivity as just another form of "working late."

Look at the letterhead of any sizeable law firm and you'll see a few names listed as being "of counsel." Attorneys that are "of counsel" are older lawyers who no longer involve themselves in the day-to-day details of clients' affairs. Instead, they make themselves available as advisers to younger lawyers. For example, my friend Boris Kostelanetz, an eminent New York tax attorney who was born in 1911, is now "of counsel." Boris's younger colleagues' job is to be smart. Boris's job is to be wise.

I believe that in these stressed-out times, every organization needs members who are "of counsel." And I'm convinced that by the time we're older, every organization will have them.

The restructuring of American corporations is being driven by paradigms of "total quality management" and "business process reengineering" that are creating organizational roles designed explicitly for possessors of wisdom. No one is better suited to take on these new roles than older people.

For example, the ten-thousand-member Association for Quality and Participation (AQP) is catalyzing the move by U.S. corporations toward "self-directed work teams." Along with the American Society for Quality Control and the U.S. National Institute of Standards and

Technology (NIST), it sponsors the annual Quest for Excellence conference, featuring presentations by each year's winners of the NIST's Malcolm Baldrige National Quality Award. One of the AQP's major thrusts is "facilitator development." "A facilitator," says *AQP Report*, "is someone who is responsible for making people aware of how they are working together, i.e., what is going on among and between them."

> The facilitator is often given the exclusive responsibility for observing and keeping the group aware of their interpersonal process. In a total quality environment, facilitator skills are needed not only by team facilitators and leaders, but also by managers. Managers in a quality environment must demonstrate the same strong interpersonal skills required of facilitators to enable people to truly contribute.
>
> Special skills are required to fulfill the facilitator role. The best facilitators demonstrate seven characteristics. They are respect, self-disclosure, self-confidence, questioning versus telling, observant, direct, and confronting versus confrontational.

In 1995 the AQP offered workshops in Baltimore, Boston, Chicago, Cincinnati, San Antonio, San Francisco, and Seattle on "Basic Facilitator Development," "Advanced Facilitator Development," and "Influencing Skills for Facilitators and Internal Consultants." "You will learn how to be an effective coach and mentor . . . ," explained the organization's brochure, "a master educator . . ."

When we're older I foresee us seeking roles in the wisdom economy not as "workers"—people who are paid to do things that are hard—but as facilitators: people who are paid to make it easier to get things done.

Will we be able to function as members of "self-directed work teams"? Dr. Matilda White Riley, born in 1911, senior social scientist of the federal government's National Institute on Aging, and chair emerita of Rutgers' Department of Sociology, and her husband, consulting sociologist Dr. John W. Riley Jr., born in 1908, have cited research indicating: "Among older workers, intellectual functioning improves with age if the work situation is challenging and calls for self-direction."

Will we have "strong interpersonal skills"? Drs. Baltes, Cornelius, and Staudinger have reported: "Another area of age-related growth and stability involves the solution of practical problems in everyday life and in reason about interpersonal dilemmas involving strong emotional content."

Will we be capable of being "direct and confronting versus confrontational?" Harris T. Schrank, a vice president of the Equitable Life Assurance Society, and Joan M. Waring, Equitable's director of corporate research, have written that older workers "feel that they have little time for playing career games—but just want to improve things and hence they are frank, honest, and direct."

Will we have what it takes to be "an effective coach and mentor" and "a master educator"? Mr. Schrank and Ms. Waring say of older people, "They can afford to be teachers, and they no longer need to be students in the workplace."

I don't know if it's true that old dogs can't learn new tricks. But I'm sure about one thing: old dog trainers can teach young dog trainers how to train young dogs.

The advent of a wisdom economy means that while such trends as contingency, automation, and globalization may be

- negative in absolute terms for American workers in general,

they'll be

- positive in relative terms for American older workers in particular.

There's already ample evidence of the negative effect. For example, the Federal Reserve Bank of Cleveland says that average U.S. manufacturing wages, expressed in 1995 dollars, were about $14 an hour in the late 1970s. Since then they've gradually declined to less than $12. The Federal Reserve Bank of New York has reported that the average hourly earnings of college graduates in their late thirties, which were $20 in 1973, are now $18.

But if we look carefully, we can see evidence of what could be called "the positive effect of the negative effect." For instance, the phenomenal growth of the do-it-yourself home-improvement industry in the last decade has been driven by the reality that fewer and fewer Americans can afford to pay someone to do it for them. The other day I was in a checkout line at my local Home Depot and saw a large sign on the wall in front of me:

TIRED OF BEING RETIRED OR JUST INTERESTED IN A CHANGE? IN YOUR YEARS OF EXPERIENCE YOU'VE WIRED, PAINTED, PLASTERED, PLUMBED,

SAWED, STAINED, WALLPAPERED, ETC. WHY NOT BRING YOUR D-I-Y EXPE-
RIENCE TO US? SALES POSITIONS ARE NOW AVAILABLE IN MOST DEPART-
MENTS. WE OFFER EXCELLENT STARTING PAY, MEDICAL INSURANCE, PAID
HOLIDAYS, VACATIONS AND MUCH MORE. APPLY AT THE HOME DEPOT
NEAREST YOU.

What I was looking at wasn't just a help-wanted sign. It could
have been headed, "Wisdom Wanted." By the time the oldest baby
boomers enter their sixties, the economic playing field for both
older and younger U.S. workers will be lower in altitude than it is
today, but far more level.

So for those of us who may want or need to "work late," it will
be possible for our sixties, seventies, and eighties to be a time of
continuing engagement with the world, not (the root meaning of the
word "retirement") withdrawal. Rather than being forced or seduced
into relinquishing a part of ourselves when we get older, we can use
the gift of time to become whole—instead of retirement . . . entire-
ment.

CHAPTER 13

FLORIDA SHOCK

If there's one state in the union where older people are supposed to be comfortably retired on a combination of Social Security, pensions, and savings, it's Florida. But in reality, plenty of people who go to Florida to retire find that they have to work to make ends meet. When we see that older people in Florida need the opportunity to work right now, it becomes clear that members of the baby boom generation are going to need it even more.

I have seen the future, and it is Florida.

The proportion of Florida's population that's age sixty-five and over today is 18.4 percent, about what the percentage for the entire United States will be in 2020, when most baby boomers are in their sixties and seventies.

Sarasota is the winter home of the Ringling Bros. and Barnum & Bailey Circus. While the lions are jumping through hoops of fire, the women and men who are about to walk the wire unobtrusively make their way around the darkened tent in their satin robes, checking the rigging themselves. Their attitude isn't, "The safety net is the management's responsibility." It's "This is my life."

In Florida, I was able to check the rigging myself. I saw with my own eyes our real safety net—the one that doesn't depend on politicians, pressure groups, or Ponzi schemes . . . on pensions that are guaranteed to be eaten away by inflation . . . on fantasies about how the typical 401(k) participant can become a money manager who performs like a cross between Peter Lynch and the Sultan of Brunei— the one that depends only on our ability to make an economic contribution when we're older.

The safety net I saw has nothing to do with a stratagem adopted by Franklin Delano Roosevelt at a time when America was threatened within and without by communism and fascism. It doesn't involve an unsustainable promise of decades of affluent leisure to the largest and longest-lived generation in the history of civilization. It doesn't rely on the willingness of tomorrow's Americans to pay higher taxes than you and I are willing to pay today. It's the bottom, so we don't have to worry about going any lower. And it isn't so bad.

At H&R Block's 418 offices throughout the state, retired doctors, lawyers, accountants, teachers, and businesspeople who spend the winter in Florida are recruited through window signs and newspaper ads to work as preparers during the January-to-April tax season, which happens to coincide with the time many snowbirds want to be there. Olsten Temporary Services, which has twenty-eight offices in Florida, has implemented a program called Mature Advantage that's designed to attract older people to work as everything from word processors and medical billers to electronic assemblers and inventory takers. Similar initiatives have been launched by the other two members of the temporary employment industry's "Big Three," Manpower and Kelly Services. Olsten's internal manual for branch managers predicts that in the near future

> Incentives for early retirement will be reduced. The median age of full retirement will rise. Retirees will be asked, on a temporary or part-time basis, to "un-retire." Mature adults will want flexible schedules to interweave work and leisure time. . . . Employers will need new and innovative recruitment and training programs that will reduce barriers for mature workers' employment. Younger and middle-aged managers will require training to work with mature adults. . . .
>
> An aging population and a growing supply of retirees who want to return to work, coupled with the decreasing number of young adults available to work, provide a sound economic basis for employing mature adults. . . .
>
> This presents a golden opportunity for Olsten to lead the way in recognizing, recruiting, and retaining mature adults to bridge the labor shortage gap of qualified workers. . . . Your Olsten office takes pride in providing your clients with quality, motivated, responsible individuals for their assignments who take pride in a "job well done." The mature adults you'll be able to recruit and retain through the Mature Advantage program will more than help you maintain your leadership role. . . .
>
> Certainly, many mature adults want to work to fill the gap between what their retirement income, savings, and Social Security provides and what they need to make ends meet. Most mature adults today are faced with the reality that additional income is needed to fund travel

and leisure activities that might otherwise be affordable due to rising costs. As Social Security becomes an even narrower financial base for later life, mature adults will find it increasingly difficult to maintain a reasonable standard of living without the income from employment.

I met a few older people in Florida who are bitter about having to work, others who accept it with equanimity, and still others who feel as glad to be working as some of the nonworking retirees feel when they arrive at a restaurant in time for the early-bird special. Mainly I discovered that in a state whose age profile is that of the America we'll be living in when we're older, a lot of work is being done by gray-haired people with lots of wrinkles. And all this work takes place without being mirrored by the media, without support even from the conventions of small-talk: When we're introduced to people in their seventies or eighties, we don't say the usual, simultaneously prying and dignifying, "What do you do for a living?" Facing our financial future will require courage, but not as much courage as older people working in Florida are already summoning to face the present.

The last place in America where older people might be expected to be working is Palm Beach County, home of Mar a Lago, Worth Avenue, The Breakers, and the Boca Raton Resort and Club. Yet I found that a significant number of the people in pastels who inhabit the dual-golf-course, guarded-and-gated enclaves of one of the richest retirement destinations in the United States are still working.

I met Sylvia, seventy-eight, a travel agent in Delray Beach, who worked while her husband was alive because she couldn't stand being in the house all day with him, and who works now that he's gone because she can't stand being in the house all day without him.

I met Hank, seventy-six, who until recently shuttled back and forth from Boca Raton to his printing business in the north, and now that he's sold a minority of the company stays in Florida full-time and logs on to its management information system daily via modem so he can consult with his new partners.

I met Al, seventy, who sold his dental office, moved to Lantana, and then discovered that with lower interest rates, his income wasn't enough to live on. He couldn't set up shop again in Florida because (a) he wasn't licensed in the state and (b) the proceeds of the sale of his practice, reduced by taxes, weren't enough to buy another practice. In order to crack the nut, he found himself working as, of all things, an usher at a funeral home. Now he's working for a medical laboratory for $10 an hour, rounding up older men for clinical drug trials.

I met Jerry, seventy-five, an accountant in Boynton Beach who says, "I didn't retire to Florida—all I did was *move* to Florida, twenty years ago. Retire from what? To what? To sitting around and watching my butt spread? When I first came down I kept all my clients in the north. I used to go up one week a month and service them. There was also a company in Pennsylvania whose books I handled. But I found that people in this area had tax returns they needed done, too. And the Pennsylvania company I'd been working for decided it wanted somebody available throughout the month. So I phased out going north and concentrated on working with clients here. People around here are willing to pay between $250 and $1,000 to have their taxes done. Most of my friends and neighbors are either retired or semiretired, still flying back and forth to the Northeast. I don't talk about my work—what's there to talk about? So they assume that I'm one of them. But actually I'm making more money now than I did before, with less work."

I met Louise, sixty-seven, who divorced her husband of forty-five years, moved to Palm Beach Gardens from Connecticut with nothing but Social Security and $5,000 she managed to extract from "the bum," bought a word processor and set herself up as a free-lance secretary, taking minutes at meetings of condominium boards, earning a living for the first time in her life.

Unless the entire baby boom out-earns, out-saves, and out-invests these silver-haired beneficiaries of the unprecedented economic growth of the decades after World War II who've made it all the way to the floodlit foliage of Palm Beach County, we can be pretty sure that plenty of baby boomers will be working long past when the culture claims they won't be.

St. Petersburg. How many other countries in the world have a whole city just for old people? "God's Waiting Room," people joke. But I've discovered that it's becoming "God's Customer Service Center." If you want to know what it's going to be like to be old in the United States in a few decades, visit Home Shopping Network's $95 million headquarters complex the next time you're in America's gerontopolis. Though I have a way to go until I'm fifty-five, the company's human resource department was kind enough to let me train to be a "Prime Timer," one of the 450 older people among the

2,500 "Network Sales Representatives" who staff HSN's call center. Anyone who thinks the "three-legged stool of retirement income" is going to be there for the baby boomers ought to spend a few days in the city that's supposed to be America's retirement capital, talking to people in their sixties, seventies, and eighties who, at what should be the high-water mark of the U.S. retirement system, have to work for $5.25 an hour taking telephone orders for the genuine-topaz-dinner-ring division of John Malone's cable empire.

Home Shopping Network is an absolute money machine. First of all, it isn't a network: It's three networks, each broadcasting live, twenty-four hours a day, seven days a week. It needs another 2,500 employees on its campuslike grounds and another 1,000 off-site to fill the orders received at the call center from 120,000 customers a day. And it isn't just selling impulse jewelry. The call center processes one-third of Amway's orders, sells tickets to sports events, does outgoing telemarketing for credit cards, handles campground reservations for the federal government, and takes orders from a catalog called "Life Way" that carries everything from food supplements to allergy medications to furniture polish. But HSN has one overwhelming problem: Working in its call center drives people bonkers.

Maybe it's the fact that Vanna White and Connie Stevens, who appear on HSN to promote, respectively, their shoe and cosmetic lines, don't jet in often enough to relieve the tedium. Maybe it's the fact that people who pick up the phone on the spur of the moment to order five-carat amethyst marquise solitaires aren't endlessly fascinating. Whatever it is that causes the annual turnover among the network sales representatives to be 50 percent a year, however, seems to be beyond mortal ken. Across a stretch of Bermuda grass from the call center, an entire glass tower full of MBAs hasn't been able to figure out what it is. Personally, I'd try paying the NSRs more. But that may be why John Malone hasn't knocked on my door to beg me to sign on as his human resource consultant; higher wages would probably only hasten the exodus by letting people save enough to quit. The bottom line is that Home Shopping Network has to train 140 NSRs a week in July and August to prevent people who experience a sudden urge to order Frankie Avalon's Health Makeover System Herbal Vitamin and Herbal Supplement from getting busy signals.

The Prime Timer program was started in 1990 to try and recruit NSRs with less get-up-and-go. The average age of an HSN Prime

Timer is sixty-three. The oldest is eighty-two. Prime Timers have to select two "anchor" days a week plus from one to three "on-call" days when they'll work six-hour shifts if HSN needs more people on the lines.

When they're hired, Prime Timers are walked in to meet with Ed Vaughn, senior vice president for human resources. The fact that seventy-five-year-old women whose husbands have just died, widows with swollen ankles who are struggling to pay their condo maintenance and have never before held a paid job in their lives, sit down with a retired army colonel who reports directly to the company's president and are asked how they like their coffee is an indication that even in a soft economy, even when American business as a whole has yet to welcome white hair in the workplace, it's possible for an older person not only to get a job but to be thanked by an officer of the corporation for taking it.

"The older people we get feel it's undignified to be seen working at McDonald's," Vaughn tells me. "If you're a Prime Timer in our call center you can hold your head up, as long as you don't tell anyone how much you're getting paid. Yo, Mike."

Enter Mike Reardon, executive vice president of operations, fifty-five, retired Marine colonel.

"I can feel the ageism out there myself. Like when I was in Vietnam. Nice, quiet, sunny day, but somewhere out there a VC has you in his sights. I'm fifty-nine, man. I'm about to be dropped from the human race."

Reardon points at Vaughn. "On the subject of aging, he's more *attuned* than I am," he drawls.

"You're aging too, you son of a bitch," says Vaughn.

"Let 'em work till they're seventy, seventy-five, I couldn't give a fudge sundae," says Reardon. "All I care is, can they do the job. They're going to need three weeks of training, whether they're twenty-five or seventy-five. If they're too old to get around, run a phone line into their house, give 'em a computer and patch 'em into the call center. The customers are ordering from home—why can't people work from home? We save money by not having to pay for brick-and-mortar and air-conditioning. Adds a security problem. But anything's better than taking money away from working people and giving it to people just because they're over a certain age."

You don't argue with this guy. All Mike Reardon needs is a few good NSRs.

I ask Vaughn how the Prime Timers stack up as employees. He shrugs. "I wish I could tell you they were the hottest thing since sliced bread. When we did a statistical evaluation comparing them with younger people in the call center, they rated slightly higher in some areas, but nothing to fax home about. We thought the numbers might show that they were better than average when it came to customer service. But there was no appreciable difference between the Prime Timers and anyone else. They can be just as mean and nasty as people half their age."

An assistant in the human resources department escorts me to the training center. She isn't young—seventy? seventy-five?—but she has no "elderly" mannerisms. She looks like a woman in her thirties wearing not-very-convincing "old" makeup.

"How do you like working here?" I ask.

"Oh, it's real fine." She smiles. A flock of crow's-feet appear at the corners of her eyes, as if she really were old. "They treat you like people. One of the best things is that they have a nurse practitioner on the premises who'll treat you for free. A lot of my friends spend half their time sitting in doctors' waiting rooms. Not me."

There is a whole floor of classrooms. In one, executives are training on new graphics that have been incorporated into the company's management information system. In another, a desktop publishing program is being demonstrated. I'm with a group of eight Prime Timers who are sitting in a darkened room in front of terminals. Two are a couple in their mid-sixties from Omaha, a retired civil engineer and his wife, a former obstetrical nurse. A man in his late sixties recently retired as a clerk for the Massachusetts Registry of Motor Vehicles. An African-American woman in her late fifties was the bookkeeper of a chain of hairdressing salons in the Atlanta area that went bankrupt. One man is a seventy-one-year-old retired high school principal from Philadelphia. A seventy-three-year-old woman who lives across the bay in Tampa hasn't worked since she was eighteen. A man from Uruguay who's been living in St. Petersburg for five years and a man who came recently from American Samoa, both in their mid-fifties, are sitting next to each other.

Our trainer is Orville Wollard, born in 1929, a former minister with an impassioned baritone and two degrees in archaeology who used to have a travel agency in Tarpon Springs, Florida. When leading two tours a month to biblical sites in the Middle East became too much for him he sold his business and took a job as an NSR as a stopgap before beginning to collect Social Security. That was when he was fifty-eight. Now he's HSN's top order-entry trainer and has no plans to retire. He begins by introducing his wife, Juanita, a retired schoolteacher who works in the call center: "I just wanted you to hear from someone who's been through this."

"I know some of you are nervous," Juanita says. "'What am I doing here? Will this be all right?' Well, I felt the same way, but it went away after a short while."

Then Orville gives each of us the 106-page *Network Sales Representative Workbook* and a copy of a document headed "The Official Home Shopping Club Order Entry Script—A Smile Can Be Heard."

As Orville begins to walk us through it, teaching us how to move our cursors from field to field and how to keyboard the data, I close my eyes.

I can hear him smiling.

1. Welcome to the Home Shopping Club. My name is Craig.
2. Would you like to order the Amcor Air Purifier and Ionizer?
3. May I have your membership number, please?
   (THE CUSTOMER IS A FIRST-TIME CALLER.)
4. May I have your phone number beginning with the area code?
5. May I have the zip code of your physical shipping address?
6. How many Amcor Air Purifier and Ionizers would you like to order? . . .

At lunch in the HSN cafeteria I ask Ruth and Zack, the nurse and engineer from Omaha, how they came to be Prime Timers.

"We saw an ad for tours of Home Shopping Network," says Ruth, "and we were bored, so we called up and made reservations. When we got here we were the only people who'd signed up, but they took us around like we were royalty. We couldn't believe they'd give such an elaborate tour to just two people."

I feel like telling them that if they hadn't shown up, Ed Vaughn and Mike Reardon probably would have come for them in an armored personnel carrier and taken them to see all 95 million dollars' worth of HSN whether they wanted to or not, but I don't say a word.

"When they took us through the call center they told us about the Prime Timer program," says Ruth. "It had never occurred to us to get jobs, but the work looked easy, and we realized it would solve a problem we were having."

"Back in Omaha we played golf every weekend," says Zack. "But when we got to St. Pete we found that now that we weren't working anymore we didn't have enough money to afford the greens fees. We weren't about to pound the pavements looking for work. But when we heard about Prime Timers, we said, 'Hey, what the heck. We'll work the phones a few days a week and be able to play golf again.'"

After lunch our group is brought into one of the three sections of the call center. It looks like an enormous aircraft hangar filled with computer terminals in which hundreds of people in headsets, of every imaginable age, sex, and ethnicity, wearing everything from suits to sweats, are sitting, standing, leaning, crouching, stretching, and pacing back and forth, while talking to people about the glories of cubic zirconia and trying to remember that A Smile Can Be Heard.

On a bulletin board I read a notice that begins:

TO: All HSN Employees
FROM: Ed Vaughn
RE: Joy Tree

As we enter the Holiday Season, many of us are filled with the joy of being able to give gifts to our loved ones, especially children. Unfortunately, there are some in our HSN family whose personal financial circumstances won't allow them to experience the joy of providing their children with gifts.

Employees are invited to give anonymous presents of Home Shopping Club merchandise, purchased at the usual 40-percent-off employee discount, to their coworkers' children. There are instructions to "families who need a hand" and "families who want to give."

Many times I've been in workplaces where gifts were being solicited for those less fortunate than the employees. This is the first time I've seen—and I realize, with a shudder, the first of many times I'll be seeing—gifts being solicited from the more fortunate employees to be given to the less fortunate employees. This is the new American workplace, the real American workplace where the bosses know that given the wages they're paying, there's an excellent chance people won't be able to afford to give Christmas presents to their children.

Each of the Prime Timers is assigned a veteran NSR to "double-jack" with. We plug our headsets into their terminals and can hear both sides of their conversations. If we feel ready, we can start taking calls. I double-jack with Liza.

Liza, born in 1929, has been living in St. Pete since 1954 and working at HSN since 1985. Her smile can be heard in a Tennessee twang as down-home as red-eye gravy. Her rheumatoid arthritis has pulled the tendons off the knuckles of both hands, which doesn't prevent her from keyboarding quickly, pecking but not having to hunt. Needless to say, she lives in a mobile home with a 110-pound dog named Killer.

"This is a great place to work," she tells me between calls, which she handles with much eye-rolling and head-shaking at the slow-wittedness of HSN customers who don't have nearly as much experience talking to her as she has talking to them. "We have excellent benefits here. I work five days, nine A.M. to three P.M. When I get tired of listening to the people who call in I take a week off—one each month. My supervisor is in her thirties. She really knows how to work with older people. It helps that I like younger people. I went to the Rod Stewart concert at the University of South Florida in Tampa the other night. I just love his album *Unplugged*.

"I've got to work because my pension ran out from Montgomery Ward, where I was a cosmetics buyer, and I got nothing from my husband. He dropped dead on the soccer field at age forty-two in 1977, leaving me with a ten-year-old son.

"I'm a painter. Florida birds, large flowers, and landscapes. I paint thirty hours a week. I keep three paintings going at once. I get two hundred to three hundred dollars a painting. My painting is as important to me as my children.

"At the doctor's office, they asked me, 'You still working at HSN?' 'Forever,' I said. They said, ''Cause we've heard some horror stories about that place.' 'Hon,' I said, 'if I had any horror stories, I'd be outta there.' I'm not saying it's perfection personified. But you've got to go with the flow. Hang loose.

"I guess if I stopped working I could live on a budget. But who wants to live on a budget? I think I'll work till I drop.

"I'm really very fortunate. God's been good to me. I used to handle the president of the company's correspondence with irate customers. I mean, in the area of irates, I was the president of Home Shopping Network. But now I'm making more money."

"They gave you a raise?" I ask.

"No." Liza smiles. "I can work more hours now without having my Social Security reduced."

Sitting in the HSN cafeteria with its signs offering KETTLE COLLECTIONS, PIZZAMORE, PASTA POT, and SWEET SURRENDERS, watching a cross-section of humanity eating and chatting—female and male, tall and short, fat and thin, straight and gay, dark-skinned and light-skinned, young and old—it suddenly came over me: *In the future this is going to be normal.*

When we're older it will be as common to see a corporate cafeteria thronged with older people as it is to see a National Park cafeteria thronged with older people today. At companies across America, people of all genders, sizes, shapes, proclivities, colors, and ages will be working together. Places like the HSN call center are going to be part of the lives of millions of baby boomers in their sixties, seventies, and eighties. It won't be necessary to fly to Florida to see large numbers of older people on the job.

If we all had picturephones it wouldn't be necessary now. Every time you dial an 800 number and reach a big call center, you're in contact with a room where older people are working side by side with younger people. But the human mix at the other end of the fiberoptic cable is hidden from us by the veil of voice-only communications. On one level this is a good thing because it provides space for a diversity that's the result of social blossoming rather than social engineering. But on another level, by obscuring the reality that so many older people already need to work, it allows us to continue fantasizing about personal futures lived in a vague neutral blur whose material aspect somehow takes care of itself.

As I boarded the plane to go back to the 1990s, I felt better knowing that if I have no choice when I'm old but to work in a virtual shopping mall, I already know the script:

25. Would you like to order the Vanna White beige kidskin pumps, our Special Purchase Item for today?
26. Please hold for the opportunity to speak with the show host.

But I also realized that if so many older people in Florida who are supposed to be in their reclining years are already finding that there's more month than money, you and I had better start planning accordingly.

CHAPTER 14

INDEPENDENT MEANS

When we're older, we're going to have to draw on personal resources to close the gap between what we'll receive from Social Security, pensions, and investments, and the income that will be necessary for us to live comfortably and creatively. Each of us needs to begin now to make sure those resources will be available.

In 1841 Ralph Waldo Emerson published an essay whose title introduced a new phrase into the English language: "Self-Reliance."

"And we are . . . not minors and invalids in a protected corner," wrote the Yankee poet and philosopher, "not cowards fleeing before a revolution, but guides, redeemers and benefactors, obeying the Almighty effort and advancing on Chaos and the Dark."

When we're older, Social Security and private pensions won't provide enough income for most of us to live on. Emerson would have chided any of us who ever believed otherwise: "And so the reliance on Property, including the reliance on governments which protect it, is the want of self-reliance." "Do your work," Emerson urged in his essay, "and you shall reinforce yourself." William M. Mercer, Inc.'s, study, *Retirement Security: Are All Bets Off?*, found that 95 percent of human resource executives surveyed said that "shifting financial responsibility to employees" was one of their companies' important objectives. To maintain our standard of living—and to be "the guides, redeemers and benefactors" we're meant to be in later life—we will have no one to rely on but ourselves.

If we find it daunting that we're going to have to be self-reliant during precisely the time of life when today's older people expect to be able to rely on others, it's because we're living in a unique politico-economic system—one that exists nowhere else, never existed before, and is about to pass away.

The United States never became a comprehensive welfare state on the Western European model. It evolved into what I call the "Retirement State": a society in which the biggest government program is a retirement plan, and the biggest segment of private capital is owned by pension funds.

Instead of taking care of its citizens from cradle to grave, the United States has been taking care of them from retirement party to grave. The welfare state was the European social democrats' way of competing with Marx's "From each according to his abilities, to each according to his needs." Their American liberal counterparts, thwarted by conservative opposition to government spending, had to settle for cobbling together a system whose motto could be "From each according to his abilities, to each according to his age."

But capitalism doesn't have to compete with Marxism anymore. We are about to see the decline and fall of the Retirement State.

The Soviet Union collapsed because the most far-seeing among its elite realized that the USSR didn't have the economic capability simultaneously to enter another round of the arms race with the United States—stealth, smart weapons, antimissile technology, space warfare—and to satisfy internal demand for consumer goods. The Retirement State will collapse because the realization is going to emerge that the United States doesn't have the economic capability simultaneously to provide affluent retirement to the baby boom generation and to meet the country's other pressing needs. Democrats will be more focused on the need for public investment (e.g., education, mass transit). Republicans will be more focused on the need for private investment (e.g., telecommunications, biotechnology). But tacit political agreement that the Retirement State must be dismantled will be wall-to-wall.

The disintegration of Russian and Chinese Communist centralism has unleashed centrifugal forces of world-historical magnitude. We are only at the beginning of a process I call "radical privatization": empires divesting themselves of nations, nations divesting themselves of enterprises, enterprises divesting themselves of individuals, individuals divesting themselves of one another.

Governments around the world are privatizing industry; industry is outsourcing all except core functions; firms to which functions are being outsourced are downsizing, wherever possible dealing with individuals not as employees (let alone unionized employees) but as independent contractors; and individuals are finding it harder than ever to maintain long-term personal relationships with other individuals. We are looking at a future in which people will be unprecedentedly on their own.

Radical privatization is going to have a profound effect on what our income sources will be in later life. Robert D. Paul is chairman of The Segal Company, a major pension consulting firm. Dale B. Grant is Segal's executive vice president. Here's an excerpt from an article they wrote titled "The Next Generation of Benefits Plans," which appeared in the Winter 1992/93 issue of the American Compensation Association's *ACA Journal:*

> The next generation of benefits will reflect the changes in economics and society that are already taking place. Perhaps the most striking societal change has been the shift from institutional to individual loyalties. Employers, unions, professions and political parties historically have provided a sense of belonging that was strong enough to persuade individuals to forego what might have been their own needs and preferences for the greater needs of the group. Today, individuals are moving toward an understanding that they must take hold of their own destinies. . . .
>
> The importance of individualism and economic needs can be seen through some interesting trends in retirees returning to work. . . . Now, as their purchasing power is being eroded by lower interest rates on fixed-income investments, many more retirees are seeking additional income through part-time or full-time employment.
>
> The thrust of individual reliance as a social dynamic has enormous implications for the next generation of benefits. And the interplay among government, business and employees will alter greatly the way programs are put together.

Each human being in the developed world is going to have to be largely self-reliant along the entire adult lifespan. In particular, the baby boom will be the first generation in the history of civilization whose members will bear individual responsibility for their own later-life income. Government will continue to play a role, business will continue to play a role, family will continue to play a role, but the buck will stop where it starts—with you and me.

Can we make and save that buck? We're going to have to, through

- Recurrent development of new competencies
- Personal entrepreneurship
- Ultra-long-term investment

RECURRENT DEVELOPMENT OF NEW COMPETENCIES

In human resource circles these days you hear about how vital it is for people who want to maintain their employability to seek out opportunities for "lifelong education." But that sounds too much like school. "Adult education"—sounds like night school. "Continuing education"—sounds like you've got to be an M.D. "Retraining" — sounds like Bowser pooped on the rug and you've got to hit him on the fanny with a rolled-up newspaper.

My friend Nicholas Rudd, senior vice president of Young & Rubicam Inc., who was the huge advertising agency's director of human resources before he metamorphosed into its chief information officer, which meant not merely learning about computers from the ground up, but becoming a world-class expert in applying data-processing technology, told me the term he's using. It's a mouthful, but it articulates the fact that, as we get older, we need to add value to ourselves, not just years: "recurrent development of new competencies" (sounds like each of us becomes a Microsoft or a Lotus, periodically issuing updated, more powerful versions of ourselves).

Professor Eli Ginzberg put it to me this way: "The basic question everyone today, regardless of age, has to ask, is, 'What kind of adjustments do I have to make to continue and enhance my personal marketability? What is it that I'll be capable of doing in the future?'"

Professor Ginzberg has been called "one of the fathers of human resource studies" and "the nation's premier health economist." His listing in *Who's Who* runs to eighty-nine lines. He has authored more than 100 books and monographs, ranging from *Studies in the Economics of the Bible* (1932) to *Human Resources: The Wealth of a Nation* (1958) to *The Road to Reform: The Future of Health Care in America* (1994). Born in 1911, he started teaching at Columbia University the year the Social Security Act of 1935 was passed, and has no intention of stopping.

"Technically I had to retire at sixty-eight," he tells me, putting in his hearing aids. There is a vigor about his white-haired, ruddy-faced, no-nonsense presentation of self that makes age irrelevant. He is wearing a black blazer and a bold red tie-of-the-moment. "But I'm actually working harder today. I'm the director of two programs—Columbia's Eisenhower Center for the Conservation of Human Resources, and the New York City Urban Development Program. I'm an urbanist too, you see."

"You seem to specialize in having a lot of specialties," I suggest.

Professor Ginzberg shrugs. "Anyone who wants to survive in the economy that's coming at us had better have a bunch."

"We're facing a fifty percent increase in potentially productive years of life," he says. "It used to be forty—now it's sixty. With every year that passes there are going to be more and more older Americans who'll need to work for a living. The problem is that the job market won't be robust enough to accommodate all the older people who'll want to continue working."

"What advice would you give people who are now in their twenties, thirties, forties, and fifties?" I ask.

"First of all, stop assuming that aging and decrepitude are the same thing," Professor Ginzberg says. "If you start with that cockeyed notion, you're going to be in big trouble.

"Second, don't count on the government to bail you out when you're older. Social Security was only meant to be so that if you didn't have any other source of income, you wouldn't starve. Americans aren't going to pay additional taxes to support a huge number of older people. Why should they? It annoys me that the City of New York gives me a card that lets me ride the bus for half-price.

"Third, you've got to come to grips with the fact that skills which aren't added to, decline. Experience alone doesn't mean a damned thing. Unless you're constantly exposing yourself to new theoretical knowledge, your skills are eroding.

"Fourth, you have to face the reality that the future is going to be in the individual's hand, not the employer's. You can't rely on the employer to send you to courses in order to keep your employability up to scratch. You've got to send yourself.

"Fifth, start thinking about what you'd do if you were self-employed. The way the American corporate culture views employment is changing drastically. Until recently, as long as you performed, the job would be there for you. Not anymore. The flip side of the shrinkage of the corporate workforce is different kinds of relationships between individuals and the labor market. Ask yourself what capacities and skills you possess that can be used in less-than-full-time self-employment when you're older."

Professor Ginzberg's analysis dovetails with what the most sophisticated voices in corporate America are telling each other. W. K.

Ketchum, AT&T's vice president for corporate labor relations, wrote recently in the National Planning Association's journal *Looking Ahead*:

Job security, the guarantee of a job for the working life of the employee as long as he or she meets certain minimal expectations, is no longer a commitment that employers can make. Job security must be replaced with a new concept that encourages employees to broaden their skill base with the intent of ensuring greater employability, internal or external to a particular company.

This new concept, sometimes called career security or career continuity, requires specific actions on the part of the employer and the employee. The employer is responsible for providing meaningful jobs, clear direction and educational opportunities that will enhance an individual's value and career options within the company and the marketplace. The employee is responsible for developing a passion for excellence, a willingness to learn and the flexibility to adapt to changing realities of the company, and for pursuing job opportunities.

Michael D. Hurd, Professor of Economics at the State University of New York at Stony Brook and one of the foremost experts on the economics of aging, gave me an excellent summation of why, from the standpoint of economic theory, it's crucial for us to take personal responsibility for our own employability. He explained that when employees work for a company, they develop "specific human capital": knowledge about the firm that simultaneously increases its productivity and their value to the firm. Knowledge that can be brought to another company is known as "general human capital." It's the difference between knowing your way around Revlon and knowing your way around the cosmetics industry.

According to Dr. Hurd, the problem for older workers is that when they change jobs after a long stint with one employer, they lose their specific human capital, and with it, part of their productivity—and part of their earning power.

"If an older worker had maintained or increased his or her general human capital," Dr. Hurd has written, "a job change would not occasion a large fall in productivity. However, most older workers probably have little general human capital: during the many years since schooling the initial stock of general human capital would have depreciated; there is little financial incentive for investment in general human capital on the part of the firm because the employee can simply leave, taking the investment to another firm."

Something Dr. Hurd told me when I visited him at Stony Brook meshes interestingly with that analysis. When I asked him how we can prepare for the decades of downward pressure on stock and bond prices that will be inevitable when pension funds and individuals will be selling assets to provide income for the baby boomers when they're older, you'll recall that, "The commodity you'd want to hold is labor."

It's not so easy for us to hold other people's labor as a commodity we can draw on for income when we're older. But there's one person's labor I already hold, and will continue to hold when I'm older, if I maintain that person's "general human capital": My own.

Let's see if we can merge the messages of Nicholas Rudd, Professor Ginzberg, W. K. Ketchum, and Dr. Hurd into an overall conception of how we can stay employable into later life:

We need to recurrently develop new competencies . . . while facing the possibility that we may have to change our relationship to the labor market . . . by continually investing in educational opportunities . . . in order to maintain and increase our general human capital.

PERSONAL ENTREPRENEURSHIP

At a 1993 conference on "U.S. Competitiveness and the Aging American Workforce," Prof. Rosabeth Moss Kanter of Harvard Business School, author of *The Change Masters: Innovation for Productivity in the American Corporation,* stated, "Overall, institutionally dependent careers are declining; self-reliant careers as professionals and entrepreneurs are ever more necessary."

Given this kind of confirmation that the Emersonian paradigm is operative, I could say, "I can't agree more with Professor Ginzberg's recommendation that people aged twenty through sixty prepare for the possibility of self-employment."

But I can agree more: The time for us to go into business for ourselves is now.

By starting as soon as possible . . .

- We can begin another career without having to abandon our first career: not a conventional second career, but a new model I call a "twin career."
- We may be able to develop a sideline that eventually becomes our main line.
- We can start on a shoestring, rather than on a short leash from the bank.
- We can use our income from employment to service a loan to bridge us smoothly into self-employment or small-business ownership by the time we're older, instead of finding ourselves suddenly out of a job and having to bootstrap a start-up on our credit cards.
- We can hedge against the onrush of contingency by being able, if necessary, to shift to self-employment earlier in life.
- We have time to fail and try again.

Carl Bach, a friend of mine in his thirties who's the manager of an auto parts store, has a twin career doing oil changes at busy people's homes for about 50 percent more than the going rate at local garages. He has far more requests for lube-oil-and-filter appointments than he can schedule, so he limits his clientele to long-time customers. If he were laid off from his day job tomorrow—or at age sixty-two, or sixty-five, or seventy—he'd still have his oil-change business, which he'd be able to expand overnight into a full-time money-earner. "Brakes on new cars are required to have two separate control systems," Carl told me. "If one quits on you, the other still works. That's what I'm doing."

Recently I met Rosie, who was born in 1930. She was a buyer for Sears until the downturn of the early 1980s made her rethink how she wanted to intersect with the economy. She quit, went to school for a year, and qualified as a licensed practical nurse. Then she spent another year studying to be a recreational therapist. "I think everyone has to become an entrepreneur," she told me. "I think of myself as having three businesses. I work as a private duty nurse in hospitals. I do bodywork out of my home. And I have a part-time job in retail."

My cousin Dick was a successful surgeon until problems with his wrist joints forced him to quit a few years ago, in his mid-fifties. Fortunately, from a small beginning in the 1970s, he'd parlayed his fascination with computers into a twin career, founding a company that writes programs that identify occupational health hazards for Fortune 500 corporations. He finds that he enjoys his present way of using his medical expertise more than he did his previous one. "At this stage of my life," he told me, "I like cutting deals better than cutting people."

A compelling reason for you to begin developing a twin career now is that any company that's smart enough for you to be working for is smart enough to be on the lookout for a way to get your job done by clicking on an icon. Ultimately, that's what a lot of today's labor-market "churn" is about, whether it's described as delayering, downsizing, rightsizing, or just plain staff reduction. If you're self-employed, whatever other challenges you encounter, at least you won't be looking to replace yourself with a software package.

The trick to being able to earn enough money in later life will be to ride the trends, not fight them. If outsourcing is the wave of the future, rather than being someone whose work is outsourced, become someone to whom work is outsourced. If switching employers when you're older will result in a salary cut because the "firm-specific skills" that made you more valuable to your previous company are worth little to your new employer, let your new employer be yourself. Your firm-specific skills will never lose value if you're the firm.

By the time we're older, companies will have far more positive attitudes about hiring, training, and retaining older employees than they do today. But if we're headed, as I think we are, toward a norm of semiretirement rather than full-time employment or full-time non-employment, most of us are going to be looking for job flexibility—ways of interacting with the economy that let us do other things besides paid work. No matter how much flex-time and flex-space are built into the future work environment, there's never going to be such a thing as a flex-boss.

The most flexible person to work for—if not necessarily the least demanding—is always going to be yourself. So I wouldn't be surprised if by the time we're older, employment by others comes to be regarded as a sort of "internship" for self-employment in later life.

In fact, it would be helpful to start thinking of yourself as already self-employed. In today's labor market, an organization you work for full-time isn't really your employer anymore. It's simply your only client. If I own a store and find that I'm down to one customer, maybe it's time to put some fliers under people's windshield wipers.

When you're ready to formally go into business for yourself, there's no better resource than the Service Corps of Retired Executives (SCORE). Sponsored by the U.S. Department of Commerce's Small Business Administration (SBA), SCORE has 750 offices around the country. SCORE's thirteen thousand volunteer counselors are retired businesspeople with an average of thirty-five years of experience. They're prepared to be mentors during the entire process of creating a successful business, from the exploratory stage through writing a business plan, obtaining financing, setting up shop, managing and growing the enterprise—even floating an initial public offering of stock.

The price is right: free. And SCORE counselors can be your conduit to all of the SBA's training services, including printed and video materials, on-line tutorials, bulletin boards, and e-mail, as well as more than six hundred Small Business Development Centers and Subcenters. But above all, SCORE will give you the opportunity to relate seriously with people a few decades older than yourself. Not only will you learn how to run a business, but along the way you'll get an idea of what life will be like for you when you're older. You might even make some new old friends.

You can arrange to meet with a SCORE counselor by phoning the SBA's Small Business Answer Desk between 9:00 A.M. and 5:00 P.M. Eastern Time at (800) 827-5722. When the recording comes on, press 1 for the menu, 3 for the counseling and training information tape, and then 3 at any time to speak with a specialist who'll have the number of the SCORE office closest to you. You can make an appointment to meet with a counselor by calling the nearest SCORE office between 10:00 A.M. and 3:00 P.M. local time. Here are the address and telephone number of SCORE's headquarters:

> Service Corps of Retired Executives (SCORE)
> 409 Third St., S.W.
> Washington, DC 20416
> (202) 205-6762

I got a good picture of what flourishing entrepreneurship in our later lives will look like when I flew to the red-rock country of Sedona, Arizona, and spent some time with Robert J. Eggert Sr.

I'd become interested in Bob Eggert when I saw the newsletter he edits, *Blue Chip Economic Indicators,* quoted in Federal Reserve publications. *Blue Chip* presents widely relied-on "consensus estimates" of fifteen figures, including GDP, CPI, Treasury bill interest rates, unemployment, housing starts, auto sales, and exports: the average of forecasts supplied by fifty-one top academic and corporate economists whom Eggert polls each month. Eggert's "cooperators," as he calls them, include experts at the Bank of America, Brown Brothers Harriman, Chase Manhattan Bank, First National Bank of Chicago, Georgia State University, GM, Metropolitan Life, Morgan Stanley, the National Association of Home Builders, UCLA, and the University of Michigan. The newsletter's subscribers are mostly government agencies, financial service companies, and major corporations. Professor Murray Weidenbaum of Washington University, a former head of the White House's Council of Economic Advisers, has called *Blue Chip* "the best available indicator of the prevailing private-sector forecast."

My original intention was to ask the man who runs this clearinghouse for economic prognostication what he believed the financial situation of the baby boomers would be in later life. I didn't know that Eggert was born in 1913 and is a one-man pilot project for the kind of entrepreneurial activity a lot of baby boomers are going to be engaged in when they're older—right down to living in a resort area and telecomputing with an office two thousand miles away.

I have a theory that a silver-and-turquoise bolo tie on a deeply tanned, smiling man with gray hair is usually a good omen. That's what Bob Eggert was wearing when he invited me into his personal office.

"I was born in Arkansas," Eggert told me. "After grad school, some teaching, and a few marketing jobs, I went to work for Ford Motor Company. That was in 1951. Eventually I became manager of marketing research, working directly for Bob McNamara. My claim to fame at Ford was that in the early 1960s my research told me younger drivers wanted a compact, muscular car. I pushed for it, and I came up with a name for it, after a book I was reading: Mustang.

"By the time I was fifty-five I'd been with Ford seventeen years. I felt like I'd reached a dead end, and I decided to take early retirement and return to university teaching. But six months later I was offered a job at RCA as vice president for economic and marketing research, and I couldn't resist taking it. I was in New York from 1968 to 1976. When I started at RCA, David Sarnoff was still chairman. Sarnoff didn't want to be presented with complications. He just wanted to know, 'What kind of economy are we heading into? Do I have a green light, a red light, or a yellow light?' That's when I started polling other economists, because it seemed logical to me that a consensus forecast would be more reliable than anything I could come up with myself.

"I retired again at age sixty-two. My wife, Betty, had chronic bronchitis, and the doctors said she'd do better in a warmer, drier climate. We'd vacationed in Sedona and loved it. So in 1976 we moved here and started *Blue Chip Economic Indicators.* When the consensus has been that the economy is going to be strong, I've printed the masthead in bright green ink. If my cooperators begin to forecast a downturn, I switch to red, and if the figures are flat, it becomes yellow—proceed with caution."

One of the things that impressed me about Bob Eggert as a model for our proceed-with-caution future was that he's working in his eighties because he needs the money, but not so he can afford to live in a furnished room and warm up cat food on a hot plate. At first he needed it to take care of his wife, and now he needs it because he has six grandkids to help through college and graduate school and into careers, and because he enjoys breeding and racing quarter horses, which has been part of his life for decades. It's certainly possible to live in the America of the 1990s on Social Security and two pensions, but will that necessarily provide you with enough income to own a grandson of Secretariat, pay his trainer, travel to racing meets throughout the Southwest, and keep your collection of classic Mustangs detailed?

I find it noteworthy that after a series of corporate jobs that were pretty financially rewarding, Eggert now has the highest purchasing power he's ever had in his life. At an age when, according to the culture, he should be fretting about interest rates, he's predicting them, sitting by the side of a road at the south end of Oak Creek Canyon, computer-to-computer with his publisher in Alexandria, Virginia, servicing more than one thousand subscribers at $498 a year.

Incidentally, I did get around to asking Eggert what the economic future of the baby boomers will be like. Over breakfast on the clubhouse terrace of the Poco Diablo golf course, he told me he thinks the age at which Social Security benefits can be received will be increased further, and that most Americans will work later into life than they do today.

"My cooperators rank slower labor force growth due to population aging as the fourth most unfavorable factor for our economic future," he said, "surpassed only by mounting structural costs such as health care, excessive debt, and high taxes, which are numbers one, two, and three, respectively. But while reduced growth in the labor force is negative for the economy as a whole, it's going to be a positive factor for older people who want to work."

"Do you have any thoughts you'd like to share with members of the baby boom generation who may want to be working for a living when they're around your age?" I asked.

"I'd tell them what Albert Einstein once wrote to a young man," said Eggert. "I've made it my personal motto: 'Do not strive for success—strive to be a person of greater value.'"

ULTRA-LONG-TERM INVESTMENT

Our idea of what constitutes a long-term investment hasn't kept pace with the longevity revolution. Is a stock or mutual fund held for ten years—a common definition of "long-term"—truly a long-term investment for people who are twenty or thirty years away from their sixties or seventies? For a woman already in her early sixties, even a twenty-year investment outlook doesn't take her to her life expectancy of just under eighty-five.

Our need to be financially self-reliant when we're older means that we have to invest not merely for the long-term, but for what I call the *ultra*-long-term. An ultra-long-term investment time horizon doesn't mean that we necessarily have to buy and hold stocks decade after decade, though fortunes have been and will continue to be made that way, and trying to time the market is generally a loser's game. But we do have to start thinking about the economic outlook in multi-decade terms, and to constantly reevaluate our investment decisions accordingly.

First we've got to ask ourselves how much current consumption we're willing to give up in order to have a chance to consume later without having to produce later. I say "to have a chance" because saving is always a roll of the dice. There's no way for us to simply postpone consumption from when we're younger to when we're older. If I refrain from spending a dollar so I can invest it and spend the proceeds in the future, I may end up losing both the dollar and the proceeds. I might be better off if I blow the dollar now on an order of buffalo wings and let the future take care of itself—or should I say, prepare to take care of myself in the future.

In other words, how much leisure do you really want to consume when you're older, given the fact that you're going to have to pay for it when you're younger?

Second, we should take advantage of any employer match that's available. Stanford University economist B. Douglas Bernheim calls his employer's defined contribution plan "extraordinarily generous." It offers to contribute $2 for every $1 contributed by the employee, up to 15 percent of salary. "But," says Bernheim, "an astonishing number of Stanford faculty—and these are well-informed, educated people—choose not to participate." Free money—must be a catch somewhere.

Third, we have to make sure that the money we do set aside will be tax-advantaged. I know people who are using after-tax income to invest in stocks via regular brokerage accounts that are subject to current taxation of dividends and gains, despite the fact that they don't make the maximum allowable tax-deductible contributions to their 401(k)s and IRAs, whose buildup is tax-deferred. This makes sense only for investors in the highest tax brackets who are planning to cash out in less than ten to fifteen years, and have to balance the fact that when capital gains from tax-deferred investments are withdrawn they're taxed at income rates against the fact that gains outside of tax-deferred accounts are taxed at the lower capital gains rate. Yet a recent survey by KPMG Peat Marwick found that while most 401(k)s allow employees to contribute up to 13 percent of their salaries, participants put in an average of only about 5 percent.

If you're maxing out your 401(k) and IRA, consider buying variable annuities, which offer selections of mutual funds wrapped in insurance policies, enabling the buildup inside them to be tax-deferred. You can put an unlimited number of after-tax dollars into vehicles ranging from bond funds to international equity funds, and start taking distributions at age fifty-nine and a half without a 10 percent tax penalty. The problem with most variable annuities is that they're weighed down with sales commissions and annual expenses that may cancel out the tax advantage, as well as "surrender fees" that further penalize early withdrawals. Two mutual fund groups, however, offer variable annuities with no sales charges, no surrender fees, and relatively low annual portfolio and insurance expenses: Scudder (Horizon Plan—about 0.6 to 1.2 percent portfolio expense plus 0.7 percent insurance expense) and Vanguard (Variable Annuity Plan—about 0.3 percent portfolio expense plus 0.55 percent insurance expense, with a $25 yearly fee on accounts under $25,000).

Fourth, we must accept the reality that not taking risks can be risky. If we put most of our 401(k) into guaranteed investment contracts (GICs), three things are guaranteed: the value of our principal, the amount of interest we'll receive, and the fact that we'll barely beat inflation. On the other hand, if we have more exposure to stocks and stock funds than we're comfortable with, we'll be tempted to unload when the market is down—which is when we should be buying.

Fifth, you should assemble a range of investments that you believe will increase in value as a result of ultra-long-term trends: processes that have already begun and are likely to continue for decades.

Sixth, we have to prepare to shift to securities capable of retaining their value during the Great Depreciation described in Chapter 8— the protracted period of downward pressure on asset prices that will result from the sale of stocks and bonds by pension funds and individuals to supply income to the baby boomers in later life.

But that's down the road a bit. For now, here are some suggestions for the fifth step:

INDEX FUNDS

A solid foundation for the ultra-long-term is to invest in "index funds," mutual funds that construct widely diversified stock portfolios whose performance will replicate broad market barometers. The logic here is that, despite aggressive stock-picking and high turnover, the vast majority of mutual funds consistently underperform the indexes.

My favorite is Vanguard Index Trust, because it offers the flexibility of being able to allocate assets among six portfolios designed to simulate the following indexes: S&P 500 Composite Stock Price (blue chips), Wilshire 5000 (total stock market), Wilshire 4500 (small and medium-size companies), Russell 2000 (small-cap companies), S&P/BARRA Value (S&P 500 companies with the highest dividends), and S&P/BARRA Growth (S&P 500 companies with the highest price-to-book-value ratio). That way, instead of putting all your eggs in one index basket, you can spread them among a variety of indexes. An additional diversification possibility is Vanguard International Equity Index Fund, the only no-load fund using an index strategy for global investment, which offers two portfolios: one paralleling the Morgan Stanley Capital International Europe (Free) Index, the other tracking the Morgan Stanley Capital International Pacific Index. The Vanguard Group is a class act that offers only "pure no-load" products with some of the lowest expenses in the mutual fund industry: no sales commissions, 12b-1 fees, or redemption charges. With more than $130 billion under management, Vanguard, the second-largest fund group in the world after Fidelity, must be doing something right.

SECTOR FUNDS POSITIONED TO PROFIT FROM POPULATION AGING

One way to hedge against the economic challenges of an aging society is to invest a portion of your assets in industries that seem likely to profit from population aging. I'd leave the choice of stocks to the managers of sector mutual funds. Fidelity Select Portfolios, Invesco Strategic Portfolios, and Vanguard Specialized Portfolios offer the following:

Brokerage and Investment Management Portfolio (Fidelity). As more and more people become aware that there's going to be a gap in later-life income, they're going to try to narrow it through more personal investment and participation in defined contribution plans. Over the ultra-long-term, securities brokers and investment management firms will benefit.

Financial Services Portfolio (Fidelity, Invesco). These sector funds are weighted mainly toward money-center banks. In addition to being repositories for individual savings, big banks own mutual fund groups (e.g., Dreyfus is a subsidiary of Mellon Bank) and are heavily involved in institutional investment management (Wells Fargo, Bankers Trust, and Mellon are among the largest investment managers in the country).

Regional Banks Portfolio (Fidelity). Regional banks are also significant players in the investment business (e.g., First Union owns Evergreen Asset Management).

Health Care Portfolio (Fidelity, Vanguard); Health Sciences Portfolio (Invesco). Even when health care reform measures are in place, population aging will drive ultra-long-term growth of U.S. manufacturers of pharmaceuticals, medical technology, and hospital supplies, which these sector funds own heavily.

Medical Delivery Portfolio (Fidelity). The same ultra-long trend applies to U.S. outpatient surgery centers, nursing homes, hospitals, home health care agencies, rehabilitation providers, and health maintenance organizations.

INTERNATIONAL HEALTH CARE FUNDS

The combined global stock market capitalization of the health care industries—including medical delivery, pharmaceutical, medical technology, hospital supplies, and biotechnology—is larger than any single nation's stock market except those of the United States, Japan, and the United Kingdom. More than half of that capitalization is outside North America. So it's sensible to seek international diversification for a portion of the assets we allocate to health care. Two specialized mutual funds invest both in U.S. and foreign health care companies: John Hancock Freedom Global Rx Fund and G. T. Global Health Care Fund.

NURSING HOMES

The projected increase in the number of people aged eighty-five and older, the fastest-growing portion of the older population and the main clientele of nursing homes, is probably the single most reliable ultra-long-term trend.

On any given day, of the 1.6 million beds in the nation's more than fifteen thousand nursing homes, 90 to 95 percent are occupied. To accommodate the anticipated number of patients, the industry will have to expand to more than 2 million beds by 2000, nearly 3 million by 2020, and 5.3 million by 2030. Yet so far in the 1990s, the bed count has actually declined slightly, because "certificates of need" are necessary to expand existing homes or to build new ones, and they're hard to get because states are trying to control the cost of Medicaid, their most quickly rising expense. Peter Sidotti, a health care analyst at NatWest Securities, said recently, "Nursing homes are the only area in health care where there is a shortage. There are not enough nursing home beds in the country, and the demand is growing."

The nursing home industry is highly fragmented, with the twenty largest companies operating only 18 percent of the facilities. The ultra-long-term trend would appear to be one of continuing consolidation, with a relatively small number of companies owning a large percentage of beds. Only sixteen companies are currently publicly owned. Among the largest, each with tens of thousands of beds, are Beverly Enterprises, Health Care & Retirement Corp., Hillhaven, Living Centers of America, and Manor Care.

EMERGING MARKETS

When I probed Dr. Hurd as to what, if according to economic theory the commodity we want to hold when we're older is labor, we should hold in practice, he told me, "You'd want a claim on the income of a young worker. That's pretty much what the tax-and-transfer system we call Social Security is. But Social Security was designed for a demographic structure that doesn't exist anymore. The problem is that it's costly to have a large number of people consuming and not working.

"As an investor, you want to invest in young economies with young workers who'll be exporting to us. My first reaction is to invest in Africa, because it has by far the youngest demographics. But I don't know if they'll get their act together in time.

"When the baby boomers get to their late sixties, you'll want to take all your money out of U.S. paper and invest it in economies with better demographics. Asia, but not Japan or Korea, which have rapidly aging populations. Mexico. South America. 'I'll buy the machines for you, and there's going to be a big demand among us older folks for the output of those machines and for your labor.'"

The strategy Dr. Hurd recommends is already being followed by some savvy investors, though for a very different reason. The rationale for what's known as the "emerging markets" play isn't the developing nations' age distribution, but their leverage upside now that the politicoeconomic lid is off the countries that have both the largest populations and the lowest wages.

The processes under way look like an economist's wish list:

- democratization
- privatization of government-controlled industries
- deregulation
- tax reduction
- deficit reduction
- tariff reduction
- inflation control
- exchange-rate stabilization
- currency-control liberalization
- foreign debt restructuring
- fostering of domestic stock markets
- opening of financial markets to foreign investors
- return of flight capital
- return of foreign-educated nationals
- increasing productivity
- increasing industrial output
- increasing agricultural output
- increasing consumer demand
- increasing exports

The probability of growth is underscored when we consider that despite all the constraints that existed until just a few years ago in the developing nations, since the mid-1960s their economies have grown at an annual rate of nearly 5 percent, compared to slightly over 3 percent in the industrial world. With the shackles off, the sky's the limit.

Emerging-market countries, which contain 84 percent of the world's people, now account for only about 19 percent of the world's economy and a scant 7 percent of the world's stock valuation. Eventually these imbalances are certain to mean enormous profits for patient investors. The baby boom generation's interest in emerging markets should be twofold. Like any other investors, they'd do well to consider immediately placing part of their assets in emerging-market equities because of the possibility that they'll go up in price on a near- or intermediate-term basis. But baby boomers should also focus on the emerging markets' ultra-long-term demographics.

When you and I are older, not only the United States but all of today's industrial countries will have high proportions of older people. It may make sense to invest in economies that will have younger age profiles, which will be associated with more recent education for people in higher-skill jobs, lower pension contributions, and fewer nonworking older people to be supported.

Here's a partial list of nations whose percentage of people under age sixty is expected to be the same as or higher than the percentage in the United States today. As you'll see, some are literally disaster areas, while others are dynamos growing at double-digit rates and have already generated sizeable returns for shrewd investors. When we're older, some of the worst-off countries may be even worse off. But other nations may pleasantly surprise us. The following nations have only one thing in common: The percentage of their population that will be below age sixty in 2020 is estimated to be 83.1 percent or more. (An asterisk indicates that the country currently has a stock market of some significance; two asterisks indicate that the country has public companies with a total market capitalization of $1 billion or more.)

Afghanistan
Algeria
Angola
**Argentina
Bahamas
Bahrain
*Bangladesh
*Barbados
Belize
Benin
Bolivia
*Botswana
**Brazil
Burkina Faso
Burundi
Cambodia
Cameroon
Cape Verde
Central African Republic
Chad
**Chile
**China (Note: The proportion of younger people in China will drop quickly after 2020 because of its low fertility rate.)
*Colombia
Comoro Islands
Congo
*Costa Rica
*Côte d'Ivoire
Dominican Republic
Ecuador
*Egypt
El Salvador

Equatorial Guinea
Ethiopia
Fiji
Gabon
Gambia
*Ghana
Guatemala
Guinea-Bissau
Guyana
Haiti
Honduras
**India
**Indonesia
Iran
Iraq
**Israel
**Jamaica
*Jordan
*Kenya
Kuwait
Laos
Lebanon
Lesotho
Liberia
Libya
Madagascar
Malawi
**Malaysia
Mali
Malta
Mauritania
*Mauritius
**Mexico
Mongolia
*Morocco
Mozambique
Myanmar (formerly Burma)
Namibia
Nepal
Nicaragua

Niger
**Nigeria
Oman
**Pakistan
Panama
Papua New Guinea
Paraguay
**Peru
**Philippines
Qatar
Rwanda
St. Lucia
Saudi Arabia
Senegal
Seychelles
Sierra Leone
Solomon Islands
Somalia
**South Africa
**Sri Lanka
Sudan
Suriname
Swaziland
Syria
Tanzania
**Thailand
Togo
*Trinidad and Tobago
*Tunisia
**Turkey
Uganda
United Arab Emirates
Vanuatu
**Venezuela
Vietnam
Yemen
Zaire
Zambia
*Zimbabwe

There are several ways you can invest in emerging markets.

• You can buy stocks listed on some developing countries' exchanges directly—through a U.S. broker with experience in international transactions, or via a foreign bank or brokerage account. Mexico, for example, now allows foreigners to buy stocks directly on its Bolsa.

• You can invest in American Drawing Rights (ADRs) of emerging-market stocks. An ADR is a claim, issued by a U.S. bank, to a share in a foreign company. ADRs are traded on the New York Stock Exchange, American Stock Exchange, and NASDAQ. The advantage of ADRs is that they can be traded by U.S. investors without the inconvenience, cost, and risk of executing transactions on stock exchanges located in countries in different time zones, operating in foreign currencies, and regulated by local laws. Corporations in such countries as Argentina, Brazil, and India now offer ADRs, with Mexican companies by far the biggest issuers.

• You can buy closed-end mutual funds—investment companies that issue a fixed number of shares, whose price is determined by the balance between buy and sell orders, like any other stock. Closed-end emerging-market funds traded on the New York Stock Exchange include "country funds," regional funds, and global funds. Closed-end funds may trade at a stiff premium over the value of the stocks they hold, which means they could decline in price even while the "net asset value" of the underlying stocks is rising. The solution is to buy only at a discount from net asset value, or a slight premium.

Among the closed-end emerging-market funds listed on the New York Stock Exchange are:

Argentina Fund
Brazil Fund
Brazil Equity Fund
Chile Fund
China Fund
Emerging Markets Telecommunications Fund
Emerging Mexico Fund
First Philippine Fund
G.T. Developing Markets Fund

Greater China Fund
India Fund
India Growth Fund
Indonesia Fund
Jakarta Growth Fund
Jardine Fleming China Fund
Jardine Fleming India Fund
Latin American Discovery Fund
Latin American Equity Fund
Latin American Investors Fund
Malaysia Fund
Mexico Equity & Income Fund
Mexico Fund
Morgan Stanley Africa Fund
Morgan Stanley India Investment Fund
New South Africa Fund
Pakistan Investment Fund
Southern Africa Fund
Templeton China Fund
Templeton Emerging Markets Fund
Thailand Capital Fund
Thailand Fund
Turkish Investment Fund

• You can buy open-end mutual funds investing in stocks of emerging countries around the globe, such as Fidelity Emerging Markets Fund, Lexington Worldwide Emerging Markets Fund, Montgomery Emerging Markets Fund, and Pimco Advisors Institutional Blairlogie Emerging Markets Fund. Open-end funds are continuously prepared to sell and redeem shares at their net asset value. Note that there are mutual funds that have the word "emerging" in their names that don't own any stocks in developing countries. "Emerging" is occasionally, and confusingly, used in fund names to refer to small companies that are thought to have growth potential. Heads up.

Vanguard has an interesting approach to diversifying among emerging-market stocks. The Emerging Markets Portfolio of its International Equity Index Fund invests in twelve developing countries in weightings designed to track the Morgan Stanley Capital International Select Emerging Markets Index.

G. T. Emerging Markets Fund is run by G. T. Capital Management, headquartered in San Francisco, one of the pioneers of the emerging-markets play. G. T. Capital is owned—through a paper trail involving a holding company controlled by a foundation—by the princely family of Liechtenstein, a sixty-two-square-mile sovereign nation tucked between Switzerland and Austria. There's something reassuring to me about being in the same financial boat with the Prince of Liechtenstein, one of the wealthiest, best-advised people on the planet—at least I can feel that I've done my best to choose solid investments. Talk about investing in emerging economies: The ancestor of the present prince bought the whole country three hundred years ago.

• You can buy open-end funds specializing in a country or region.

"China will be the greatest market opportunity of our lifetimes," says Nicholas Bratt of the Scudder group. But though dozens of mutual funds have "China" in their name, none invests just in the People's Republic, because there aren't enough purely Chinese investments available. "China" means mostly Hong Kong stocks for the time being.

Take a look at Fidelity Southeast Asia Fund, T. Rowe Price New Asia Fund, Scudder Pacific Opportunities Fund, and Strong Asia Pacific Fund. Be cautious with John Hancock Mutual Funds' Freedom Pacific Basin Equities Fund: Almost half its holdings are in countries with high age profiles, including Australia, Japan, New Zealand, and Singapore.

India has a highly evolved securities market, with nearly eight thousand companies listed on twenty-three stock exchanges. The country is closed to individual foreign investors, except Indian citizens living abroad. But you can get still get into the party—for example, through Eaton Vance Greater India Fund, which has holdings in India, Pakistan, and Sri Lanka.

If the Arabs and Israelis can finally get down to business, Americans will be able to profit in a region with a low age profile. For example, in 1994 Africa-Israel Investments, one of Israel's major corporations, signed a contract with Triangle, a Jordanian company, to build hotels at the northern shore of the Dead Sea. If you think the odds favor Mideast peace, you can put some money on the table by going into Israel Opportunities Fund, which is available through Bank Leumi Trust Company of New York, Barnett Bank, First Chicago Bank, and Shawmut Bank of Boston.

At last the United States is finished with the Monroe Doctrine, the Good Neighbor Policy, the Alliance for Progress, and all the other patronizing gringo initiatives it's been pushing on Latin America since the early nineteenth century and settling down to plain old capitalism. And guess what? It works. Check out such funds as Fidelity Latin America Fund, G. T. Latin America Fund, T. Rowe Price Latin America Fund, and Scudder Latin America Fund.

• You can buy emerging-market debt instruments. The easiest way to diversify is through open-end mutual funds, e.g., Fidelity New Markets Income Fund and G. T. Global High Income Fund.

All the positives of investing in emerging markets couldn't exist without some negatives. One is currency risk—the possibility that an inflation-prone developing country's exchange rate could fall relative to the dollar, as when the Mexican peso nose-dived in the winter of 1994–95. And because transaction costs are higher in developing nations, emerging-market fund expenses tend to be 1.5 percent or more, reducing total results.

But the biggest problem is volatility. Emerging equity markets are "thin"; that is, they have a small number of traders, so prices are hypersensitive to the activity of individual investors. And they're "narrow," with most of the trading volume concentrated in the stocks of very few companies. Emerging markets' lack of "depth" and "breadth" causes their stock prices to be much more volatile than those in developed countries.

The relatively low capitalization of emerging markets results in high "liquidity risk." Small inflows of cash can cause a big rise, small outflows, a big fall. Sought-after shares can carry outlandish premiums. Huge run-ups have been followed by dizzying corrections. Declines in the net asset value of open-end mutual funds trigger redemptions. Fund managers have no choice except to sell stocks owned by their funds—a maneuver known in the industry as "selling against yourself," which drives prices still lower. The question is, how do you get out of, say, Turkey, Brazil, or Indonesia when everyone else is trying to get out at the same time?

Low depth, breadth, and capitalization make emerging markets particularly vulnerable to external financial shocks. For instance, during November 1987, the month after money-center stock markets crashed, several major Mexican stocks didn't trade for days at a time—a disturbing sign of the lack of liquidity in emerging markets.

By the time we're older and it becomes necessary to jump into emerging-market investments with both feet, the financial markets of today's developing countries will have grown enough for their stock prices to be relatively stable. But in the meantime, for us to build positions in emerging-market equities means accepting volatility. The pace at which you and I can accumulate emerging-market holdings will depend on how much volatility we can withstand. There's no way to time an emerging market, because wide swings make technical analysis impossible. You've got to be in for the duration, or not at all. Investors who feel that if they hit a pothole they're going to want to jump out of the car don't belong on this road.

My personal approach would be to begin modestly and increase my emerging-market exposure as volatility drops. With emerging-market stocks now representing about 7 percent of the value of all the stocks in the world, I'd limit my exposure to about 7 percent of my assets for the time being.

The sixth step outlined above—switching to investments that will be able to ride out the Great Depreciation—will be the ultimate test. At some point in the early decades of the twenty-first century you and I are going to have to get out of the broad market before it starts on the downgrade in anticipation of massive pension-fund selling. The same goes for sectors benefiting from population aging: Pension funds and individuals will be strongly invested in them, and at a certain point will have to begin liquidating their positions to support the population that has aged.

It's less clear how emerging-market stocks will fare during a multidecade period of general pressure on asset prices. Pension funds and far-seeing individuals will have accumulated huge emerging-market holdings well in advance of 2024, the year after which, according to the econometric model created by Sylvester J. Schieber and John B. Shoven, the pension system will stop being a net purchaser of financial assets. Holders of emerging-market equities will be inclined to continue holding them in order to take advantage of the younger demographics of the developing world. And there's every reason to believe that the emerging economies will still be growing briskly when the baby boomers of today's industrial countries are in their sixties, seventies, eighties, and nineties. But there's no way of telling, at this early date, what the balance of asset-pricing forces will be between the positive fundamentals of the "younger" countries in one pan of the scale, and, in the other pan, the downward drag on paper values in the financial markets of the "older" countries.

For example, there could be a collapse of developing-world stock prices if the emerging markets were to become perceived as over-bought by Americans, Europeans, and Japanese seeking a safe har-bor, triggering a cascade of sell orders.

Alternatively, there could be enough buying of American stocks by residents of today's developing countries to counter downward pressure on U.S. financial markets when we're older.

All you and I can know for sure right now about the ultra-long-term future of emerging-market stocks is that we're going to have to be psyched to get out of them immediately, if and when necessary.

It's conceivable that when it's time for us to take the sixth step, we'll be able to weather the storm by going into financial instru-ments we can't even imagine today. But for now, we should be thinking about:

SHORT-TERM GOVERNMENT SECURITIES

Bank accounts and CDs? Deposit insurance would be paid out too sluggishly during the avalanche of claims we could have in a Great Depreciation. Money market funds holding CDs and commercial paper? They could go below $1 a share if the economy falls out of bed. Bonds? Not with interest rates rising—and bond prices falling—as they would be if there's "dissaving," as predicted by the Schieber-Shoven model. That leaves short-term government securities.

U.S. Treasury bills aren't issued in certificate form. We'll be able to hold them in "book-entry" accounts at our regional Federal Reserve Banks, in the custody of our bank or broker, and via money market mutual funds that buy only T-bills, with no repurchase agree-ments, on which there have been defaults when conditions were much more favorable than they may be in the future (e.g., The Ben-ham Group's Capital Preservation Fund).

GOLD

Gold may be able to play its historical role as a "store of value" dur-ing the Great Depreciation because of an interesting coincidence.

Few citizens of countries that will be aging swiftly have sizeable personal holdings of gold. But the two countries with the most people—China and India, which together have an astounding 40 percent of the world's population—both happen to have relatively young demographic profiles, and both happen to have traditions of individual hoarding of gold, to the point where they're the two largest gold-buying nations.

When we're older, China will be developing dynamically. Chinese culture emphasizes saving (the savings rate today is about 30 percent), astronomical numbers of people will have higher incomes from which they'll be able to save more, and part of that extra saving is likely to go into gold coins and bullion. The proportion of China's population that will be age sixty and above in 2020 is projected to be 16.5 percent, slightly lower than the proportion of Americans sixty and over is today, and one-third lower than what the U.S percentage will be in 2020.

India is another vast, rapidly developing nation with what economists call a "taste" for gold as a savings medium. India's population in 2020 will be younger than China's, with only about 10.4 percent age sixty and above.

So at a time when the populations of the "older" countries won't be selling much gold, the populations of the two biggest "younger" countries will very likely be buying a lot of gold. This asymmetry could put a floor under the world gold market, protecting the value of gold owned by ultra-long-term-oriented U.S. citizens.

How much gold should we own? One leading Swiss private bank recently recommended to its clients that they keep 3.5 percent of the total value of their investment portfolio in physical gold as an "insurance" position; that seems about right to me.

INTERPERSONAL BIOTECHNOLOGY

B. Douglas Bernheim leans toward me: "Would you like to know an investment strategy you can implement in the near future that will provide excellent insurance against the uncertainties of later life?"

A hot tip from a Stanford economist. I palm my pocket phone, poised to call my broker. Embeddos? Swaptions? Inverse floaters? Fax Hong Kong! E-mail Zurich!

"Have children," says Dr. Bernheim. "Make sure they love you so they'll want to take care of you when you're old. See to it that they become productive, so they can afford to. That's what people have done from the beginning of time and still do throughout the developing world. The reason people had eight or nine children was so that three or four would survive till they were old and needed to be supported." He leans back.

"Are you following your own investment advice?" I ask.

He beams. "Three daughters."

"How old?"

"Sixteen, eight, and four."

"So you're . . . laddering your maturities," I suggest.

"You could say that."

"I met an eighty-year-old guy in Florida who said I should make sure to have some sex in my book," I tell him.

Dr. Bernheim laughs. "Well, now you've got it."

CHAPTER 15

PRESSING ON ALL THE BUTTONS

There are plenty of things you can start doing right now to make life better for yourself and others when you and they are older. They involve influencing public policy, talking with your employer and fellow employees, and taking personal action. You don't have to move on all the items in this chapter. You may want to pick a few suggestions that especially appeal to you and concentrate on them. Or you may decide to "press on all the buttons" and see which ones make you feel that you're having an impact.

I've formed an organization called Future Elders of America (FEA) to enable younger people to act now to create an economic, social, and cultural environment in which they'll be able to thrive when they're older.

FEA's purpose is to raise awareness among baby boomers—and anyone else who's planning on getting older—about the inevitable collapse of the "three-legged stool of retirement income" and the need for each of us to prepare to prosper despite it. FEA is working to inform and inspire the public about the kind of measures described in this chapter, and to encourage Americans of all ages to come up with more ideas about how we can assure ourselves of a later life that will be worth living.

Watch for FEA's op-ed pieces, media events, talk show appearances, on-line user groups, speaking engagements, workshops, and seminars. We're going to open a lot of eyes and, hopefully, a lot of hearts.

If you're interested in joining FEA, please write to:

Mark Schauerte
Executive Director
Future Elders of America
P.O. Box 201095
Yale Station
New Haven, CT 06520-1095

Each "button" below is followed by a suggested way you can "press" it:

(Policy)

Believe it or not, your legislators care about what you think—at best because they really do want to represent you, at worst because they don't want you to give them "early retirement."

The most effective way to influence your congressional representative, senator, or state legislator is to make a hefty campaign contribution, followed by a personal visit. If you're not in a position to write a sizeable check, even a small one—$25, say—will get you some respect: Legislators are businesspeople, and every customer counts.

A distant second best is to register your views by letter, fax, or phone. Lawmakers' staff members keep a tally of communications received on various issues and will bring interesting ones to the attention of a senior aide, or even the boss. Legislators pay little attention to individual messages, but a lot to the numbers.

To write to your congressional representative, the address is:

The Hon. _____
U.S. House of Representatives
Washington, DC 20515

Dear Mr./Ms. _____:

To write your senator, the address is:

The Hon. _____
U.S. Senate
Washington, DC 20510

Dear Senator _____:

To phone, call the Capitol switchboard at (202) 224-3121.

Another way to make an impression on a lawmaker is to write a letter to the editor that includes your target's name. Effective politicians have interns or services that try to compile clippings of every mention they get in the press. Their content is analyzed and tabulated, and lawmakers take the resulting spreadsheets seriously as indicators of what they should do if they want to keep their jobs. So getting your thoughts about Social Security, pensions, savings, and employment opportunity for older people into the letters pages of your newspaper can be a way of sharing them with elected officials.

Talk radio is an essential forum for blowing away the retirement myth. If there was ever an issue that requires the kind of shift in national consciousness that can be activated by call-in radio, it's the need for public policy to come to grips with the imminent collapse of the "three-legged stool of retirement income." Even if you've never dialed for dollars with the phrase that pays, it's time for you to pick up the phone and fill the airwaves with demands that if the politicians can't help us, they should at least get out of the way.

(Workplace)

Keep up the infield patter where you work and sooner or later the back office will have to take notice. Human resource executives in particular tend to be on the leading edge of the issues raised in this book. The more you talk with them about ways to improve pension plans and to make it possible for people to continue working regardless of age, the more ammunition they'll have to use on top management.

(Personal)

There are plenty of things you can do without anyone else's permission to improve your future and other people's present.

ALTRUISTIC SELF-INTEREST

What goes around when we're younger will come around when we're older.

• **Every baby boomer should make helping inner-city residents lift themselves out of poverty a crucial generational project.** We need to turn people into producers and savers not as an exercise in humanitarianism, but as a hardheaded personal survival strategy. Each of us can think of a way to participate in rebuilding the life of urban America, whether by political action, donating money, or volunteering our services. When we're in our sixties, seventies, and eighties, the government simply isn't going to have enough money to deal simultaneously with the problems of younger people who never made it into the middle class and older people who've been squeezed out of it. As Dr. Robert N. Butler told me, "It's not just altruism—it's self-interest. We're heading toward a society with an entirely different ethnic mix than we're used to. Inner-city and minority youth are the people we're going to have to depend on to run the economy when we're old."

The National Association for the Advancement of Colored People, in a new emphasis on "economic empowerment" as a main civil rights goal, has embarked on a "youth entrepreneurship" program to teach young African Americans the importance not only of business but of saving and investment. This is the kind of effort where we can lend a hand. *(Policy) (Personal)*

• **Do something immediate and concrete to make sure homeless people in your community can get shelter.** Homelessness isn't simply a matter of there not being enough "affordable housing." It's the result of an inability to function in society. When we're older, a lot of members of our generation are going to crack under the financial strain and end up sleeping under the bridge. We're going to need to know how to help each other. *(Policy) (Personal)*

• **Become involved in developing shared housing as an option for older people.** Help start, financially support, or pitch in at a group shared residence for older people or an intergenerational home-sharing program. If we want to have a range of affordable living arrangements available to us when we're older, it makes personal sense for us to incubate those options now. *(Policy) (Personal)*

• **Work to change zoning regulations that discourage group shared housing for older people.** Harvest House, a handsome colonial with a swimming pool shared by six men and women in their eighties and nineties in a Long Island suburb of New York City, looks like an upscale bed-and-breakfast. But Sister Jeanne Brendel, who founded Harvest House in 1989, told me, "When the neighbors found out what we were planning, they complained to the town government. We had to spend four years fighting the zoning board in the courts before we could get a permit." *(Policy)*

• **Broaden your understanding of extended families.** When you travel to places where it's still common for extended families to live together—the Caribbean, Latin America, Africa, Asia—make a point of visiting people's homes and seeing how the generations get along under the same roof or in the same compound. A lot of us will be living multigenerationally when we're older. *(Personal)*

• **Convince your school system to teach the young about the old.** Elementary, middle, and high school students should be learning about the history, sociology, physiology, psychology, politics, and economics of aging. If you're involved in academia, catalyze the establishment of interdisciplinary undergraduate programs in aging studies. As the United States enters the "Age of Aging," college students need to learn how to encounter older people—and how to encounter themselves as they grow older. *(Personal)*

• **Become an amateur gerontologist.** Everyone today has to be an amateur film critic, wine connoisseur, sports coach, etc. But our gerontological literacy isn't all it could be. It's time for us to bring ourselves up to speed on the demographics, economics, sociology, and psychology of human aging. Go to a university library from time to time and browse periodicals like

Age and Aging
Aging
Aging and Society
Aging Today
Annual Review of Gerontology and Geriatrics
Canadian Journal on Aging
Employee Benefit News
Employee Benefit Plan Review
Generations: Journal of the American Society on Aging

Geriatrics
The Gerontologist
Gerontology News
Industrial Gerontology
International Journal of Aging and Human Development
Journal of Aging and Human Development
Journal of the American Geriatrics Society
The Journal of Gerontology
Milbank Quarterly
Modern Maturity
Pensions & Investments
Psychology and Aging
Social Security Bulletin
(Personal)

• **Volunteer to work with older people.** You can help out at a senior center, a meals-on-wheels or group nutrition program, or a nursing home, or simply help an older neighbor shop for groceries or visit the doctor. Everything you do to make more real to yourself the fact that you'll be old someday will help you be ready for it. *(Personal)*

• **Become involved in creating a project in your area to help older people go into business for themselves.** Professor Rosabeth Moss Kanter of Harvard Business School told a recent conference, "Many people in so-called retirement from large organizations already start their own small businesses, whether an antiques store in the garage on Cape Cod or a franchise that they have always wanted to buy. But while there are many programs for youth entrepreneurship, from Junior Achievement to An Income of Her Own, there is notable absence of help for those at the other end of the life cycle—even though their maturity should improve their business judgment. . . . Imagine the payoff a community could get if it mounted a Senior Achievement Program alongside Junior Achievement, aimed at new business formation." It would be nice for such programs to be around when you and I are old enough to make use of them. *(Personal)*

• **If there's a medical school in your area, donate or raise money to enable it to establish a department of geriatrics.** Robert

N. Butler, M.D., who heads the nation's only medical school geriatrics department, wrote recently: "The baby boomers, the largest
generation in U.S. history, which comprises one-third of our population, will become a huge cohort of older persons between the years
2020 and 2030. In the judgment of most people in gerontology and
geriatrics, our society is ill-prepared to meet the challenges that this
increase will bring. Therefore, the baby boomer generation is very
much at risk, as are the generations that follow."

"Where are all the doctors who know how to treat older people
going to come from by the time the baby boomers are older?" Dr.
Butler asked me. "And right now there are only a handful of teaching nursing homes—we at Mount Sinai are associated with one. So
is Harvard Medical School. Baby boomers should become involved
in creating and funding hundreds of such facilities. They're a generation that's extremely interested in fitness. Well, there are three
types of fitness: physical fitness, which can be maintained by exercise; intellectual fitness, which can be maintained by lifelong education; and a third kind of fitness which I don't know that I've found
quite the right word for—let's call it 'purposive' fitness. We've
found that people who have a purpose for living live longer. Baby
boomers need to get involved now in purposive projects. I can't
think of a more purposive project than setting up programs to train
the physicians who'll be taking care of them in the future." *(Personal)*

• **Support government and private research into diseases
associated with aging before you come down with one of them.**
For every $1,000 now being spent on caring for the chronically ill
aged, $1 is being spent on research into their chronic illnesses.
"There are problems that require a lead time to solve," Dr. Butler
explained to me. "Osteoporosis. Alzheimer's. Stroke. By the time
baby boomers start experiencing them, it'll be too late for them to
do anything to help themselves. Alzheimer's is the polio of aging. If
we can get rid of Alzheimer's, we won't need half the nursing home
beds in America. We need to spend the millions now that will prevent conditions that will cost billions to treat. Baby boomers have to
use their political power and their dollars now to make sure that
their increased life expectancy will give them added years of social
and economic productivity." *(Policy) (Personal)*

• **Support research into enhancing the abilities of older people.** Down the road, we'll benefit directly if scientists can find ways of improving short-term memory, problem-solving speed, reaction time, and hand-eye coordination. *(Policy)*

• **Support R&D specifically designed to lower the cost of delivering high-tech health care to older people.** Huge sums are invested in cutting the "cost-per-function" of computer chips—a function being one logic switch or bit of memory. As a result, chip prices have been falling every year by 25 to 30 percent, and we don't seem to be facing a national "computer crisis." "If baby boomers don't want to have a hard time receiving technologically sophisticated medical treatment when they're older because it's too expensive," Harold L. Sheppard, Professor Emeritus of Gerontology at the University of South Florida, told me, "they should be advocating research targeted explicitly at reducing the cost of the technology." *(Policy) (Personal)*

• **Make fostering the development of the Third World—especially Africa—a top national priority.** As the continent with the highest proportion of younger people, Africa has the potential of becoming a huge market for U.S. securities by the time baby boomers reach their sixties, seventies, eighties, and nineties. We need to increase the productivity of less-developed countries so that there will be enough people able to buy U.S. stocks and bonds from American pension funds with obligations to baby boomers, as well as from mutual funds and individuals, so that our financial markets won't go into a tailspin.

If developing Africa seems impossible, consider that not too long ago the idea that we'd be seeing "Made in India" on labels in Kmart would have seemed highly unlikely. We no longer have the luxury of sitting back and letting African nations continue to be international basket cases. If today's less-developed countries don't become capable of investing in the financial assets of today's industrial countries in the decades ahead, we'll be the ones who need CARE packages.

In Europe, later life is called the Third Age. If we want to live well during our Third Age, we've got to help develop the Third World. *(Policy)*

• **Be a generational peacemaker and peacekeeper.** Don't buy into any we/they "generational warfare" scenarios. What this country needs isn't intergenerational conflict, but a transgenerational strategic partnership. Today's retirees played fair and shouldn't be faulted for winning—if they've actually won, which plenty of them haven't. The group that makes the Retirement State unsustainable isn't them: it's you and me. *(Personal)*

SOCIAL SECURITY

Don't be spooked by end-of-the-world types who insist that you'll never see a cent from Social Security. No matter what happens, you'll get a check or an electronic funds transfer every month. The question is, how old will you be when you start getting it, and how much will it be for? It's absolutely certain that you won't be able to collect full cash benefits at the age people do now, because the age of complete eligibility has already been increased. It's probable that the age will be raised again—though how much, and in what time frame, no one knows. Also, your benefits will probably be a lower percentage of your earnings: Not so low that busloads of white-haired baby boomers will handcuff themselves to the White House fence and sing "We Shall Overdraw," but low enough to keep a human chain of baby busters from going limp across the Florida Turnpike.

• **Support incorporating a voluntary public service program into Social Security.** I've come up with the idea that people should have the option to simply collect Social Security cash benefits, as recipients do now, or to choose to receive exactly the same amount of money as their salary for working for nonprofit organizations and for local, state, and federal government agencies that deliver human services. This pay could be made tax-free (in contrast to Social Security payments, which are taxed if income is high enough) in order to attract people to the public service jobs.

I believe that the tax break would be more than made up for by improved health among the people who'd be working, which would result in lower costs to Social Security's Medicare program. But even if there were no tax advantage, I think a significant number of older people would jump at the opportunity to do stimulating work.

If only 1 percent of today's Social Security recipients were to participate in such a program, we'd have an additional 350,000 experienced brains and pairs of hands available to work in areas like education, health care, law enforcement, drug treatment, and environmental protection. By the time you and I are old enough to collect Social Security, I wouldn't be surprised if a substantial number of us choose to receive government checks because we're using our talents to help people rather than because we consider ourselves "entitled" to receive them in return for past "contributions," which were in fact taxes that supported our parents' generation.

When people on Social Security do this kind of work for free today, the younger public doesn't perceive a connection between the fact that they're being supported by tax revenues and the fact that they're available to volunteer. The sight of hundreds of thousands— possibly millions—of recipients working for the public good as an integral part of Social Security, reducing the need for other government expenditures, would help protect the program as a whole from deeper cuts. *(Policy)*

• **The Social Security "earnings test" ought to be scrapped immediately.** First, it's unfair. Receiving interest, dividends, and pension payouts doesn't reduce Social Security benefits, yet work does. So the earnings test doesn't direct benefits away from people with higher incomes—it directs benefits away from people who need to or want to work.

Second, it's counterproductive. It literally counters the productivity of older Americans.

Third, it's crazy. To be warning young single mothers on one entitlement program that they'll lose their benefits unless they work, while warning older couples on another entitlement program that they'll lose their benefits unless they don't work is just plain nuts.

The earnings test docks recipients $1 for every $2 earned over a limit of about $8,000 from age sixty-two to sixty-four, and for every $3 earned over about $11,000 from age sixty-five to sixty-nine. According to the House Ways and Means Committee, abolishing it would cost the Social Security Administration around $6 billion a year, with 10 percent of that figure offset by higher payroll tax receipts. But the $5.4 billion cost would be far outweighed by the benefit of getting rid of the strange set of signals we're sending ourselves— that it's okay to work until age sixty-two, not okay to work from sixty-two to sixty-four, fairly not okay to work from sixty-five to sixty-nine, and all clear again starting at seventy. No one has calculated the cost to society of rules that send us the message that at some time in our sixties our government wants us to stop producing goods and services, but in America's $6 trillion economy, it has to be a lot more than $5.4 billion. *(Policy)*

• **Employees should be able to take out loans against their future Social Security benefits to finance "recurrent development of new competencies."** Professor W. Andrew Achenbaum of the University of Michigan Institute of Gerontology has advocated that employees be able to borrow money to pay for "training that will enhance their worth and longevity in the labor force," with a portion of their future Social Security cash benefits going to pay back the loan.

This is a smart and politically feasible idea. University of Washington anthropologists Pamela T. Amoss and Stevan Harrell have gone even further, proposing that the government pick up the entire cost of education for a second career. In this era of high deficits, I doubt whether it's practical to talk about creating a new entitlement. But in general, baby boomers and younger generations should be supporting initiatives that will encourage "productive aging." With increasing longevity, financial aid for lifelong education is as justifiable as financial aid for elementary, secondary, and college education. The cost of educating adults to enable them to continue working if they want to or have to will be far less than the cost of not educating them. If Generation X doesn't want to eventually find itself confronted with a vast bloc of "dumpies"—destitute unemployed mature professionals with obsolete skills clamoring to be supported by taxpayers—its members should be thinking of ways to encourage "productive aging" among baby boomers. *(Policy)*

PENSIONS

Harold L. Sheppard, born in 1922, was the first research director and staff director of the U.S. Senate's Special Committee on Aging, served in the White House as President Carter's Counselor on Aging, and was then responsible for the landmark study of pension issues conducted by the National Council on the Aging called "Aging in the 80s." He was the mentor for AARP's Dr. Sara E. Rix, with whom he wrote the prophetic 1977 book *The Graying of Working America: The Coming Crisis of Retirement-Age Policy.* Over lunch at the faculty club of the University of South Florida in Tampa, where, although formally retired from the Department of Gerontology, he's still teaching, Dr. Sheppard told me, "There appears to be an unexamined assumption that the proportion of workers assured of adequate private pension benefits will rise. There's no guarantee of that at all."

• **Support adjusting defined benefit (DB) pensions to reflect increases in the cost of living.** "The federal government should require some degree of indexing of pension benefits," M. Cindy Hounsell, staff attorney and coordinator of the Women's Pension Advocacy Council at the Pension Rights Center in Washington, told me. "In today's job-hopping economy," said Hounsell, who as a former Pan Am cabin attendant knows what it means to switch employers, "when someone who's vested in a defined benefit plan moves to another company at, say, age thirty-five, she may have to wait thirty years to start collecting benefits. Her pension benefits stay frozen as a percentage of her final salary, but inflation marches on. Three decades later, the amount she'll receive will have fallen in purchasing power by more than seventy percent. After she begins to receive her payout, she may live another thirty years, so she'll lose another thirty percent. So postretirement benefits should be at least partially indexed."

The Pension Rights Center is an outfit with a markedly liberal agenda, so it's noteworthy that the National Retirement Income Policy Committee of the nonideological American Society of Pension Actuaries issued a similar call in 1994 for employers to be required to "inflation-protect all private pension benefits": "If possible, the increase rate should be linked to the actual CPI. For practical reasons, it may be necessary to establish a fixed annual rate of increase (e.g., 4 percent). An employer might be permitted to choose between these options."

Sound utopian? In Britain companies have to index accrued pension benefits for inflation until an employee retires, with a cap of 5 percent a year; Ireland has a 3 percent cap; and Germany requires full cost-of-living adjustments. *(Policy) (Workplace)*

- **Support changing IRS regulations that keep employers from making prompt contributions to their DB plans to adjust for anticipated future inflation.** Such contributions should be encouraged, not prohibited. *(Policy)*

- **Support expanded pension coverage.** One reason to do so has been highlighted by The Wyatt Company's Dr. Sylvester J. Schieber: to head off a decline in financial markets caused by the sell-off of pension assets to pay benefits to baby boomers by increasing the flow of money into pension funds. "If possible, pension coverage should be broadened through incentives," Dr. Schieber told me. "For example, new legislation could allow executives with high salaries to receive bigger pensions when their companies' plans include all employees. But we may have to put in a requirement that every employee be covered. I've never liked the idea of making pension coverage mandatory, but I'm coming with great reluctance to the conclusion that we may have to go that way."

The American Society of Pension Actuaries' National Retirement Income Policy Committee advocates universal coverage, coming from a different angle: to provide more income in later life. While Dr. Schieber sees incentives and mandates as two options listed in order of desirability, the ASPA panel would like both approaches to be implemented at once: "Instead of dwelling on preventing discrimination in favor of the highly-compensated, we should focus on preventing discrimination against lower-paid people. Our major concern should be providing coverage for all employees." One of the actuaries' recommendations is to "remove all existing benefit and contribution limits for highly-paid executives," with "benefit levels available to higher-paid individuals increas[ing] as rank and file benefits increase." Another is "Require all employers to provide base level pension benefits equal to 15 percent of final salary."

Baby boomer David Certner, an attorney who's senior coordinator for economic issues in the Federal Affairs Department of the AARP, told me, "Under current law a company can 'carve out' thirty percent of its lower-paid employees. Our position is that if you have a pension plan, you should have to cover everyone—even part-timers." *(Policy) (Workplace)*

- **Simplify regulations that discourage employers from providing DB pensions.** Replace the tangle of laws and regulations that make it hard for employers to offer and operate pension plans with a single piece of legislation whose only purpose is to see to it that employees will get the money they've been promised. The Employee Retirement Income Security Act of 1974, known as ERISA, was supposed to do the job. Instead, its rules have made it less attractive for companies to offer pensions to their employees. Ted Barna of the pension consulting firm of Kwasha Lipton told me, "You know what we say those letters actually stand for? 'Every Rotten Idea Since Adam.' " And since ERISA's passage, eighteen other laws affecting pensions have been put on the books that either reduce tax incentives for employers to provide pensions, or add to the paperwork.

The government keeps changing the rules in the middle of the game. As a result, since 1981, the expense of administering a typical DB plan with seventy-five participants has gone from 8 percent of total costs to 33 percent—money that companies could otherwise be putting aside for their employees' old age.

Martha Priddy Patterson, director of employee benefits policy and analysis at KPMG Peat Marwick's National Compensation and Benefits Practice, testified recently before the House Social Security Subcommittee about a survey she'd conducted in which pension plan sponsors said frequent changes in the law are "more troublesome than actually complying with the law and about twice as troublesome as actually trying to fund the plan."

"Without spending one additional cent," Patterson said, "Congress could greatly improve the baby boomers' employer-provided retirement income. Congress simply needs to stop changing the law regulating these plans. Employers are more troubled by changes in the law than any other aspect of retirement benefits. The more income the baby boomers can anticipate from employer-provided benefits, the less pressure they will exert on the Social Security system." *(Policy)*

  • **Support establishing a single federal agency to oversee pension plans.** Right now pension sponsors have to deal with the Pension Benefit Guaranty Corporation (whose regulations put pressure on employers to make higher contributions to their plans), the IRS (whose regulations put pressure on employers to make lower contributions to their plans), and the Department of Labor's Pension and Welfare Benefits Administration (whose regulations put pressure on employers to comply with its regulations). Every dollar your company spends coping with three bureaucracies instead of one is a dollar that can't be invested in your future well-being. *(Policy)*

* **Support continuing to defer taxes on pension funds.** The so-called tax expenditure on pensions—estimated by the congression: Joint Committee on Taxation at $61.3 billion for 1995—isn't an expenditure in any sense. The taxes aren't lost forever, as with the mortgage interest deduction. They're just deferred until participants are old enough to receive their payout, at which time the federal government (and our taxpaying kids) will be very happy to see those revenues come onstream. According to the U.S. Department of Commerce, for every $1 of taxes "expended" on pensions, the plans pay more than $4 to older Americans and their families.

The notion that this "tax expenditure" primarily benefits the wealthy is untrue. A Census Bureau study found that the biggest beneficiaries of pension tax deferrals were people earning between $15,000 and $50,000. They received 61 percent of pension benefits, but paid only 36 percent of federal income taxes. People earning over $50,000 paid 61 percent of federal taxes, but received only 38 percent of pension benefits. But pension tax deferment isn't on employers' short list of issues to push—too many other matters have a higher priority for them. Individuals are going to have to carry the water on this one. *(Policy)*

P.S. Is it just me, or does it make you feel like belting people inside the Beltway when they refer to the money they don't take away from us as a "tax expenditure"?

* **Support phasing out the provision of the Pension Protection Act of 1987 that allows companies that didn't have enough assets in their pension funds to meet their obligations at the time the law was passed to delay full funding of their plans.** As Gregg Richter, actuary with the pension consulting firm of Sedgwick Noble Lowndes, puts it, "ERISA was enacted to eliminate persistent underfunding of pensions, not to encourage its long-term continuation." The act's "grandfather" provision could end up cramping your lifestyle when you have grandchildren. *(Policy)*

* **Support lowering the threshold above which an employer must add to its pension fund when it increases benefits.** Compa-

nies shouldn't be able to make promises to their employees that are backed up by nothing except more promises. *(Policy)*

• **Support making the federal government responsible for insuring DB plans in which the payout comes from annuities bought by employers.** The AARP's David Certner pointed out to me that when Executive Life Insurance went belly up and was taken over by the state of California, the annuities it had sold to pension funds, which were being relied on by 86,000 retirees in forty-six states, were cut by 30 percent. The Pension Benefit Guaranty Corporation had no statutory responsibility for the loss. *(Policy)*

• **Support raising the maximum amount of compensation that can be included in pension contribution and benefit calculations.** The 1993 budget act reduced it from $235,840 to $150,000, which sounds like only people making six figures were affected. In reality, as a result of unbelievably complex pension regulations, lowering the limit weakens DB coverage of employees making around $35,000 and up because it forces companies to delay contributions to their plans.

R. Theodore Benna, president of the 401(k) Association, tells me that companies have been terminating their 401(k)s as a result of the limit. Benna is a legend within the pension community for having "invented" the 401(k), named after a clause in the Revenue Act of 1978 allowing pretax employee contributions to profit-sharing plans. Benna, then a pension consultant, realized it would take more than a tax break to motivate employees to contribute. In 1981 he got IRS approval for the first plan in which a company committed to matching its employees' contributions. Today more than 17 million people participate in 401(k)s. "The problem with the $150,000 limit," Benna told me, "is that it doesn't just hit people who make more than $150,000. Because of its impact on another government regulation, it lowers the amount employees who are earning more than $64,245 can put into their 401(k)s to about five percent of their salary. Three thousand dollars a year isn't a whole lot to be able to put away toward your retirement when you're making that kind of money."

Rather than discouraging 401(k) contributions by higher-paid employees, we should be working to make it possible for every American employee to make tax-deferred contributions to a 401(k).

A 1992 study by economists James M. Poterba of MIT and Steven F. Venti and David A. Wise of Harvard found that participation in 401(k) plans adds to total savings. The total amount saved by 401(k) participants inside and outside their plans is higher than the savings of people who don't have 401(k)s. *(Policy)*

• **Accelerate vesting schedules.** Vesting after being on the job for five years should be required in multiemployer pension plans such as those in the construction, mining, and trucking industries. About 6.5 million employees still have to work for ten years to become vested, despite the fact that single-company plans have had to vest within five years since 1974. *(Policy) (Workplace)*

• **Make DB pension formulas age-neutral.** "Backloading" rules that give more weight in calculating defined benefits to working years closer to eligibility age should be changed. In some pension plans, the years worked between fifty-five and sixty-five may be worth four times as much as the years between twenty-five and thirty-five. Many younger employees let go in downsizings have discovered that their benefits are microscopic. *(Policy) (Workplace)*

• **Push for getting rid of caps on the number of years of employment that can be counted toward a pension, and on total benefit levels.** A 1986 law requires that employees over sixty-five continue to be credited with pension benefits, but still allows such caps. Those limits are a form of age discrimination and should be abolished. *(Policy)*

• **If your employer has no pension plan because administrative expenses are too high, suggest that it set up a Simplified Employee Pension (SEP) plan.** SEPs don't require any annual paperwork. All a company has to do is make sure that each of its employees over age twenty-one with three years of service opens an Individual Retirement Arrangement known as a SEP-IRA. Your company (or you, if you're self-employed) can contribute up to 15 percent of your salary to your SEP-IRA each year, or $22,500, whichever is lower. You pay no taxes on that amount until you begin taking distributions, which can begin at age fifty-nine and a half, or sooner if there's hardship.

If your company has twenty-five or fewer employees, and at least half of them want contributions taken out of their salaries, it can also set up a Salary Reduction SEP, known as a SARSEP, which enables you to contribute up to about $9,000 out of your paycheck, reducing your currently taxable income. Total SEP and SARSEP contributions can't be more than the 15 percent/$22,500 limit. You get to manage your own investments, and if it's okay with your employer, you can choose any mutual fund group you want to handle your account(s). *(Workplace)*

• **Support restoring the annual ceiling for SEP and SARSEP contributions to $30,000.** That's what it was until the 1993 budget package was passed. If we're concerned about fat cats getting too much, it makes more sense to raise their income taxes than to prevent them from saving. The problem with soak-the-rich approaches like limiting tax-deferred pension contributions is that if we want to increase our national savings rate to foster investment, productivity, and growth, and to reduce the impact of the huge asset sell-off that's sure to take place when the baby boomers are older, the last thing we want to do is discourage the rich from saving, because they're the ones who have the money. *(Policy)*

• **Consider what kind of pension plan a company has before going to work for it.** "If all you cared about were your retirement benefits," says KPMG Peat Marwick's Martha Priddy Patterson, "and if you could do it, the way to really maximize your lot in life is to work for a defined contribution plan sponsor in your early years and sock in all the money you possibly can. Then, when you're about fifty, move to an employer that provides a defined benefit plan. That's the way you would make the most money." But keep in mind that receiving a lump-sum distribution from a defined contribution plan won't help you later if you spend it immediately, or if your investments go sour. And the advantage of defined benefits— that they're fixed in dollar terms—has the flip side of exposing them to reduction by inflation. *(Personal)*

• **Try to work for a company that not only offers a generous DB plan, but offers a 401(k) to which it contributes.** According to the Employee Benefit Research Institute, 29 percent of employers don't offer an "employer match." *(Workplace) (Personal)*

- **Another option is to work for an employer that has a "target benefit" defined contribution (DC) plan.** In target benefit plans, companies make contributions designed to provide employees with a specific—but not employer-guaranteed—percentage of final pay. Employer contributions are calculated according to a formula that takes into account the employee's current pay, age, and years of service. *(Workplace) (Personal)*

- **If you're in your forties or fifties, consider working for a company with an "age-weighted profit-sharing plan."** These plans allow employers to make higher contributions for older employees. *(Personal)*

- **If you're doubtful about how long you'll be with a company, you may prefer an employer with a "cash balance" DB plan.** Employees are credited each year with a percentage of pay, plus interest determined by the prevailing market rate. The total amount is paid out as a lump sum when the employee leaves. Cash balance plans give a higher payout to shorter-term employees than conventional DB plans, because the number of years of service isn't a factor in computing benefits.

  An interesting variation on this theme is the "minimum balance" plan, which provides employees with the larger of a DB pension based on the average of several years of final salary or a lump sum based on percentage-of-pay contributions plus interest at market rates. These plans are designed to provide more accumulation in the early years than a traditional DB plan. The idea is that short-service employees will find the minimum balance feature more lucrative, while long-term employees will prefer a traditional DB payout. *(Personal)*

- **One way of avoiding erosion of defined benefits by inflation is to work for an employer with a "life cycle" pension plan.** The benefit is paid as a lump sum based on a percentage of the employee's final average salary multiplied by years of service. While you're working under such a plan, you'll have no "investment risk" because the employer has to pay you the amount determined by the formula. After you leave, you're on your own if your investments lose value. But if you make the right investments, your returns can beat inflation. *(Personal)*

• **If you have a 401(k) or similar plan, contribute as much as you can.** Every year, you either use your opportunity to contribute to your DC plan or lose it. Use it—especially if your employer will match it. When considering how much to contribute to a 401(k), follow the priorities suggested by Stanford savings expert B. Douglas Bernheim: "A household ought to max out on anything they get matching contributions to. Then, generally, they should max out on voluntary plans like 401(k)s, even when there isn't an employer contribution." *(Personal)*

• **If you receive a lump-sum distribution from a 401(k) or DB plan, hold on to it.** According to the Employee Benefit Research Institute, 71 percent of people who receive a lump-sum distribution don't roll any of the money into an IRA to provide later-life income. They spend all of it—minus the 20 percent penalty the IRS charges for not rolling it into an IRA. If you receive a lump-sum distribution, either roll it over into a tax-deferred account or spend it on something that will improve your later-life productivity, like developing new competencies or financing a sideline business. *(Personal)*

• **Before you jump out of an "early retirement window," make sure your stunt crew has inflated the big pillow down below.** If you're an older employee planning to leave a company with a DB plan, and you see higher inflation coming, you may want to delay your departure to raise the final average salary that will be used to compute your benefits. *(Personal)*

• **Work for an employer whose 401(k) allows you the widest range of investments.** Or persuade your employer to select a 401(k) provider that works with a number of investment managers and offers a variety of financial vehicles. For example, such providers as Charles Schwab and State Street Bank & Trust enable 401(k) participants to buy not only guaranteed insurance contracts and mutual funds but also individual stocks. Ideally, you should have the ability to weight your 401(k) with assets that are likely to benefit from population aging, such as health sector funds. And you want to be able to shift, when the time comes, toward securities that can withstand downward pressure on prices caused by the inevitable sell-off of pension assets. *(Workplace) (Personal)*

• **Ask your employer to make "emerging-market" mutual funds available in your 401(k) plan.** Otherwise, when the time comes for you to cash out, you may find that your cash is already out. *(Workplace) (Personal)*

SAVINGS

A penny saved, after thirty-five years at the stock market's inflation-adjusted 7 percent real rate of return since 1926, is eleven pennies earned.

• **Support innovative concepts like the "Premium Savings Account" (PSA) proposed by Stanford's B. Douglas Bernheim and economist John Karl Scholz of the University of Wisconsin.** To contribute to a tax-deferred PSA, individuals would have to qualify by saving specified percentages of earnings. Contributions above that amount would be tax-deferred up to a ceiling scaled by income, as would dividends and interest earned in the PSA.

PSAs would avoid the main obstacle to further expansion of IRAs: the claim that instead of encouraging higher-paid people to save more, Individual Retirement Arrangements allow them to shift amounts they've already saved into tax-deferred accounts. A 1993 study by economists James M. Poterba, Steven F. Venti, and David A. Wise found that in reality, "most of the contributions to these programs represent new saving that would not have occurred otherwise." But even if the claim were true, the 1986 tax law's remedy— canceling IRA eligibility for couples with pension coverage who earn over $50,000—was like treating a headache by cutting off the head. IRA contributions have fallen by about 75 percent since the 1986 legislation took effect—a net loss of much-needed savings and investment.

Instead of simple-mindedly depriving high earners of a tax incentive for saving, PSAs would require them to save more before becoming eligible for the incentive, while lower-income people would begin to receive the tax advantage after saving less. There's plenty of latent political support for ideas like this. A 1993 survey by the Employers Council on Flexible Compensation asked employees, "Do you think the government provides adequate incentives through tax advantages for the average working person to save for their retirement needs?" Eighty-two percent said no. *(Policy)*

• **Saving should be encouraged regardless of income level.** Reinventing welfare should include reinventing saving among poor people, which used to be one of the main ways Americans boot-strapped themselves out of poverty. The Savings and Investment Incentive Act introduced in 1994 by Senators William V. Roth Jr. (R-Delaware) and John B. Breaux (D-Louisiana) called for recipients of Aid to Families with Dependent Children (AFDC) to be able to save up to $8,000 in special accounts that would allow withdrawals for buying a home or for improving employability through such means as education and training, buying a car or home, or relocating. Would conservatives object to changing the law that denies welfare to people who have savings? Listen to former member of Congress and HUD secretary Jack Kemp, cofounder of the conservative group Empower America: "We should end the criminalization of saving among the poor. Right now, the most basic act of faith in the future—saving for your children, or for a home, or for your education—is a crime under our AFDC laws." *(Policy)*

• **Support restoring the $400 dividend exclusion from taxable income that was eliminated in the 1980s.** It's another "soak-the-rich" attempt that has ended up mainly soaking the middle class. *(Policy)*

• **Support the revival of Individual Retirement Bonds.** The Treasury suspended the little-known program in 1982 because of lack of demand, so it would seem that to have it reinstated, all we should have to do is demand them. Each bond was like a miniature IRA: Interest accumulated tax-deferred; they weren't transferable; they couldn't be pledged as collateral; there was a 10 percent penalty for redeeming them before age fifty-nine and a half; and they stopped earning interest after age seventy and a half. *(Policy)*

• **Push for the Treasury to issue long-term bonds with interest indexed to inflation.** Such securities have already been issued by Sweden and Britain. The jury is still out in Sweden because the first indexed bonds were issued in 1994. They've been holding down the British government's borrowing costs because of the

United Kingdom's success in controlling inflation. As economists Zvi Bodie of Boston University and Robert C. Merton of Harvard have observed, "Over the years, a number of economists have considered it desirable, if not essential, for the U.S. government to issue inflation-linked bonds in order to lay the foundation for private inflation insurance. Indeed, Nobel laureate economists Milton Friedman, Franco Modigliani, and James Tobin, who often hold very different opinions on other issues, are united in their enthusiastic support for the idea of the U.S. Treasury's issuing CPI-linked bonds." *(Policy)*

• **Support continuing tax deferments on the build-up of assets within life insurance policies and variable annuities.** Such deferrals are frequently under attack inside the Beltway. The deferment for earnings inside new variable annuities and additions to existing annuities was on the verge of being eliminated during the last year of the Bush administration. If the government tries to increase today's revenues by getting rid of the few tax incentives for saving that are still in place, it will end up having to spend tomorrow's tax revenues to prevent starvation and homelessness among baby boomer "dumpies" who were unable to save. *(Policy)*

• **Stimulate insurance companies to offer group annuities with payouts based on market interest rates through your professional, trade, fraternal, and labor organizations.** Actuary Mary S. Riebold, a former managing director of the employee benefits consulting firm of William M. Mercer, Inc., pointed out to me that the payout from today's annuities generally isn't as high as the return available from other investments. But if insurers see a market for competitive annuity products, they'll offer them. (I'm referring here to annuities providing "fixed installments for life," not variable annuities, which are actually tax-deferred investment accounts.) *(Workplace) (Personal)*

• **Give serious consideration to the proposal by Senators Sam Nunn (D-Georgia) and Pete Domenici (R-New Mexico) for a "consumption-based tax code."** "The core of our proposed alternative—which we call the Universal Savings Allowance (USA)—is the elimination of taxation on personal savings and business investment," Senator Nunn explained to me. "Under the proposal, individual income would be defined much the same as it is today, but taxpayers would subtract the amount they saved and invested from what they earned during that year. The balance would be subject to progressive tax rates just as taxable income is today. And to ensure fairness, we would provide a generous exemption for spending on essentials as well as a credit to low-income Americans for payroll taxes withheld to finance entitlement programs.

"Senator Domenici and I believe that saving and investing are how we provide for our future. The current tax code actually discourages savings and investment by taxing them more than other uses of our income. As a result, the level of savings is less than it would be if all uses of income were taxed the same. The current tax system is broken and it cannot be fixed. We must completely replace it and start from the beginning." *(Policy)*

• **Aim for a savings target that's within your range, and do your best to hit it consistently.** There are several ways you can choose a target. One could be to equal the average percentage of disposable income saved between 1975 and the recession of the early 1990s by Japan (17), France (16), Germany (13), Canada (13), or the United Kingdom (10). These figures are all higher than the U.S. average for the period of 7 percent—let alone our current abysmal savings rate of less than 5 percent. Another might be to follow a guideline suggested by B. Douglas Bernheim: "Even relatively young households (thirty-five to forty-five years old) generally need to save 9 to 19 percent of their after-tax income, and individuals who are not covered by private pension plans should be even more frugal. On average, a household in the thirty-five-to-forty-five age bracket that does not expect to be covered by a private pension should save between 13 percent and 25 percent of after-tax income, and this figure should rise with age." *(Personal)*

• **Promote savings education in the schools.** Work through your PTA to suggest to school administrators that learning to save be made part of the curriculum at the elementary, middle, and high school levels. We need to teach young people to be savers and investors not only for their own good, but so they'll be able to afford to buy our personal and pension plan assets when we're older. To do that, they're going to have to be wealthier than we are on a per capita basis. Otherwise, since there are fewer of them than there are of us, we'll have to unload what we own at fire-sale prices. *(Personal)*

• **Support a national public/private campaign to encourage saving.** More saving results in more investment, and more investment results in more productivity and economic growth, both of which we urgently need to support the baby boom generation as it ages—not to mention the generations after it. We often read that the Japanese save at three times our rate, but we're seldom told that in the 1920s and 1930s they saved at a lower rate than we did. Tokyo began to tackle the problem after World War II by setting up a Savings Promotion Center in the Ministry of Finance and a Savings Promotion Department in the Bank of Japan. The overall effort is coordinated by a Central Council for Savings Promotion. The program includes advertisements, brochures, pamphlets, posters, and seminars. It's time to stop complaining about our wretched personal savings rate and start doing something about it. *(Policy)* *(Workplace)*

WORKING LATE

Two things that happened in 1935: (1) An interview with Picasso was published in *Cahiers d'Art* in which he said, "Work is a necessity for man. A horse does not go by itself between the shafts. Man invented the alarm clock." (2) The Social Security Act, which paid older people to stop working, was passed.

Interviewed in 1952 at age eighty-five, the architect Frank Lloyd Wright said, "This matter of age you see in the provinces is one of the things that's quite the matter with our culture. They think a chicken has so many eggs to lay, at a certain age a horse has so much more work to do and they begin to put human beings in the category of the animals, which has put us in the position of really making old age a disqualification when it should be a qualification. If any damning count can be brought out against civilization, our culture is just that—that old age is a disqualification."

It's up to each of us to become an advocate for opportunity for older workers, because in the not-too-distant future, we're likely to be older workers ourselves. Members of the baby boom generation have always prided themselves on their willingness to stay at the office after 5:00 to get the job done. I believe that continuing to work when we're older will become yet another form of "working late."

• **Support what I call "human-investment tax credits" for developing new competencies.** Gerontologist Harry R. Moody has pointed out that education to improve skills we can use in our present occupation is tax-deductible, but education for a new occupation isn't. It's irrational for the tax code to penalize people for taking steps to adapt to today's rapidly evolving economy. *(Policy)*

• **Support making it illegal for employers to exclude people over age forty from apprenticeship programs.** The Equal Employment Opportunity Commission has dithered on this issue, first interpreting the Age Discrimination in Employment Act as allowing exclusion, then voting unanimously to eliminate it, then voting to go back to permitting exclusion. Congress should clarify the law so that midlife and older employees will be able to obtain the vital new job skills they'll need to remain marketable members of the labor force. *(Policy)*

• **Support making it possible for unemployment insurance to be paid in a lump sum if it's used to start a business.** This is already the law in several states. Any measures that open the way to personal entrepreneurship will make life better for us when we're older. *(Policy)*

• **Support granting tax credits to companies that employ and train older workers.** Such credits are advocated by figures like Dr. Richard S. Belous, vice president and senior economist at the National Planning Association. Gösta Rehn, former director of the Swedish Institute for Social Research and director for manpower and social affairs at the Organization for Economic Cooperation and Development, wrote recently: "It is noteworthy and peculiar that so many governments have given higher priority to using taxpayers' money to persuade workers not to work instead of using that money to create more work and higher productivity." It'll be cheaper in the long run for taxpayers to subsidize productivity among older people than to subsidize leisure. *(Policy)*

• **Support elimination of the "health earnings test" that discourages employers from hiring people aged sixty-five to sixty-nine.** That's what Urban Institute economists C. Eugene Steuerle and Jon M. Bakija have aptly called it: "Medicare now has rules requiring that it be made a 'secondary payer' relative to health insurance provided by employers of twenty or more workers. If an employer provides health insurance to employees and their spouses in general, it must also cover any elderly employee and spouse. The Medicare system will pay for health services only to the extent they are not already covered under the employer plan. . . . Since older persons have higher health expenses, of course, the mandate requires that the amount spent on the health benefits of elderly workers be greater than the amount spent on other workers. . . . Since [the employee] already had Medicare, the additional $6,000 paid out to buy a duplicate insurance policy operates like an additional earnings test or tax. The employer might have been willing to hire him for a higher cash wage if Medicare had remained the primary payer."

The consulting firm of ICF Inc. has calculated that if the "health earnings test" didn't exist, the cost to companies of health insurance for employees sixty-five and over would be lower than the cost for those aged nineteen to sixty-four, because they're covered by Medicare. *(Policy)*

• **Make it illegal for employers to ask job applicants to disclose the dates they attended educational institutions.** Employers, afraid of age discrimination lawsuits, no longer ask for your date of birth on a job application. But many companies require that you give the dates you went to school, which lets them estimate your age within a year or two. Insisting on an answer to this question has been made illegal in California. That's a step in the right direction. But the question itself should be banned, because not answering has to put an applicant at a disadvantage. The day will come, hopefully, when employers will stop asking how old people are—and when prospective employees will have no reason to be wary of revealing their age. Until then, your age is nobody's business but your own. *(Policy)*

• **Encourage your company to employ a specialist to develop programs to encourage hiring and retaining older workers.** ITT Hartford was a pioneer in assigning an officer to oversee the function the insurance company called "corporate gerontological development." Merrill Lynch recently put a gerontologist on staff. An executive with responsibility for issues connected with aging makes sense because aging is something everyone in every company is constantly doing. *(Workplace)*

• **Work for a company with a tuition reimbursement plan and ample opportunities for you to upgrade your skills.** Companies that are now unilaterally redrafting the "unwritten contract" that once provided some degree of job security have been talking about a new version under which they will supposedly guarantee "employment security." Let them walk the talk by getting them to offer you concrete help with your personal program of "recurrent development of new competencies." *(Workplace) (Personal)*

• **Encourage your company to allow "phased retirement."** Older employees should be able to gradually cut down on their hours or days through part-time work or job-sharing rather than making them stop cold turkey—what human resource professionals aptly call "cliff retirement." *(Workplace)*

• **Make sure the Americans with Disabilities Act is used to protect everyone with a handicap, regardless of age.** For example, an older worker with "normal" arthritis has just as much of a right to be accommodated by her employer as a teenage worker with juvenile arthritis. *(Policy) (Workplace) (Personal)*

• **Keep in mind that if you're over forty, it's illegal under ADEA for an employer to terminate you because of your age.** So you don't have to accept a take-it-or-leave-it Early Retirement Incentive Plan (ERIP) with a gun to your head in the form of a "time window." You've got plenty of leverage to negotiate a better package: Use it with help from a lawyer specializing in employment issues. (You can get a referral from the National Employment Lawyers Association, headquartered in San Francisco.) Sweeteners can include higher severance pay, extended health benefits, not having to sign a noncompete agreement, and strong reference letters if merited, or a written agreement to decline comment about you to prospective employers who ask for references. *(Personal)*

• **If you're a manager, let your employees know that ageism is no longer profitable.** Help your staff learn how to benefit from the special strengths of older workers while compensating for difficulties they may have, such as impaired vision, hearing, or mobility.

Age discrimination in employment is a function of gatekeepers' perceptions of who is "old." Forty-six percent of American executives today are baby boomers, so for now, we're the gatekeepers. It's time for us to use our position to set new standards of opportunity for older workers—because many of us are going to be older workers ourselves. *(Workplace)*

• **Fight what I call "chronological harassment."** If, for instance, you ever find yourself the butt of "good-natured" jokes about how old you are, pleasantly but firmly help the supervisor or coworker who's hurting your feelings realize that one of these days they're going to be your age. And make sure as many people as possible in your workplace and among your friends know where you stand. According to the U.S. Bureau of Labor Statistics, more than half of today's workforce are baby boomers. If we talk the issue up, it won't be long before there's a pervasive awareness of the damage that can be caused even by the most subtle forms of age discrimination. I can foresee the day when chronological harassment will be as unacceptable as sexual harassment. *(Workplace) (Personal)*

• **Each of us has to face up to any negative feelings we may have toward older people and deal with them.** We're surrounded by age bigots, and many of those age bigots are us. As matters now stand, it's not okay to discriminate against someone because her skin is brown, but it's okay to discriminate against someone because her skin is wrinkled. AARP Executive Director Horace B. Deets told a recent conference that human resource managers responding to his organization's surveys report that while employees under thirty get along well with older workers, baby boomers tend not to: "They are critical of the baby boomers for not accepting older workers, for being ageist in their attitudes." Age bigotry is incomparably the dumbest form of prejudice imaginable. If we're European American we aren't going to become African American. If we're Anglo we aren't going to become Latino. But if we're young, the chances are high that we're going to become old. To discriminate against a group that one is involuntarily going to turn into a member of is very, very dumb. *(Personal)*

Whatever actions you take now to make life better for others and for yourself when you're old, keep in mind these words of the late anthropologist Margaret Mead: "Never doubt that a small group of thoughtful, committed citizens can change the world; indeed, it's the only thing that does."

CHAPTER 16

OWL MOUNTAIN

From the beginning of time, societies have called older people to continue to contribute to the life of the community. The first stirrings of a new, intergenerational aging movement, in which younger people help empower older people, while older people convey their wisdom to younger people, are being felt. It's essential that members of the baby boom generation begin now to become involved in this effort, so that by the time they're older, there will be a widespread appreciation of the importance of enabling elders to contribute—in the form of paid work, if they need it—far into later life.

This desert is so long it can take a lifetime to go from one end to the other and a childhood to cross at its narrowest point.

—Ibn Khaldun (1332–1406), Tunisian historian;
epigraph to the novel *The Process*
by Brion Gysin (London: Jonathan Cape, 1969)

Many years ago I was given a blessing whose full meaning I believe I have finally come to understand while writing this book.

In January of 1973 I received a very formal letter from the ruling elder of a tiny village called Jajouka in a mountainous region of Morocco. The letter invited me to the *Aid el-Kebir,* the annual Great Feast that would be held in the village a few days later. It had been dictated to a scribe by Malim Abdsalam Attar, the head of the priestly brotherhood responsible for presenting the yearly ritual drama portraying the power of the principal deity of Moroccan folk religion, Bou Jeloud, god of flocks.

I was astounded to be informed by an African village elder that a piece of music criticism I'd written in *The Village Voice* several months before had found its way to him. In my article in the New York weekly, I'd noted that the late Brian Jones, one of the original

Rolling Stones, had visited Jajouka in 1968 to experience African music as performed by the village's holy men, who for centuries had been the court musicians of Morocco's sultans. I'd heard the tapes he made there. They sounded like the greatest hits of an unbroken chain of precursors of Stravinsky who had composed not only the rite of spring but the rites of every season of the year, every season of the soul. The polyrhythmic bass undertow was so ominous it made the muffled drums of John Kennedy's funeral seem about as somber as the petty percussion of a cocktail-hour rendition of "It Was Just One of Those Things." I'd speculated that Jones had played the tapes for his fellow band members, and that it was this infusion of African roots that prodded the Stones' music, until then mostly a bad-boy revision of Chicago blues, to jump the groove into the magisterial barrage of anthems that bombarded arenas across America during their 1972 U.S. tour, which I covered in so many cities that my ears are still slightly traumatized—a music, as William Blake might have described it, "rifted with direful changes," an elegiac grand finale in which each of the hopeful and idealistic themes of the 1960s and early 1970s was restated and negated. The elder told me that what I had written was indeed so, and that my presence in his village was therefore desired.

The invitation—actually it read more like a subpoena—called on me to drop everything and report immediately to an address in Tangier, where I would be met by a total stranger and escorted in the dead of night to a hilltop in the middle of nowhere. If such a summons were not intriguing enough in itself, there was the legend of Jajouka to consider.

Jajouka could be described as the world's most secret famous place. Long before I received Malim Abdsalam's letter, I'd known that Jajouka was where one of the major streams of the post–World War II cultural revolution of Western society originated—the mass marketing of bohemianism: loose living not, as it was previously, as a way of life, but as a style.

The line leads back to the Beats, and especially to Allen Ginsberg, who was not only a central Beat figure, but the Beats' living link with hippiedom, and who continues to be revered in "alternative" circles. Ginsberg's mentor was the author William S. Burroughs, who was in turn strongly influenced by his friendship and collaboration with the late Canadian novelist and painter Brion Gysin, the first foreigner to "discover" Jajouka.

Gysin recognized in 1950 that he'd stumbled onto one of the last places on earth where the most ancient ceremonies, from the time of the Phoenicians and earlier, still survived. He was a Byronesque romantic who believed that the truths conserved by the villagers for thousands of years could reenergize Western art. It didn't happen, of course . . . but something else, perhaps more consequential, did. If you're interested in the details, you can find some of them in a 1993 book called *Jajouka Rolling Stone* by the journalist Stephen Davis. Otherwise, suffice it to say that a lot of things would be different if it hadn't been for a Moroccan village by the name of Jajouka.

Cut to my arrival on a starlit mountaintop in Africa, entering the brotherhood's meetinghouse, being hugged and kissed by a wizard in a turban and a golden earring as if I were his long-lost grandson, and finding myself at a kind of Apalachin meeting of hip. Bill Burroughs was there . . . Brion Gysin himself . . . a prominent French author . . . a familiar face on the BBC . . . several fabled wayfarers along what was known as the Hash Trail, the transformation super highway for seekers and loafers . . . an American film director . . . the actor Don Johnson . . . the jazz virtuoso Ornette Coleman . . . I could go on.

That week I found out what one does at a Great Feast: One eats a lot.

And each night the members of the brotherhood and the few hundred people who lived in the village assembled around a bonfire in the smaller of Jajouka's two squares. The brotherhood's musicians played oboes and drums—how trivial that word "played" seems when I remember the serpentine discord of the reeds, the insistent roar of the taut skins; there was nothing playful about what those men were doing. They were engaged in the serious business of calling on the god of flocks to help this little village of goatherds get through the coming year. They invoked him with progressions of conflict, crisis, and catastrophe, arousal, orgasm, and ejaculation. Men of the brotherhood dressed in goatskins, every one a Nijinsky, appeared in the firelight and took turns dancing the presence of Bou Jeloud as if everything depended on it, which according to their way of understanding things, it did. Though these people were nominally Muslims, the most impressive building in their village wasn't the mosque but the brotherhood's meetinghouse. Allah to them seemed too important, too abstract, too far away to care much about a village with no electricity, no telephone, no running water, no toilets, no school, no clinic. If the king of Morocco didn't care, why should the king of the universe?

While I was in Jajouka, a little boy fell off a donkey, hit his head on a rock, and after several days in a coma, died. I found out about this only when I saw his relatives burying him in a white shroud. When I asked them why they didn't ask one of the Westerners to drive him to the district hospital, they lowered their eyes shyly and said, "We didn't want to bother you."

I think they didn't want to bother Allah either. The thing about Bou Jeloud was, he didn't care very much about you, busy as he was embodying the confluence of all the forces of nature in the gift to humankind of herds of healthy goats, but at least you didn't have to worry about bothering him.

On the last night of the festival whole families had traveled to Jajouka from other villages and set up camp. A tent was set up for us delicate Westerners at the edge of the village's main square. One of its sides was left open, and we sat on carpets facing the fire.

This time the music was even more urgent than before, but Bou Jeloud did not come. Instead, a boy of perhaps twelve materialized in the distance, skittering wildly toward us. A vortex of pure power was coming for me and I was completely defenseless.

Within seconds the boy was whirling directly in front of our pavilion. It wasn't like watching someone dance—it was more like watching someone have a seizure. Yet instead of a seizure of lost consciousness it was a seizure of exorbitant consciousness. Instead of a fit of lost control it was a fit of absolute control. Instead of a convulsion of spasticity it was a convulsion of grace.

I've seen Nureyev, Villella, Baryshnikov, Plisetskaya, Fonteyn, Makarova. But this was by far the greatest dancer I had ever seen— the strongest, most graceful child on a continent, plucked from the cradle by the brotherhood of sorcerers and groomed for this moment. He was the personification of human vitality. He was the half of Elvis that Ed Sullivan couldn't show. He was the young Aretha, the young Janis, the young Jagger, the young Otis, all swirled into one body and one gender and raised to the nth degree.

His dance said, "I am the most alive thing you have ever seen or ever will see. I am you the way you would be if you could shed your lethargy, your fatigue, your laziness. Now that you finally know what a living being looks like, you have to acknowledge that I cannot go on like this, that I am doomed to decline—that you are doomed to decline. Watch me and exult; watch me and weep."

The reeds shrieked, "This is the highest of all heights." The drums pummeled, "This is the deepest of all depths."

We poor Westerners began to sob, to pant, to groan. I looked around me, gasping for air. It was too far out for Ornette Coleman! It was too naked for William S. Burroughs! Brion Gysin grinned like the organizer of a surprise party when the guest of honor finally catches the drift. The boy writhed and quivered. The music wailed and pounded. The speechless moaning in the tent said, "How could I have been so stupid? How could I have been so blind?"

It was then that we were formally blessed. The youngest priest stepped among us and sprinkled rose water on our foreheads from a silver bottle. As detached as a physician unmoved by the sight of blood, he was not a brain surgeon but a mind surgeon, a spiritual surgeon, an existential surgeon, slicing away the most reassuring and dangerous illusion from which anyone can suffer: that I am exempt from mortality, that contrary to everything I know rationally, somehow I will never grow old, weaken, wither, and die.

Then the boy danced away from us and aged sixty years in a few seconds.

His knees and elbows stiffened. His head and hands shook. His shoulders slumped. His chest sank. His back bent. He clutched a staff and leaned wearily on it. The music slowed, its mainspring winding down. It was terrifying. This was going to happen to each of us.

So here was the great obvious secret, the one that could only be revealed to us blockheaded Westerners using every artifice of the Muses: "One of these days you're going to be old; deal with it."

And then the drumbeat picked up and the boy began another dance.

It was the phone call from the governor's office. It was the search plane returning and starting to circle. It was your car's frozen engine coming to life on the last feeble crank from its dying battery. It was unadulterated mercy. It was the dance of old age.

He was jaunty. He was dapper. He was spry. He synchronized his tremor to the rhythm of the music, and instead of hindering the dance it became part of it. He twirled his stick like an old vaudevillian.

It was a dance not of strength but of persistence. It was a dance not of potency but of contentment. It was a dance not of evanescent sparks but of coals still glowing.

The boy's eyes had been glazed with ecstasy. The old man's eyes twinkled with irony.

The dance of youth had been a sprint. This was the marathon.

If that was our future, we might not relish it, but it was something we could accept. A few of the people in the tent got up and joined the dance. The villagers laughed and clapped and shouted encouragement. It was amazing that Westerners could have so much money, considering how silly they were.

Finally the boy who had become old danced into the darkness. The music stopped. The feast was over.

I knew I had been taught a lesson, but I couldn't fully grasp its meaning. The performance was symbolic, and symbols speak to the deepest self that learns but does not divulge what it has learned until the time comes.

There was plenty to do in the meantime. Because Bou Jeloud's supreme gift is fertility, my wife and I went back to America and made four children.

Then one night while I was writing this book it occurred to me that every child of that village far from any other village, growing up as each did among swarms of children, outnumbering the adults, needed to be reminded every year that youth was fleeting and that old age had constantly to be kept in mind. Those children in a place without a doctor would be fortunate to reach old age, but unfortunate also. They had no prospect of ever receiving a check in the mail from anyone, least of all a government. If they wanted to be supported ungrudgingly when they were old, they would have to continue to contribute to the life of the village. From the time they were infants it had to be literally drummed into them that they must be prepared to keep on keeping on.

I had thought that the blessing bestowed on me in my twenties was to know not merely cerebrally that someday I would be old, but to know it in my bones. Now I realized that the lesson of the dance of old age was not that I would be old, but how I would be old. The boy who turned into an old man had mimed the qualities I would need down the road—shrewdness, perseverance, tenacity. If I kept his firelit image in mind, I'd be able to step out in style.

I remembered the 1992 testimony before the Senate Special Committee on Aging of Howard "Sandman" Sims, born in 1918, who pulls the losers off the stage of Harlem's Apollo Theatre on Amateur Night and has been dancing professionally since age three: "Most people's hearts are manufactured to dance. Not everyone does it, but it's never too late to dance your dance."

The message of Jajouka was that it's never too early to learn that it's never too late to dance your dance.

I recalled the words of Oliver Wendell Holmes Jr. (1841–1935), who served on the U.S. Supreme Court until he was ninety-one. In a radio address on his ninetieth birthday Justice Holmes told the nation: "The riders in a race do not stop short when they reach the goal. There is a little finishing canter before coming to a standstill. There is time to hear the kind voice of friends and to say to one's self: 'The work is done.' But just as one says that, the answer comes: 'The race is over, but the work never is done while the power to work remains.' The canter that brings you to a standstill need not be only coming to rest. It cannot be, while you still live. For to live is to function. That is all there is in living."

The message of Jajouka was that the work of comprehending that the work never is done—never is done.

Mass retirement is on its way to becoming a historical curiosity. With the fall of communism it is no longer necessary for capitalism to compete by offering workers a pot of gold at the end of the rainbow; a longer rainbow will have to do. With the rise of global economic competition it will be impossible for the U.S. public or private sectors to afford to compensate Americans with decades of later-life leisure when this country's workers are already paid more in an hour than workers in Mexico earn in a day, more in a day than workers in China are paid in a month. Vast numbers of baby boomers are going to need to work part-time or full-time when they're older.

Happily, the intellectual infrastructure that will enable us to have the option to work when we're older is already in place. Foundations such as the Commonwealth Fund, the Villers Foundation, and the Retirement Research Foundation have been sponsoring studies and projects designed to promote the acceptance of older employees in the labor market. Academic centers like the University of Massachusetts Gerontology Institute, the Andrus Gerontology Center at the University of Southern California, Cornell University's Institute for Labor Market Policy, and the Pepper Institute on Aging and Public Policy at Florida State University have been in the forefront of research on the future role of older employees.

Among the think tanks and corporate forums, the Southport Institute for Policy Analysis has spearheaded research into employment prospects for older women. The Hudson Institute has done landmark studies of the changing age structure of the future labor force. The Urban Institute is deeply involved in examining the economic prospects of tomorrow's older Americans. The International Leadership Center on Longevity and Society has been founded by Dr. Robert N. Butler with offices in New York and Tokyo to develop policies for "aging populations, their needs, and their productivity. The Conference Board has sponsored important research by such scholars as Kathleen Christensen, one of the foremost experts on changing workstyles, Audrey Freedman, who has examined the implications for older employees of the decline in literacy and numeracy among younger workers, and Shirley Rhine, who has explored management attitudes toward older workers. And the National Planning Association and the Washington Business Group on Health, each a pioneer in its own right, have created a Joint Project on U.S. Competitiveness and the Aging American Workforce, with the support of companies of the caliber of Chrysler, Kodak, Federal Express, Ford, General Mills, General Motors, Goodyear, IBM, Levi Strauss, Mobil, PepsiCo, Procter & Gamble, 3M, Westinghouse, and Xerox. Such organizations as the AARP, the Older Women's League, and the National Council on Aging are deeply involved in studying older-worker issues as well as in pressing for more opportunity for older employees.

Some advocates of increased employment opportunity for older people have become discouraged that while more and more companies are expressing support for the idea that older workers should be hired and retained, few have gone beyond lip service. But given the one-two punch of the weak economy of the early 1990s and the advent of downsizing, it would be surprising if employers were chasing after older workers. The consensus among university and think tank experts that working late will be good for employees, good for business, and good for the federal budget isn't going to be enough to induce companies to change their practices. What's been called the "older worker movement" or "extension of work-life movement" won't spread beyond academic and policy circles until it dawns on members of the baby boom generation that the need for job opportunities when they're older is too serious to leave to the professionals. The "older worker movement" will take off as the realization spreads among baby boomers that if they don't become personally involved in combatting ageism in employment, they may well end up as impoverished "dumpies."

The "older worker movement" is going to evolve into a key element of a comprehensive "aging movement" that will emerge as the great societal upheaval of the early decades of the twenty-first century. Everything the baby boomers have touched has become a phenomenon, and this huge, articulate generation's experience of old age can be relied on to trigger as remarkable a modification of consciousness as did its experience of youth.

When the aging movement attains critical mass it will release as much cultural energy as any previous coming-together of the baby boom generation, if not more. The aging movement will not only reharness the moral impetus that propelled the previous movements of the baby boomers, but will be driven by an additional force—economic self-interest: fear of destitution, and the desire to thrive.

In musical theater the climactic moment is the reprise, the culminating reappearance of an almost-forgotten melody. I predict that as the baby boomers enter their sixties and early seventies there is going to be a reprise of the endemic sense of excitement of the 1960s and early 1970s. A generation dismayed by feelings of loss, frustrated by a sense that in adjusting to the necessities of adulthood it somehow sold out, will get a second wind.

This mass invigoration will be the exact opposite of *Big Chill* wistfulness about the minority of our generation who have died prematurely. The tone of the cultural crescendo of our sixties and seventies will be delight at the survival of the scores of millions of baby boomers who will live longer than any generation in history. You and I are on our way to an unexpected harvest festival.

A key factor that permitted the 1960s and early 1970s to happen will be there for the baby boomers when they're older: a financial cushion. Many of those who were involved in the ferment of that time felt free to take risks because they had something to fall back on: help from parents and an ebullient economy. When the baby boomers are older, the cushion will be provided by Social Security, pensions, and savings. While vast numbers will need or want to do paid work, these three income sources will provide downside support for interpersonal openness, artistic creativity, and spiritual development.

Those who shared an ecstatic vision in their youth of life as it could be will be enabled to reconvene in later life and pick up the threads of their dreams. Where is it written that everything must be accomplished in our twenties, thirties, forties, and fifties? The gift of the longevity revolution is that there can still be time in our sixties, seventies, eighties, and nineties. Those who sought "expanded consciousness" will venture into the realm of extended consciousness.

They will put the overtired "inner child" to bed and allow themselves to be consoled and enlightened by the inner grandparent. They will discover that there is a wise elder struggling to grow out of each of us.

Just as the baby boomers became famous for their "youth culture," in later life they will develop an age culture. The youth culture had two dissonant strains: a hedonistic celebration of the collective self, crosscut with rage against various others, often defined as "anyone over thirty." The motifs of the age culture will harmonize: joy at having survived, with eagerness to share the experience of a lifetime with anyone over zero.

What can people who are now in their thirties, forties, and fifties do today to build the aging movement that will help sustain them in later life? They can actively support those among today's older people who are searching for ways to make their lives richer in every sense of the word.

The establishment of contexts in which this joining of the generations can take place has already begun. I was present in October 1994 at the second Conference on Conscious Aging, held at the Sheraton Stamford Hotel in Connecticut. It was convened under the auspices of the Omega Institute, whose Rhinebeck, New York, campus is the main East Coast center of the human potential movement, and which conducts retreats across the country. Omega presenters include the actress Olympia Dukakis, physician Bernie Siegel, poet Anne Waldman, novelist Marge Piercy, singer-songwriter Rosanne Cash, baseball pitcher Bill Lee, biologist Rupert Sheldrake, drummer Babatunde Olatunji, psychotherapist Claudio Naranjo, physicist Fritjof Capra, Zen monk Thich Nhat Hanh, psychologist Jon Kabat-Zinn, playwright Jean-Claude van Itallie, musician Paul Winter, basketball Hall of Fame member Bill Walton, author William Least Heat-Moon, and Sufi teacher Pir Vilayat Inayat Khan.

The three-day conference was designed, according to its prospectus, to give "people of all ages the opportunity to develop a new understanding of aging that considers the practical issues of health, finances, housing, families, and other realities in the elder years, as well as the creative and spiritual possibilities of celebrating maturity, honoring elders in the society, mentoring, and positively integrating aging into every stage of our lives."

The master of ceremonies was Ram Dass, born in 1931, known in a previous manifestation as Richard Alpert, Ph.D., who as a young member of the Harvard psychology faculty got himself canned for experimenting with hallucinogens and teamed with his colleague Timothy Leary to popularize LSD in the 1960s; now his hair is white. Clearly he was enjoying his personal sixties as yet another altered state of consciousness. Initiated into the mysteries of meditation by an Indian guide three decades before, he jokingly described his most recent initiation—at the hands of a railroad conductor in Westport, Connecticut, who asked if he wanted to buy a senior citizen's ticket. The conference's pivotal figure was Rabbi Zalman Schachter, Professor Emeritus of Judiac Studies at Temple University and author of *From Aging to Saging,* who has founded the Spiritual Eldering Institute to foster growth in old age and during the conference received Omega's first Conscious Aging Award. Among the keynote speakers were Betty Friedan, author of *The Fountain of Age,* and cardiologist Dean Ornish, M.D., author of *Stress, Diet, and Your Heart.*

Workshop leaders included Thomas Cole, Professor of History and Medicine at the University of Texas and author of *The Journey of Life: A Cultural History of Aging in America*; Margaret Harmon, director of the National Shared Housing Resource Center; gerontologist Dr. Ruth Harriet Jacobs, former chair of sociology at Clark University, now with the Wellesley College Center for Research on Women, author of *Older Women Surviving and Thriving;* psychotherapist Myrna Lewis, coauthor with her husband, Dr. Robert N. Butler, of *Love and Sex After Sixty*; and gerontologist Dr. Harry R. Moody of the Brookdale Center on Aging at New York's Hunter College. The ovations given Ram Dass and Betty Friedan, each of whom has a track record of having helped instigate a tectonic shift of American culture, were a portent.

More than one thousand people paid $240 to attend, not counting accommodations and meals. The visual tone was Lands' End/L. L. Bean/Orvis/Eddie Bauer, with a dash of Santa Fe and Cuernavaca. More than half the participants were women, a majority in their sixties and seventies. Some were in their eighties and nineties. One, a woman a few weeks from her one-hundredth birthday, was lifted out of her wheelchair by fellow members of the Young at Heart Chorus of Northampton, Massachusetts, and, gripping a mike stand for support, belted out a ballad.

Many of those who cheered her were in their twenties, thirties, forties, and fifties. A number of younger registrants were there at least partly in a professional capacity: I spotted Amelia J. Dyer of the AARP's Programs Division and Prof. Robert C. Atchley of the Scripps Foundation Gerontology Center at Ohio's Miami University, author of the standard social gerontology textbook *Social Forces and Aging,* now in its seventh edition. Others were there because, as one man in his twenties put it to me, "When you think about it, we're all aging, aren't we?"

For many, the motives were as multiple as the ages of the attendees. I met a pharmaceutical executive who was interested in developing a mentoring program within his company. A woman from California who described herself in a workshop as a baby boomer who didn't think she'd ever have enough money to stop working and had gone back to graduate school to learn how to counsel people in their sixties who can't afford to retire and are going through "career transition" was there with her mother. I came hoping to get a sense of where retaining the option to work in later life will fit into the aging movement; I found myself at one point massaging the neck and shoulders of a sixty-four-year-old Egyptian orthopedic surgeon in a business suit. He'd flown in from Cairo because, as he explained, "I want not only to heal the damaged knee of the older person, but to heal the older person." When yoga teacher Lillias Folan, fifty-eight, described herself during a plenary session as an "apprentice elder" and asked how many present thought of themselves that way, more than a third raised their hands.

Several sessions emphasized the role that continued work can play in "conscious aging." Therapist Ilana Rubenfeld, who combines touch with talk, conducted a session called "Growing Old Is Forgetting to Retire" in which she told about an eighty-two-year-old woman who'd informed her that she was considering a career change. Rubenfeld highlighted lessons she learned from mentors Pablo Casals, Fritz Perls, and Buckminster Fuller in their productive old age, and said, "If you want to be able to stay on the job when you're older, make sure there's an element of playfulness in your work." Management consultants Phoebe and Jack Ballard gave a seminar titled "Beating the Age Game: Redefining Retirement," which stressed employment and entrepreneurship as necessary alternatives to "the obsolete goal of a twenty-five-year vacation, which can get to be a bit of a bore" and advocated a blend of learning, work, and play in what they call "the third half of life."

One of the conference's most stimulating events was a "Council of Elders." People aged sixty and older were asked by Zalman Schachter to sit in a circle, speak only when they felt they had something to say, holding up the council's feathered and beaded "talking stick"—according to Native American tradition, while carrying it, one can tell only the truth—"and stop when you hear the first whiff of bull-shit." A second ring of chairs was set up around them where people under sixty could sit. Every so often, a member of the "outer circle," as it came to be called, would take the talking stick and, in a tone of profound respect that seemed to be called for by the occasion, address the "inner circle." The council began at 1:00 in the afternoon, and, after breaking for dinner, continued until 9:00 at night. Each statement began with "and," to signify that the speaker was adding to what had been said, and ended with the words, "I have spoken." One of the earliest rounds of statements went like this:

"And I feel that my rainy day is now," a woman in her sixties said. "I don't have so many demands on my schedule. I can do what I want to do without having to go to a nine-to-five job anymore. I have spoken."

A woman in her mid-seventies eagerly took the talking stick. "And I've just gotten a new nine-to-five job," she said proudly, "with a very young boss to whom I'm able to bring a wealth of valuable experience. I have spoken. Don't make me say it again!"

"And as a result of errors and bad judgment I find myself in the position of needing to work for a very long time," said a psychotherapist in his early sixties. "I have no idea where retirement income would come from. I make quite a good living, but I won't be able to stop.

"At first I was intensely ashamed of this. I'd be with friends who were talking about their houses in Bermuda. They'd turn to me and ask what my retirement plans were, and I'd be extremely embarrassed and terribly jealous of them. Part of it was related to how I'd defined my masculine role—just as I'd been expected to provide for my family, now I was expected to provide for my retirement. And I wasn't able to, which was very painful.

"I began to look for a therapist for myself. I wanted to talk to someone older than myself, preferably in their late seventies or eighties. I thought there would be plenty of such people in my area. To my surprise, there were none at all. Suddenly I realized there was a future for me—that I could be that older therapist. That's when I began to pull out of my depression.

"Now I'm enjoying the fact that I need to work. It forces me to take good care of myself. Above all, I'm glad that I have no choice except to continue to help others. The prospect of having to work continues to be a good thing for me and to open all kinds of wonderful possibilities. I have spoken."

"And I want my elders in the inner circle to know that there are many of us who passionately need you," said a woman in her twenties. "Maybe some of the younger people in your lives who you thought would pay attention to what you have to say have turned away from you. But I want you to know that there are many of us who want to learn what you have to teach. I have spoken—and I'm listening."

And yes, it was all very touchy-feely. But I must tell you that I was touched, and that I felt. Sitting there, hearing the truth-telling, I reflected that the seating arrangement in that hotel function room was a model of how the aging movement would build: the younger ones first joining the outer circle to learn from the elders, then, as the years pass, gradually accepting their ordained places in the inner circle. It is crucial that each of us act now to make sure that by the time we're older, there will be an aging movement in place formidable enough to ensure that we have the opportunity to do paid work if we need to or want to. It is time for us to take our places in the outer circle. I have spoken.

In the dialect of Morocco's Rif country the word "Jajouka" means "Owl Mountain." The village is the primordial sanctuary of this particle of wisdom: that there are two periods of life that can only be seen clearly through the speculum of the highest drama.

There is youth, during which the succession of small developmental steps and missteps blurs and obscures the most salient aspect of the overall twenty-year picture: an animal vitality so extreme that, when seen in isolation and concentration on a sacred peak at midnight, it makes men and women who think they've been there and back moan and pant as if they were suddenly forced to give birth to themselves.

And there is old age, during which the change of appearance, loss of stamina and agility, attenuation of the senses, and alteration (not necessarily deterioration) of some mental functions, can cause younger people to experience "confusion" and "forgetfulness" about the fact that there are certain things a human being can find out only by living a long time, and that a culture which glorifies youth and rejects age will not know those things anymore, will become "mentally incompetent," will inevitably "lose gray matter."

What I saw that night on Owl Mountain so many years ago was a ritual preserved since the most ancient times . . . since before Rome . . . since before Greece . . . since a time when there were only villages in the middle of nowhere . . . speaking to us across the millennia in the tender voice of our parents' parents' parents' parents'. . .

• Calling younger people to let go of their angst . . . to rejoice in their God-given strength . . . to live to the limit while they're young because someday they'll be old . . . to have compassion for today's aged because, to paraphrase Pogo, "We have met the enemy, and they are us, older."

• Calling older people to endure . . . to refuse to shuffle off meekly into exile from the society they have built . . . to proclaim, in the words of the classic blues lyric, "Hand me down my walking cane!" . . . to continue their bittersweet dance as long as the last ember glows.

Bringing it all back home: There is no possibility that the vast majority of baby boomers will be able to quit work at an arbitrary age and be supported in idle affluence for decades. For most, there will be two alternatives: Many will continue paid work, will be considered semiretired or not retired at all, and will live in comfort and dignity. Others will end their lengthened days scraping by on a shrinking dole.

If enough of us free ourselves from the retirement myth and embrace models of "productive aging," "resourceful aging," "conscious aging," the baby boom generation will be said to have at last outlived its narcissism and to be taking care of its unfinished business. We will have enough income to concentrate on our outcome. We will be be able to transcend the petty work of paying the rent and become engaged in the great work of healing the world. We will be said to have solved once and for all the chronic U.S. budgetary crisis by showing those after us that it is unnecessary for America to bankrupt itself by mindlessly mandating ever-growing spending on older people while constricting the share of public resources available to every other generation.

If too many of us remain in denial, we will be remembered as a generation that began as self-indulgent hippies and self-righteous yippies, turned away from trying to liberate itself and others to become self-aggrandizing yuppies, and then overstayed its welcome to degenerate into self-pitying "dumpies," a fringe of moochers and scroungers squeegeeing windshields at the edges of a globally unforgiving socioeconomy.

We have before us the possibility of redeeming our generation's promise, or of showing that promise to have been a delusion.

Which will we choose?

NOTES

Page 8. "A 1994 Urban Institute report": C. Eugene Steuerle and Jon M. Bakija, *Retooling Social Security for the 21st Century* (Washington, D.C.: Urban Institute Press, 1994), p. 57. Steuerle, an economist and senior fellow at the Urban Institute, was a Deputy Assistant Secretary of the Treasury and spearheaded the Treasury's 1984–86 tax reform project. Bakija, an economist, was a research associate at the Urban Institute.

Page 8. "an analysis": John B. Shoven, Professor of Economics, Stanford University; Michael D. Topper, Assistant Professor of Economics, College of William and Mary; and David A. Wise, John F. Stambaugh Professor of Political Economy, John F. Kennedy School of Government, Harvard University, "The Impact of the Demographic Transition on Government Spending." Paper presented at a conference, "The Economics of Aging," sponsored by the National Bureau of Economic Research, St. John, Virgin Islands, May 8–9, 1992. Computed from Table 4A.

Page 9. "2.1 . . . to 1.9": *The 1994 Annual Report of the Board of Trustees of the Federal Old-Age and Survivors Insurance and Disability Insurance Trust Funds* (Washington, D.C.: U.S. Government Printing Office, 1994), p. 58.

Page 9. "771,000 . . . 35 million . . . 72 million": Ibid., p. 156.

Page 10. "Chater told *AARP Bulletin*": January 1994, p. 14.

Page 10. "Nathan Keyfitz": *Funding Pensions: Issues and Implications for Financial Markets—Proceedings of a Conference Held at Melvin Village, New Hampshire, October, 1976* (Boston: Federal Bank of Boston, 1977), p. 27.

Page 11. "According to the Social Security Administration": *The 1994 Annual Report of the Board of Trustees of the Federal Old-Age and Survivors Insurance and Disability Insurance Trust Funds*, p. 119.

Page 11. "in the ballpark": According to ibid., p. 107, the percentage of annual taxable payroll that would be needed to pay cash benefits at today's levels in 2030, when people born in 1963 will turn sixty-seven and thus become eligible under current law to receive full benefits:

- 17.22 percent under the Social Security Administration's "best estimates," "intermediate" scenario—39 percent higher than today.
- 20.59 percent if the "more pessimistic," "high-cost" scenario prevails, with economic performance somewhat lower and fertility and life expectancy somewhat higher—66 percent higher than today.

Page 11. "Franco Modigliani": *Funding Pensions: Issues and Implications*

245

for Financial Markets—Proceedings of a Conference Held at Melvin Village, New Hampshire, October, 1976, p. 202.

Page 12. "the 1994 Urban Institute report": *Retooling Social Security for the 21st Century,* p. 241.

Page 12. "In *Status of the Social Security and Medicare Programs: A Summary of the 1994 Annual Reports*": (Washington, D.C.: U.S. Government Printing Office, 1994), p. 14.

Page 13. "about 25 percent": *Income Security and Health Care: Economic Implications 1991–2020—An Expert Panel Report to the Advisory Council on Social Security* (Washington, D.C.: Advisory Council on Social Security, 1991), p. 19.

Page 13. "dramatic": Ibid., pp. v, x, 15.

Page 13. "alarming": Ibid., pp. v, x, 17.

Page 13. "dire": Ibid., p. vii.

Page 13. "31.57 percent": Ibid., p. 76.

Page 14. "slower than the past decade" and "significant slowing": Ibid., p. 8.

Page 14. "26.50 percent": Ibid., p. 76

Page 14. "14.96 percent": *The 1994 Annual Report of the Board of Trustees of the Federal Old–Age and Survivors Insurance and Disability Insurance Trust Funds,* p. 168.

Page 14. "1 percent": *Income Security and Health Care: Economic Implications 1991–2020—An Expert Panel Report to the Advisory Council on Social Security,* p. 76.

Page 15. "roughly 3 to 1" and "about $1,300": *The 1994 Annual Report of the Board of Trustees of the Federal Supplementary Medical Insurance Trust Fund* (Washington, D.C.: U.S. Government Printing Office, 1994), p. 1.

Page 15. "Urban Institute summed up": Ibid., pp. 55–56.

Page 16. "For the combined OASI": *Status of the Social Security and Medicare Programs: A Summary of the 1994 Annual Reports,* p. 7.

Page 17. "Here's what researchers told a conference": Sylvester J. Schieber, director, Research and Information Center, The Wyatt Company, and John B. Shoven, Professor of Economics, Stanford University, September 15–16, 1993.

Page 20. "the Urban Institute reports": *Retooling Social Security for the 21st Century,* p. 125.

Page 20. "26 percent less": Ibid., pp. 107, 111.

Page 23. "Liberals have portrayed": *Abundance of Life: Human Development Policies for an Aging Society* (New York: Columbia University Press, 1988), pp. 24, 107.

Page 23. "Robert B. Hudson": "Social Contingencies, the Aged, and Public Policy," *The Milbank Quarterly* 71, no. 2, p. 258.

Page 24. "a Senate report": Special Committee on Aging, *Developments in*

Aging 1992—Volume 1 (Washington, D.C.: U.S. Government Printing Office, 1993), p. 2.

Page 34. "One study": Performed by James H. Schulz, Professor of Economics and Ida and Meyer Kirstein Professor for Planning and Administration of Aging Policy, Heller School, Brandeis University, and a former president of the Gerontological Society of America. It is cited in Dr. Schulz's *The Economics of Aging*, 5th ed. (Westport, Conn.: Auburn House, 1992), p. 231.

Page 34. "The average . . . $4,830": *Income Security and Health Care: Economic Implications 1991–2020—An Expert Panel Report to the Advisory Council on Social Security*, p. 25.

Page 34. "A 1993 study": Zvi Bodie, Professor of Finance, Boston University, and Robert C. Merton, Professor of Business Administration, Harvard University, "Pension Benefit Guarantees in the United States: A Functional Analysis." In Ray Schmitt, ed., *The Future of Pensions in the United States* (Philadelphia: Pension Research Council, Wharton School of the University of Pennsylvania, 1993), p. 221.

Page 35. "A 1993 study analyzed": Sylvester J. Schieber and John B. Shoven, "The Consequences of Population Aging on Private Pension Fund Saving and Asset Markets." Paper presented at a conference, "Public Policy Towards Pensions," sponsored by the Association of Private Pension and Welfare Plans and the Center for Economic Policy Research, Stanford University, Washington, D.C., October 7–8, 1993, pp. 6–7, 12, 14.

Page 38. "C. Eugene Steuerle and Jon M. Bakija": *Retooling Social Security for the 21st Century*, p. 147.

Page 40. "what *CFO* has to say": Ted Moncreiff, "The Furor Over PBGC Reform: The Debate Over Unfunded Pension Liabilities Begs the Question. Can the Pension System Itself Endure?", April 1993, p. 73.

Page 45. "A 1995 study": "Myopic Loss Aversion and the Equity Premium Puzzle," *Quarterly Journal of Economics*, February 1995, in press.

Page 50. "less than 5 percent": *Federal Reserve Bank of Cleveland Economic Trends*, May 1993, p. 13.

Page 52. "around 16 percent": Ibid., February 1994, p. 9.

Page 51. "*Saving for Prosperity*": (New York: Twentieth Century Fund Press, 1990).

Page 60. "A 1993 report": *Reductions in Mortality at Advanced Ages* (Odense, Denmark: Center for Health and Social Policy, Odense University, 1993), p. 2.

Page 60. "In a 1993 study": *The Future of Mortality at Older Ages in Developed Countries* (Odense, Denmark: Center for Health and Social Policy, Odense University, 1993), p. 22.

Page 60. "Vaupel and Lundstrom note": Ibid., p. 2.

Page 65. "a high chance of divorce": According to the Census Bureau, 35.2

percent of women aged forty-five to forty-nine have been divorced after a first marriage, while another 36.4 percent have divorced again after remarrying. See U.S. Census Bureau, *Current Population Reports*, Series P23, No. 180.

Page 66. "the liberal Urban Institute": *Retooling Social Security for the 21st Century*, p. 250.

Page 67. "We have facetiously described": "Lessons from Canada." In Theodore R. Marmor, Timothy M. Smeeding, Vernon L. Greene, eds., *Economic Security and Intergenerational Justice: A Look at North America* (Washington, D.C.: Urban Institute Press, 1994), p. 321, note 2.

Page 70. "*The Lancet*": November 28, 1992, p. 1343.

Page 74. "*British Medical Journal*": A. J. Wing, "Why Don't the British Treat More Patients with Kidney Failure?", October 22, 1983, p. 1157.

Page 74. "*New England Journal of Medicine*": William B. Schwartz and Henry J. Aaron, "Rationing Hospital Care: Lessons From Britain," January 5, 1984, p. 56.

Page 74. "*Hastings Center Report*": James Childress, "Ensuring Care, Respect, and Fairness for the Elderly," October 1984.

Page 75. "Bluntly speaking": Jonathan Greenberg and William Kistler, *Buying America Back* (Tulsa, Okla.: Council Oaks Books, 1993), p. 370.

Page 76. "How might we devise": "Aging and the Ends of Medicine," *Annals of the New York Academy of Science*, June 15, 1988, pp. 125–32.

Page 77. "we are incurring much greater costs": "Paying the Real Costs of Lifesaving." In Nancy S. Jecker, ed., *Aging and Ethics* (Totowa, N.J.: Humana Press, 1991), pp. 296, 303.

Page 81. "two of the foremost authorities on pension economics": Dr. Schieber, a vice president of The Wyatt Company and director of its research and information center, was previously research director of the Employee Benefit Research Institute, and before that, deputy director, Office of Policy Analysis, Social Security Administration, and deputy research director, Universal Social Security Coverage Study, U.S. Department of Health and Human Services. Dr. Shoven is Charles R. Schwab Professor of Economics and Dean of the School of Humanities and Sciences at Stanford University, a research associate of the National Bureau of Economic Research, and author of *Return on Investment: Pensions Are How America Saves*.

Page 87. "a 1993 Wharton School study": Marshall E. Blume and Stephen P. Zeldes, Finance Department, The Wharton School of the University of Pennsylvania, "The Structure of Stockownership in the U.S." Paper presented at the Wharton/New York Stock Exchange Roundtable on Stockownership, March 15–16, 1993.

Pages 88–98. "The consequences of the change": "The Economic Status of the Elderly," *Scientific American*, May 1989, p. 663.

Page 90. "N. Gregory Mankiw . . . and David N. Weil": "The Baby Boom, the Baby Bust, and the Housing Market," *Regional Science and Urban Economics* 19, pp. 235–58.

Page 90. "Prof. Patric H. Hendershott": "Are Real Housing Prices Likely to Decline by 47 Percent?," Ibid. 21, pp. 553–63.

Page 91. "Recently Dr. Hendershott": Richard K. Green and Patric H. Hendershott, *Demographic Factors and Real House Prices* (Cambridge, Mass.: National Bureau of Economic Research, 1993), pp. 13, 15.

Page 91. "a study for the U.S. National Institute on Aging": Daniel L. McFadden, "Demographics, the Housing Market, and the Welfare of the Elderly." In David A. Wise, ed., *Studies in the Economics of Aging* (Chicago: University of Chicago Press, 1994), pp. 225–85.

Page 100. "Societies are afraid": "Dispelling Ageism: The Cross-Cutting Intervention," *The Annals of the American Academy of Political and Social Science* 503 (May 1989), pp. 141–42.

Pages 104–5. "In the future": Employee Benefit Research Institute, *Pension Evolution in a Changing Economy*, (Washington, D. C.: Employee Benefit Research Institute, 1993), pp. 21–22.

Page 105. "a report prepared for the federal government's Administration on Aging": *An Employer's Guide to Older Worker Employment and Retirement Transition Programs* (Washington, D.C.: Washington Business Group on Health—Institute on Aging, Work & Health, 1991), p. 57.

Page 106. "a study by Dr. Barth and economist William McNaught": "The Impact of Future Demographic Shifts on the Employment of Older Workers," *Human Resource Management*, Spring 1991, p. 34.

Page 108. "wealth had hardly any effect": "Past and Current Trends in Retirement: American Men from 1860 to 1980," *Federal Reserve Bank of Atlanta Economic Review*, July/August 1988, p. 23.

Page 108. "held steady at about 75 percent": Ibid., p. 19.

Page 108. "25 percent": "U.S. Retirement in Historical Context." In Abraham Monk, ed., *The Columbia Retirement Handbook* (New York: Columbia University Press, 1994), p. 15.

Page 114. "W. Andrew Achenbaum": *Social Security: Visions and Revisions—A Twentieth Century Fund Study* (New York: Cambridge University Press, 1986), p. 117.

Page 130. "W. Andrew Achenbaum": "U.S. Retirement in Historical Context," p. 14.

Page 134. "typing—has been found to be unaffected": Timothy A. Salthouse, "Effects of Age and Skill in Typing," *Journal of Experimental Psychology: General* 113 (1984), pp. 345–71.

Page 146. "Studies of printers . . . and quality inspectors": Mildred Doering, Susan R. Rhodes, and Michael Schuster, *The Aging Worker: Research and Recommendations* (Beverly Hills: Sage Publications, 1983), pp. 61–82.

Page 146. "the cognitive mechanical system": "Aging of Intelligence," *The*

Annals of the American Academy of Political and Social Science 503, (May 1989), p. 48.

Page 146. "the performance of older people": Jeffrey Sonnenfeld, "Dealing with the Aging Work Force," *Harvard Business Review* 56, November–December 1978, p. 85.

Page 148. "Epstein wrote in 1933": *Insecurity: A Challenge to America*, 2nd ed. (New York: Random House, 1968), p. 270.

Page 148. "According to James H. Schulz": *The Economics of Aging*, p. 122.

Page 149. "Gösta Rehn": "Flexibility and Free Choice in Working Life." In Jack Habib and Charlotte Nusberg, eds., *Rethinking Worklife Options for Older Persons* (Washington, D.C. & Jerusalem: International Federation on Aging & JDC–Brookdale Institute of Gerontology and Adult Human Development in Israel, 1990), p. 207.

Page 175. "*Looking Ahead*": "Education and Training for the American Labor Market: A Business Perspective," *Looking Ahead* 13, nos. 1/2, p. 11.

Pages 175–76. "Dr. Hurd has written": *The Effect of Labor Market Rigidities on the Labor Force Behavior of Older Workers* (Cambridge, Mass.: National Bureau of Economic Research, 1993), p. 31.

Page 205. "Robert N. Butler, M.D., . . . wrote recently": "Education, Clinical Services, and Research on Treating Older People: A Decade of Experience," *Mount Sinai Journal of Medicine,* November 1993, p. 458.

Page 215. "A 1992 study": *NBER Reporter*, Fall 1993, p. 18.

Page 220. "Jack Kemp": *Imprimis*, August 1994, p. 4.

Page 221. "Zvi Bodie . . . and Robert C. Merton": "Pension Benefit Guarantees in the United States: A Functional Analysis," p. 223.

Page 222."B. Douglas Bernheim": *Is the Baby Boom Generation Preparing Adequately for Retirement?* (Princeton, N.J.: Merrill Lynch, Pierce, Fenner & Smith, 1993), p. 1.

Page 231. "Frank Lloyd Wright": Patrick J. Meehan, ed., *The Master Architect* (New York: Wiley-Interscience, 1984), p. 274.

Page 223. "Gösta Rehn": "Flexibility and Free Choice in Working Life," p. 200.

Page 225. "C. Eugene Steuerle and Jon M. Bakija": *Retooling Social Security for the 21st Century*, p. 248.